Gardens of
Use & Delight

OTHER BOOKS BY JO ANN GARDNER

The Old-Fashioned Fruit Garden (1989)

The Heirloom Garden (1992)

Heirloom Flower Gardens (new edition, 2001)

Living with Herbs (1997)

Herbs in Bloom (1998)

Gardens of
Use & Delight

Uniting the Practical and Beautiful
in an Integrated Landscape

Jigs & Jo Ann Gardner

Illustrations by Elayne Sears

Fulcrum Publishing
Golden, Colorado

Library of Congress Cataloging-in-Publication Data
Gardner, Jigs.
   Gardens of use & delight : uniting the practical and beautiful in an
integrated landscape / Jigs & Jo Ann Gardner ; Illustrations by Elayne
Sears.
        p. cm.
Includes bibliographical references.
   ISBN 1-55591-324-5 (pbk.)
  1. Gardening. 2. Nature craft. 3. Cookery. 4. Gardening—Nova
Scotia—Cape Breton Island. 5. Gardner, Jigs. 6. Gardner, Jo Ann,
1935– I. Title: Gardens of use and delight. II. Gardner, Jo Ann, 1935–
III. Title.
   SB455.G365 2002
   635'.09716'9—dc21

                                                          2001006712

Printed in China
0 9 8 7 6 5 4 3 2 1

Editorial: Marlene Blessing, Michele Wynn, Daniel Forrest-Bank
Cover and interior design: Constance Bollen, cb graphics
Front cover image: Elayne Sears

Fulcrum Publishing
16100 Table Mountain Parkway, Suite 300
Golden, Colorado 80403
(800) 992-2908 • (303) 277-1623
www.fulcrum-books.com

To our children,
Seth, Jesse, Nell, and Curdie,
who helped to lay the foundations.

—

The proper caretaking of the earth lies not alone in maintaining its fertility or in safeguarding its products. The lines of beauty that appeal to the eye and the charm that satisfies the five senses are in our keeping. . . . To put the best expression of any landscape into the consciousness of one's day's work is more to be desired than much riches . . . the farmer does not have full command of his situation until the landscape is a part of his farming.

—Liberty Hyde Bailey, *The Holy Earth*

Contents

Contents

Introduction

—

WE COULD CLAIM that the needs of a growing family—four children born between 1955 and 1960—and the low salary of a college teacher in those days forced upon us a regime of self-reliance for the first seven years of our marriage, and perhaps that's part of the truth. When colleagues looked askance as Jigs picked dandelions on the library lawn for wine, and when he was told that tenure would elude him so long as he rode a bike and kept a flock of hens, that was his defense. Too many people will readily accept economic justifications when they would scorn arguments based on what we think are weightier considerations, like pleasure and independence. Those were the real motives that sent us after wild fruit on obscure byways—what delicious jams and jellies we made!—that drove us to plant ever larger vegetable gardens with consequent orgies of canning, that made us search old books for wine and beer and soap recipes (then hard to find). We were curious, we were fascinated by the processes, and no failures in performance damped our zeal; if the thing could be made, we made it—and well. It took us, for instance, nearly ten years to learn to make Farmer's cheese (akin to cheddar) right every time. We loved every aspect of providing for ourselves, and the feeling of independence it gave us was very gratifying—but unfortunately it also gave us swelled heads, leading us to take the drastic step of moving to a farmhouse in northern Vermont in September 1962. At the time, this was not the fashionable move it would later become, when hordes of young people, usually with trust funds, would flood Vermont to "live off the land," so it was not surprising that our families and friends, shaking their heads at such perversity, washed their hands of us. The rent was paid for two years, we had a cow, a pig, a borrowed horse, a dozen hens and a rooster, and $300. Self-reliance with a vengeance!

If we thought we knew something about it, our ignorance was soon painfully exposed. The first year, when the firewood ran out, the water froze, and our food nearly gave out, was very, very hard. That we survived and even thrived is a testimony to our ability to learn—as well, of course, to our stubbornness. There was more to the experience than utilitarianism because the owner's wife, with her seemingly insignificant plantings, had made the site beautiful, and during our sojourn there, we felt its effect on our life and half-consciously absorbed its lesson. This book is not that story, but those two years determined the rest of our life. Their consequences, working themselves out on what can best be described as marginally productive land on an island in the North Atlantic, form the basis of this book.

To put them somewhat aphoristically, these interlocking principles underlie everything herein. Necessity—practicality—seems a hard taskmaster, but learning and keeping its laws can be deeply, even aesthetically satisfying. Simplicity of means is the beginning of subtle and profound effects. Without a sense, however unconscious, of beauty in our landscape, our lives are impoverished.

We moved to a remote farm, untilled for eight years, on Cape Breton Island in April 1971, and our struggles with poor soil, long damp winters, no spring, ferocious winds, and summer droughts, as we worked to create a productive farm that was also a beautiful place, taught us much that we could never have learned in a more favorable environment (we are in Zone 4). Although the struggle itself has a certain interest, the emphasis in these pages is on the lessons we learned about how to combine the aesthetic and practical in what we call the integrated landscape—and these are lessons that can be applied anywhere. That's the point of this book, and we have taken pains throughout to draw general principles from our specific experience.

Chapter One describes the farm as it is today, so the reader will have a clear picture of the domestic area, that is, the acre separate from the barnyard and fields. Chapter Two goes back to the beginning in 1971 to show the blank canvas, so to speak, and proceeds, chronologically, to show in some detail the changes we made, and why and how we made them. Nor do we overlook our many mistakes, instructive in themselves.

In ensuing chapters, the heart of the book, a variety of gardens of "use and delight" are described in detail to show how plantings were developed and integrated into the general landscape. These chapters begin with the establishment of a vegetable garden, then fruit and herb plantings, and include descriptions of our garden sites and design, growing techniques, and specific plants selected for their beauty, vigor, adaptability, fragrance, and not least of all, versatility: Blueberries, for instance, are beautiful shrubs in their own right; lungwort, usually regarded as a ground cover, can be grown as a weed-smothering hedge around flower gardens, providing nectar for the season's first humming-birds. Combining practical needs within a pleasing, aesthetic framework where we live and work is a major theme.

Part Three "The Integrated Landscape," offers the gardener the wisdom of our forty years' experiences, a lengthy span for any growing guide. Topics here include: growing zones; successful germination; no-dig gardening; plant maintenance and harvesting; managing water resources; and sensible disease and insect control.

The final chapter summarizes the principles and lessons discussed throughout the book: creating fluid outdoor living spaces that grow from life, that unite practical need and aesthetic vision by the simplest means available to every gardener. ●

PART ONE

The Whole

*Herb garden in foreground
and vegetable garden in background,
cold frame and meatcase hotbed in lower right.*

CHAPTER ONE

The Farm Today

—

A VISITOR TO OUR FARM undergoes an experience on the way that prepares him, willy nilly, to be more than usually receptive to the beauty of the farm, to respond, at the first glimpse, with wholehearted warmth. He has weathered an unusual passage. It begins when, leaving the Trans-Canada Highway, smooth, broad, spacious, indistinguishable from any of the myriad superhighways that criss-cross North America, he turns onto a secondary road, a two-lane affair not so smooth or manicured, passing scattered houses, woods, a few overgrown fields, a somewhat rundown rural background, and after a couple of miles he turns onto a more recently paved road, here and there touching the shore of the Bras d'Or Lake, a little more populated than the last, modern houses occasionally interspersed with older farmhouses standing in the midst of empty fields—only one functioning farm is passed—and for the final four miles he turns onto a wretched, potholed, graveled road winding through dense woods, seeing only two houses, crossing a railroad track, watching anxiously for the next turn marked on the sketch map he's been given, and now the road is worse, narrower, not a single sign of habitation, and when, after a couple of miles, he crosses the tracks again, the road is suddenly more constricted, a dark tunnel overarched by trees. Increasingly dubious, peering at the map, proceeding cautiously, at last he spots our mailbox and a crude sign nailed to a tree:

Butter Eggs Cream Jams & Jellies
Herbs Milk Buttermilk
Curds Smoked Bacon

Reassured by the tub of bright flowers beside the mailbox (Figure 1), he turns onto the very narrow lane, wholly enclosed by woods, hoping he'll meet no one coming the other way. How long is this lane, he asks himself (it's a half mile), thinking there'd better be something

Figure 1.
The mailbox scene.

good at the other end. Down a hill between steep wooded banks, he turns, crosses a small bridge, and suddenly rampant wilderness begins to give way to cultivation. Brush beside the road is mown, a rail fence enclosing a pasture begins at the bridge, there are scattered groves of tall spruces, and for the first time in four miles the visitor sees open, tended fields. Rounding a curve beneath a venerable apple tree, climbing a hill for the last one hundred yards, there is a barn in the distance, the house at the top of the hill before him, and in May and June, thousands of daffodils of all sorts line the lane on either side, thickly scattered in the grass around lilacs, a pear tree, and three old apple trees (Figure 2).

Emerging from the car, a visitor's almost invariable first remark is, "Boy, this is a hard place to find!" A little tired of the line, we always respond, "The best things are never easy." A little taken aback by our failure to apologize for where we live, he looks around and then he says, "What a beautiful farm," struck by its appearance as a cultivated oasis in the midst of wildness (Figure 3).

The beauty is not an illusion created by the effort to get here—that merely enhances the first impression. The farm is beautiful because we have made it so, sometimes by accident, often with mistakes and failures, but largely deliberately, working always to blend two ends, function and aesthetics, necessity and beauty, in a harmonious whole— the integrated landscape.

Figure 2.
Spring daffodils in bloom.

Figure 3.
The panorama of the farm.

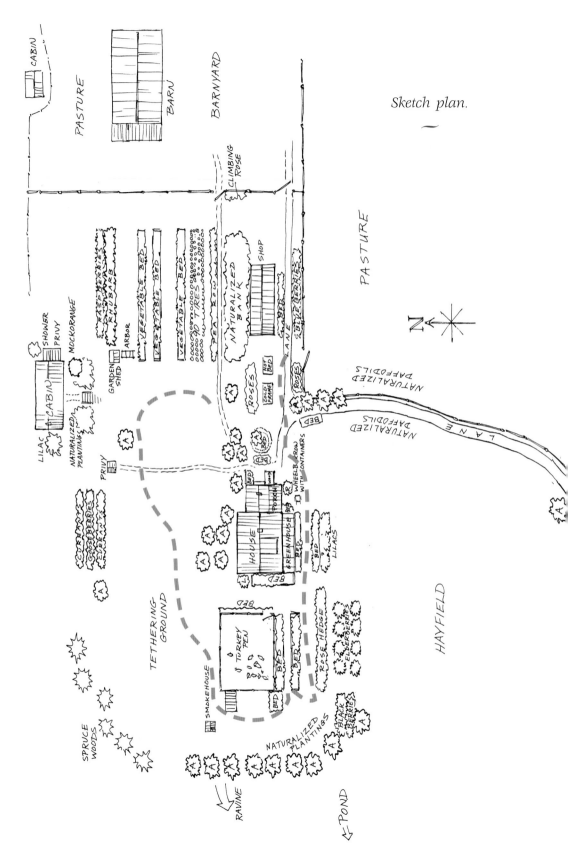

Sketch plan.

Figure 4.
Approach to the barn.

A dotted line on the sketch map on page 20 shows the route we shall follow as we take a closer look at the scene. On the east side at the top of the lane we are confronted by a thick hedge of roses (*Rosa rugosa* 'Rubra Plena'), a forsythia bush carpeted with blue scilla (followed by blue forget-me-nots) at the end almost beneath the apple tree, a tub of golden-edged hosta (*H. fortunei* 'Aureo-marginata') and white sweet alyssum (*Lobularia*) in its midst. Walking a little way down the barn lane toward the shop (Figure 4), those are highbush blueberries on the right, with a flower bed under the shop windows and a hop vine (*Humulus lupulus*) at the corner. Stepping back to the top of the lane

Figure 5.
House and rose hedge.

and looking to the northeast (see pages 12 and 13), we see the flowering herb garden in the foreground, and beyond it coldframes and the meatcase, ca. 1940, that serves as our hotbed, planted in front to Sedum 'Autumn Beauty' surrounded by a frilly gray mat of the Roman wormwood used to flavor vermouth (*Artemisia pontica*), with a clump of old-fashioned golden-glow (*Rudbeckia laciniata* 'Hortensis') at the end. A low, wide hedge of the Apothecary's rose (*Rosa gallica* 'Officinalis') is on the slope above, the Russet apple tree to the right, vegetable gardens right rear, and that's the classic white rugosa 'Blanc Double de Coubert' at the far right. Turning back toward the house, the flowering herb garden is on the right, Curdie's tulip bed is in the middle distance, there are gardens around the back door, and flowers in containers in front of the woodshed and porch. Proceeding along the lawn before the house

(Figure 5), a hedge of the native *Rosa virginiana* fronts the porch, there's a small garden in the corner by the greenhouse, with containers of herbs and flowers on the stone terrace. Straight ahead (Figure 6), looking west, there are three lilacs with a bed of shade-lovers at their feet, dominated by Solomon's Seal (*Polygonum multiflorum*) and hostas, with a facing bed

Figure 6.
Looking west at elderberry hedge.

Figure 7.
Rose bed and surrounding plantings.

of sun-loving annuals edged with lamb's ears (*Stachys byzantina*) in front of the greenhouse.

Walking along beyond the house corner, we come upon an extensive scene, our "secret" gardens invisible from the front of the house, always a delightful surprise to visitors. On the far left, extending along and running down the steep bank, is a tall, dense planting of cultivated elderberries (*Sambucus canadensis* 'Nova'), just above them a line of specimen plantings of shrub roses, the rose trial bed straight ahead, and the harvest bed on the right against the turkey fence. Against the house is the west bed of silvery and blue plants. The illustration (Figure 7) is from the end of that vista, facing east, harvest bed on the left, rose trial bed center, shrub roses to the right. The area where the artist was standing shades gradually into the wild as elderberries give way to the rampant growth of cultivated blackberries on the bank, a 'Cortland' apple tree, a wild hawthorn tree, and wild apple trees with naturalized plantings of cowslips, lungwort, and wild geranium in their shade.

Continuing our tour around the turkey house, we pass the smokehouse, cross a bit of grassland where we tether calves, skirt the old apple orchard, passing on our left three mint beds and rows of red currants, black currants, and gooseberries. A dense black-currant hedge in front was originally established as a place to heel in currant shoots for sale. They quickly grew up thickly, as black currants will, and now we pick the fruit for wine and juice after we've picked the others for jam and jelly. It proved very useful when our big Jersey bull got loose one day and evaded capture until Jigs, running beside him, edged him into the hedge to slow him down and was able to grab his collar. There followed, as he says, "The fastest three or four seconds in my life," until he managed to reach around with his other hand to seize the bull's nose ring, stopping just short of the smokehouse. The integrated landscape also means a place where we and our animals interact!

Passing under the huge old apple tree, a striking feature in our landscape, the big cabin (Figure 8) is due north at the edge of the woods. There are naturalized plantings by the bridge and in front of the cabin, and a mock orange bush on the lawn. Walking back toward the house, across a grassy area used for tethering cows, we stop in front of the laneway leading to the barnyard (Figure 9), garden shed on the left,

Figure 8.
The big cabin.

golden-glow beside it with a barrel of climbing nasturtiums supported by the wooden slab wall, a rustic arbor with a red 'Dorothy Perkins' rose ('Excelsa') and a hop vine, the raised rhubarb bed extending to the barnyard gate, raspberries behind. Stepping on a little farther, Figure 10

Figure 9.
Garden shed and arbor.

Figure 10.
Vegetable garden.

reveals the raised vegetable beds, the planted tires, and the pea row on the right. Down the bank to the right are naturalized ground covers and flower plantings lightly shaded by two wild apple trees severely pruned of their bushy lower growth.

The tour is intended to give the reader a general acquaintance with the whole cultivated area. In Chapter Two, "The Evolving Landscape," we shall consider specific areas in detail, describing not only the plants and their arrangement, but also their place in the landscape, their contributions as groupings, as parts of vistas, to the aesthetic pleasures of the whole. Even with this cursory tour, however, the reader should begin to see the harmony of the place where we and our animals live and work, the integrated landscape of use and delight.

CHAPTER TWO

The Evolving Landscape

—

WHEN WE WERE RENTING the small farm in northern Vermont nearly forty years ago, the owner put it up for sale and we showed it to a lot of people, mostly from the Boston area. This was an eye-opening experience that taught us how not to assess rural property, because, without exception, these folks concentrated their attention on inessentials—the furnishings, whether the house needed repairs, and so on, the things that would be important if they were considering a suburban property. As we tramped around the fifty acres, pointing out the breathtaking view of the valley below and the far hills, the well-tended woods and fields, the big maples by the house, the beautiful perennial plantings, the perfect setting of the house, the finest garden location we've ever seen (rich loam on a southern slope, protected on the north by a six-foot stone wall sheltering currant bushes), we were amazed that they had no eye for these things. We learned then that the features to look for in rural property are the permanent or long-term things that cannot be significantly changed or created in your lifetime—the overall look of the place, the view, big trees, fruitful soil, location of the house. Other things one can easily change.

Looking to buy a farm in Nova Scotia, we advertised in weekly papers across the province, and with the replies in hand Jigs drove here in October 1970 and went from farm to farm. Of the twenty he visited, only one had all the permanent features we wanted—the bones as it were—but it was far beyond our means. Finally he crossed the causeway to Cape Breton Island to look at three places. One had been sold, one had no buildings or fields, but when he drove into the lane to this place, he knew this would be our farm (Figures 11, 12, 13). Looks pretty bleak, doesn't it? But he saw the bones: apple orchards near the house, the good location of the house (unlike so many he had looked at, down in a hollow or standing stark, treeless, in the middle of a field), the attractive way the lane wound its way up to the house, and, knowing how Jo Ann yearned for flower gardens, hitherto precluded by our frequent moves, he saw things that would give her heart: the lilacs, the mock orange, a circle of lungwort (*Pulmonaria*), a fragrant rose by the porch, wild yellow iris in a clump beside the cellar door, daylilies. He knew our time and labor would supply the rest. No one was here—the place had been empty for a year—but he peered in the windows to make sure the house was intact, and went away to make an offer to the real estate agent. *That's* how to buy rural property!

Our elder son, Seth, fifteen, was settled in here in April 1971 with another boy, camping out in the house, learning domestic skills like baking bread, working hard on the tasks necessary to bring the farm back to life. There had been no farming here for eight years. Fence posts had to be cut, the stables had to be gutted, a pen for the hens

Figure 11.
The house, May 1972.

Seth had with him had to be built in the barn, and so on and on. Jigs made seven trips from April to June, moving everything we had, all our furniture and domestic goods, two horses, a cow, two calves, chickens, dogs, cats, our antique farm equipment, more children. A sort of Kid's Republic was set up, wistfully canceled after we came in June to reestablish parental authority. The children worked very hard and did a splendid job.

To say that necessity dictated the jobs we tackled that first summer would imply that afterward our choices were largely unfettered, and that's nonsense; what we should say is that we were so preoccupied with the looming survival problem of the coming winter that we concentrated on tasks relevant to that—shelter for the animals, cutting hay, growing food, cutting firewood. Trees were felled to be hauled to the local sawmill so we could rebuild the barn; the rotting porch was rebuilt and extended; a skidway for loading logs on the wagon was built on the front lawn beside the lane; extensive vegetable gardens, plowed in May, were put in, the main one covering the area from the present pea row back to the woods by the big cabin (See Figure 14, page 36), another behind the house from the path to the privy to the smokehouse, and one on the west side of the house comprising the area from the row of specimen roses back to half of the present turkey pen. Jo Ann made her very first flower garden—now called the flowering herb garden—using many roots and cuttings, mostly herbs, from Vermont, in a spot twenty yards from the house where rocks and debris were piled against an old apple tree. In the fall we dug up wild roses (*Rosa virginiana*) growing beside the road and planted them in front of the porch.

To understand our plans for the next year, the reader must know this much about our past: From our marriage in 1955 until our move to Cape Breton in 1971 we had moved more than a dozen times, from one rented place to another. Somehow, somewhere, we managed every year to plant a vegetable garden, but flowers and fruit had to come with the property, which happened only twice. We made up for the lack, in some degree, by scouring the countryside for miles around for wild fruit, and bouquets of wildflowers often graced our table—but now we wanted to grow all those fruits and flowers we had missed, a wish common to smallholders everywhere (for a very funny instance, see

Chekhov's "Gooseberries"). What's important to the reader is how we carried it out, and our peculiar past experience played a part in that.

We had been keeping animals of various sorts since 1960, sometimes in restricted circumstances (once we used a garage for a cow stable), and we were used to tethering cattle on the lawn. Of course we were going to use the large pastures on our new farm, but we also planned to tether calves near the house where they would be easy to see and keep an eye on (and where they'd be able to get loose and eat Jo Ann's flowers). So the area around the house would be mixed grass and plantings. Nor would all the fruit be planted in a block, because in the back of our minds we kept a memory of that first place in Vermont, where the raspberry patch was at one side of the vegetable garden while currants and tall hollyhocks lined the wall on the other side, and the cow was tethered nearby under an apple tree. We had never liked arrangements where the woman's realm (house and flowers) was genteelly fenced off from the man's (farm, vegetables, fruit); our plantings would be mixed and scattered in the area around the house. The final purpose we would serve would be fending off the wild. It is an old principle in farming, especially in an area like this where the wild presses so closely and some fields had already been abandoned to brush, that if the land is not used it will quickly revert to its natural state, so we meant to tend all cultivated or once-cultivated land on the place. We ordered a long list of fruit trees and bushes from a mainland nursery in late winter 1972 and set them out in spring.

Five dwarf and semidwarf apple trees were planted on the periphery of the clearing around the house, plum and pear trees lined the lane coming up to the house; highbush blueberries went where they are

Figure 12.
The house, July 1971.

now, currants and gooseberries on the north-facing slope out back, rhubarb beside the smokehouse, elderberries on the hill where they remain, blackberries beside them, strawberries and raspberries in the garden land beside the house. Mistakes were made, to be discussed in due course, but most of the plantings were successful, and we could see already how scattering the plantings made our immediate living area attractive. Elderberries on the steep slope near the house largely

Figure 13.
The barn from front lawn, May 1972.

eliminated that barren look with their tall, arching shapes and foliage, presenting a glorious swath of creamy blossoms in July, and by adding pears and plums to the three old apple trees on the east side of the lane, and planting more across the lane, we gave the lane definition, an avenue of approach marked by graceful tree forms. Everywhere we went there were fruiting plants with their distinctive forms, foliage, blossoms, and fruit, variety that added interest to every prospect. From the point of view of use, this pattern of planting insured that we would see these fruiting plants every day and could keep our eyes on them, so we would know if and when diseases or pests appeared, in time to intervene, just as we would know as soon as fruit began to ripen, important knowledge for jelly making, because pectin decreases as fruits get riper.

Furthermore, all plantings were easily accessible by horse and wagon, the way we spread manure. In that connection, we should note that the distance between the plantings right against the house and nearest gardens is maintained at about ten feet, room enough for the team to maneuver. That has a pleasing aesthetic effect, also; the gardens are close, but there's a feeling of spaciousness around the house, too.

Over the next few years, the evolution of the landscape was mainly a story of buildings and their consequences. We put up the two log cabins to earn money by renting them to summer guests, but they looked so stark and bare that Jo Ann planted flower beds in front. The one at the big cabin was a difficult site that gave us trouble for years until she found the solution, described in Chapter Eight, "The Art of Naturalizing." We built the wagon shed addition to the barn to house our equipment, and the shop for the repair and rebuilding of everything. Compare Figure 13 and Figure 15 (on page 38) and note the improvement in the vista; the staring blank wall is mitigated by a structure that could have been equally dull, were it not for the shallow arches over each bay. Old horse-shoes over the double doors of the shop make a striking decoration, an iron flower. Once again, Jo Ann saw a place for flowers along the shop wall, facing the blueberries across the lane. For the first few years, we raised our early plants, like tomatoes, peppers, and some flowers like petunias and marigolds, in hotbeds heated with horse manure, but we were developing local demand and we needed more room, so we built a very simple greenhouse from old storm windows across the south front of the house. Directly across the narrow front lawn were the three lilacs—two white and one purple—planted here in the 1920s with Solomon's seal at the base of one, a clump of daylilies at the next, and a circle of lungwort at the third. Jo Ann had dug a long, narrow bed in front of the lilacs for tulips and daffodils and had transplanted the lungwort to its edge, a move full of large consequences later. To match that bed, she made a narrow one along the front of the greenhouse, and there she transplanted the wild yellow iris we had found growing in a dump by the porch. A small flower bed was tucked into the corner

Figure 14.
Jesse disking the garden with the team.
Note the rubbly nature of the clay soil.

between the greenhouse and house. The last building project that resulted in a garden was the relocation of an old shed on the east side of the house to the garden as a shelter for bee equipment and garden tools. Curdie wanted a flower garden of her own, so we dug up the old site of the shed for that.

By the mid-1970s the children were leaving home, and in just a few years we were alone. We still had summer guests and visitors, but we didn't need so many vegetables anymore, so we thought perhaps it was time to scale back the gardens. By 1979, the big potato patch in the hayfield was gone. Now, however, we noticed that production, no matter what we did, was falling year by year, and we were forced to acknowl-edge that our unremitting efforts to improve the soil in our vegetable gardens, working tons of manure and compost into the hard clay, had failed. We began to experiment with raised beds filled with made soil (rotted manure), converting the gardens behind the house first. After some mistakes, we finally moved all our vegetables, rhubarb, strawber-ries, and raspberries to the raised beds where they are now. The whole process is explained in detail in Chapter Three, "The Kitchen Garden."

Our guest business began to decline in the mid-1980s, as fewer and fewer people wanted to vacation in a log cabin without running water and electricity, and the old-fashioned farm meals (lots of butter, cream, and meat) became anathema. We had never made much money, we had no savings, and our income now was negligible. We had always sold jam at the farm along with other farm products, and in an extremity, a kind friend set Jo Ann up at a craft sale where she sold thirteen cases of jam and twelve pounds of a product she'd recently dreamed up—Herb Salt. She never looked back. Naturally, this led to more products—herb jellies,

Figure 15.
New wagon shed addition to the barn,
the workshop, and hotbeds, fall 1975.

teas, other herb blends, potpourri, dried flowers, and so on—which required more production from the gardens and relentless harvest. Finally, Jigs put his foot down: "We have more flowers drying in the stove than we have left in the gardens!" So the Harvest Bed, a raised bed, was constructed, and soon thereafter, when coyotes made their appearance and we could no longer let the turkeys wander freely about the fields (also, Jo Ann objected to them eating her petunias), the turkey pen was built and fenced with slabs, enhancing the appearance of the Harvest Bed and enabling Jo Ann to grow climbers like runner beans, as well as tall sunflowers.

One last need led to the creation of all the rest (save one) of the flower beds and plantings: Jo Ann's growing interest in heirloom plants, which resulted in *The Heirloom Garden*. The bed along the west side of the house was added, then the Rose Bed opposite the Harvest Bed, and all the other rose plantings—above the elderberries, at the top of the lane, behind the cold frame—because heirlooms led her into trialing roses, old and new, that could survive our climate and soil conditions.

The only purely gratuitous garden is the one along the bank between the pea row and the back of the shop, and that came about because Jigs, reading one of Gertrude Jekyll's books one winter night, was impressed by her condemnation of "unsightly places" and thought at once of the bank, then an impenetrable thicket of wild raspberries, burdocks, thistles, and jewelweed. How it was transformed is told in Chapter Four, "An Old-Fashioned Fruit Garden."

We had three goals when we set out to plant the household acre— vegetable and fruit production, integration of animals and plants, beautification—all soon achieved. But nothing remained fixed for long. The children grew up and left, market demand changed, production had to be shifted to raised beds, new structures went up, and so on, and plantings were accordingly changed and added (never subtracted!). The evolution of our landscape, until very recently, has always been a response to material needs or facts. Obviously, we could never have planned it beforehand; any scheme drawn up by a landscape architect in 1971 would soon have been abandoned. No preconceived plan, no matter how aesthetically inspired, could have foreseen and allowed for all the changes that are part of any life. The pattern of beauty was not imposed here—it has grown out of the use of the landscape.

It would be an affectation, however, to pretend that the aesthetic result just "happened"; we made it happen, at least to a degree. We had one humble virtue—doggedness. Many of our initial plantings were opportunistic, hasty improvisations—a strip of flowers beside a building, a way to fill in a corner—and if they didn't wholly work out, as they often didn't, we worked at them, sometimes for years, until we learned what would make them successful. Too much of our energy at first was expended in trial-and-error efforts, but as our knowledge grew—of the needs of plants, of characteristics of this soil, of successful defensive techniques—our touch became surer and less time- and labor-consuming. Of course, we must have had a rudimentary aesthetic sense when we came here or we would not have seen the possibilities, but there is no question that we have developed it since. If Jigs sees the larger effects, the placement of plantings in relation to the whole pattern, Jo Ann has trained her eye in the subtleties of color, probably the most important single tool to bring to the making of beautiful gardens. One of her training exercises is bouquet recording: whenever she picks flowers for the house, she writes down the colors of each flower as exactly as she can (no easy feat in itself), turning the vase this way and that to note harmonies and discords. Finally, the fact that Jo Ann has been writing about gardening since the mid-1970s has certainly increased her knowledge and sensitivity.

The brief description in this chapter of what we've done, to be examined in detail in later chapters, should be heartening to the reader: It was not until the late 1980s, after we had been laboring here for more than fifteen years, that we had learned enough to be fairly certain of what we were doing and could begin to make it clear to ourselves—and then to the reader. Out of ignorance has come knowledge, and now you are the beneficiary: The lessons in this narrative should make it easier for you to achieve something like what we have done, no matter the scale, though without so many false starts and mistakes. ●

PART TWO

The Gardens

The tire garden at full growth.

CHAPTER THREE

The Kitchen Garden

—

WHEN WE PLANTED OUR FIRST vegetable garden in 1957, a gardening friend converted us to the concept of organic gardening, and we followed its precepts in all our gardens until the mid-1980s. It did no harm, because until we moved to Cape Breton all the soils we worked—in Wisconsin, Maryland, Massachusetts, and Vermont—were productive, and we were never in one place for more than four years. We had an innocent faith in soil, ignorant of the fact that there are soils that do not respond significantly to organic additions, soils that are not only infertile but also rife with other problems.

The first thing we noticed when we plowed the land in 1971 was the soil texture: hard reddish clay, so hard that the children, who planted the seeds before our arrival, told us they had to scrape up bits of soil here and there to cover the seeds. You could only work it when it was quite dry—but not too dry, because then it was rock hard. If you ran the disc harrow over it when it was damp, it dried into a rocky rubble (see Figure 14, on page 36). Wet, it was sticky and greasy. It never developed a fine tilth. Hoeing it in any state was a wretched labor, and the roots of weeds were impossible to get at. We had prided ourselves on our luxurious gardens free of weeds, thanks to a system we initiated in Vermont of pulling two bushels of weeds a day to feed our chicken flocks. If there's a dual purpose in weeding—cleaning the garden as well as feeding chickens or building a compost heap—then weeding becomes a regular part of the routine and the gardens will be clean. Now, no matter how hard we worked, the gardens were always full of weeds. Furthermore, they grew faster than the vegetables, which hardly grew at all until mid-July, due to the combination of no spring—a few warmish days in May, then a cool summer in June—chill winds off the ice pack around the island, and a cold, dank soil that took forever to warm up.

There's another reason for the phenomenal success of weeds here. Wild plants and wild grasses are, generally speaking, low in nutrients, hence they are undemanding and thrive in poor soil to which they are well adapted. They love Cape Breton soil. Cultivated annuals, like most vegetables, are relatively rich in nutrients, so they need good soil to thrive. Since this soil, leached of nutrients by glaciation, is relatively inhospitable to microorganisms and worms, those great tillers of the soil, manure takes a long time to rot, making the release of its nutrients, its chemicals, to plant roots agonizingly slow. When we first spread manure on the hayfields, it was still discernible a year later. When vegetables are planted in good soil, they quickly outgrow weeds; the reverse is true here.

We saw these difficulties at once, and the answer, we thought, was more; more manure, more compost, mulching with paper and cardboard, more plowing, more cultivating, more hoeing. The gardens improved, both in fertility and tilth. All our vegetable plots, the big garden that ran from where the pea row is now back to the woods by the big cabin, the gardens behind the house, and a potato patch in the hayfield, amounted to 30,000 square feet, and they fed us throughout the year, but never so bountifully as in Vermont, where we fed twelve people, eight of them growing boys, from less land. And the vegetables themselves, their foliage a pale sickly green, lacked the rich juiciness and taste we were used to. Our experience has shown that adding *lots* of organic matter and plowing the land regularly will improve this soil—temporarily. A dramatic example is the pasture behind the barn. The soil, probably untouched for a generation, was hard gray clay. When we set the team with the sulky plow to it, the share would go no deeper than four inches, and the only topsoil was a thin brown smear at the grass roots. We plowed it as best we could, disked it, manured and limed it, kept cows and horses on it, and when we plowed it again three years later, the plow went down eight inches and there was noticeable topsoil. After a few years, however—and this is as true of our fields as it is of the vegetable gardens—whatever fertility the soil has accumulated in its long fallow years has been used up, and manure and compost alone cannot restore it; fertilizer must be added, too.

By the early 1980s, the yields were falling drastically. With our children grown and gone, we needed less, so we sowed the top part of the big garden, from the laneway where the arbor is now to the woods, to timothy and trefoil for pasture and concentrated our efforts on the lower part, which wasn't as bad. The garden behind the house was declining, too, and there we began experimenting with raised beds. We built two, each four feet wide by sixty feet long, using six-inch boards set on edge, held in place by short stakes, filled with a mixture of soil and rotted manure. Dark and friable, it warmed up quickly in June, weeds pulled up easily, and yields improved. But weeds, especially deadly witchgrass, riotously invaded the beds from underneath. Next spring, removing the soil from end to end, shovelful by shovelful, we pulled out every witchgrass root, probably our stupidest exercise in futility. Of course, the witchgrass came back as strong as ever. The year following, we removed all the soil, lined the beds with old plastic grain bags, and replaced the soil. Better, but now witchgrass entered from the sides, under the boards, and also crept in via gaps between the bags. And the boards, in this damp climate, were rotting. Meanwhile, yields in the lower part of the old big garden were falling inexorably.

Our experiment convinced us that raised beds with made soil were the answer to our problems, but we had to make improvements, and we had to do the job in a thorough, comprehensive manner. In the fall, we felled poplar and spruce trees no thicker than ten inches at the butt, cut them off where they dwindled to six inches, and skidded them full length with Pookie (the skid horse) to the old garden area. We made two beds, ten feet apart in order to leave room for the team to haul manure, lining them with plastic grain bags that extended under and beyond the logs for added protection against intrusive weeds (Figure 16).

Now we produce an abundance of composted manure for all our needs—hotbed, gardens, cold frame, raising seedlings in the green-house—using a total of 900 cubic feet per year at the outside. A certain amount of manure is generated every day in the stables during the summer by pigs, hens, and horses when they're kept in during horsefly

Figure 16.
Smoothing the raised bed.

time. Since manure is not spread on the fields then, we dump one
wheelbarrow each day in a heap across from the stable door in the
barnyard, a heap enclosed by timbers on three sides, with piles of
sawdust and rotted hay next to it that we use to cover the manure, thus
keeping down flies and helping to make the compost. We turn it in fall,
and by next spring, it's ready to use.

The first two raised beds we made were each sixty feet long and
four feet wide. We laid down a row of plastic grain bags, overlapping
them six inches on each side, and rolled the logs onto them, leaving
six inches of bag sticking out the side. We did the same thing on the
opposite side. The bags didn't quite meet in the center, so we covered
the gap with another line of bags, again overlapped. Of course, a single

sheet of thickish plastic would have been better, but the bags were all we had, and they have been satisfactory. Put another way, we're cheap. The beds were filled to a depth of six inches with rotted manure, and if it was heavy, dank, and thick, as with cow manure (horse manure is lighter), we added sawdust and shavings from the local sawmill, ten wheelbarrow loads per bed. We mixed everything thoroughly with a deep rake (four or five curved tines, six inches long), sprinkled lime over the bed to balance the acidic manure, added fertilizer, 0-20-20 because there was plenty of nitrogen in the manure, and deep-raked it again. We tamped the whole bed flat, then spread a couple of inches of sifted, composted manure over the top. Seeds need fine soil for germination. The beds were then ready to plant.

We used logs because we have them, but stone, cement blocks, or timbers or two-inch boards would be fine. We like long logs because, except at their joints, there are no cracks for weeds to creep in. The breadth of a log is nice to kneel on when working in the garden. Poplar logs, which rapidly rot, were a mistake, and we replaced them with spruce, but even so, they lasted five years. In the fall, we check the logs and replace any that are rotten. After harvest, we go over each bed on our knees and pick out every smallest weed for the hens. The soil settles, and of course the vegetables use it up, so in October, when the cows and horses are stabled at night, we collect a wheelbarrow of fresh manure at noon, wheel it to the garden and dump it where it's needed to maintain the depth of soil. We also add a few loads of sawdust or shavings to keep the mixture light and loose. During the winter, we spread ashes from our woodstoves over all beds, including flower beds. That helps to keep the soil sweet and adds phosphates. In spring, after deep mixing, we add lime and fertilizer as described in the previous paragraph, substituting 6-12-12 for 0-20-20 if we added little fresh manure the fall before. The beds are raked smooth, ready for planting. Naturally, the beds are not planted all at once—lettuce goes in two or three weeks before beans, for instance—and now's the time to watch for and pull out emerging weeds in the prepared but as yet unplanted sections. Just before planting the first seeds, we spray around the outside of the logs with Roundup, holding the nozzle close to the ground so only a narrow band of weeds is suppressed. Sometimes, in an especially rainy season, we have to spray again late in the summer. We mow the grass around the beds each week. Inside the beds, we weed by hand, using buckets to collect for the hens, as needed, about two or three times in the season. All three beds can be done in two hours.

The advantages of these plastic-lined raised beds were immediately apparent. No more persistent invaders like witchgrass. Weeds were easy to pull from the friable soil. The richness of the soil allowed us to plant everything so close together that weeds were shaded out. The warmth of the soil meant that we could plant earlier, the seeds germinated quickly, and the plants shot up. One startling effect we had not antici-pated was that the plants assumed their natural variety of colors—all the different shades of green, yellow, and red we had forgotten during the years when there was only one pale green hue in our gardens. Beds of healthy growing vegetables are beautiful. Now we had abundant harvests of succulent vegetables from a much-reduced area with less effort.

For the first couple of years while the three raised beds were being established, we continued to plant corn and potatoes in the ground between the first bed and the present pea row, a strip about fifteen feet wide, but beds with our made soil were so superior to the clay that we decided to try tires. A friend was enthusiastic, claiming the tires absorbed the sun's heat, warming the soil within. A farmer gave us a lot of heavy black plastic he had used for putting up haylage, and we spread that over the ground and lined up three rows of thirty old tires in each row with two feet between the rows (Figure 17). They were filled with the same mixture we used in the raised beds, limed (do not lime the tires where potatoes are planted), and fertilized. After experimenting with different vegetables, we finally settled on green peppers, potatoes, cucumbers, zucchini, tomatoes, and a few herbs, including garlic. The tires are topped off with a shovel or two of manure and sawdust in the fall. In midseason, we heap shavings up at the base of the potato plants to prevent sunburn (see pages 42 and 43).

Figure 17.
Preparing tire garden.

Winds, especially from the northwest, are fierce here. They not only damage plants but retard growth by chilling, stressing them and drying them out. We wanted to make a flower bed by the back door, and because the raised vegetable beds were so successful, we made one there, but without the plastic lining since perennials put down deep roots. As a decorative element, we built a high slab fence (sawmill refuse, the four outside slices from a log) on the north side, not realizing it would create a protected area, a microclimate out of the wind, exposed to the south and east. We immediately had great success with plants that had hitherto led a frail life of struggle out in the open. The next spring, we built a seven-foot slab fence along the northern edge of the last raised bed, and we extended a fifteen-foot wing at an oblique angle on the west end. It primarily shields the bed it's next to, but some protection is afforded to the other beds, too, and it is a tremendous asset. Before its advent we had watched not only corn being blown to the ground but also cabbage and broccoli plants.

Three-fourths of that fenced bed is taken up with eighty to one hundred tomatoes, our favorite vegetable (well, fruit, we suppose), from which we make Garden Special, catsup, juice, sauce (see recipes that follow beginning on page 65), not to speak of eating them fresh from late August to January (stored to ripen in the cellar). They are trained and tied to tripods made from saplings and pruned once a week for the largest, quickest-ripening fruit. Pruning also helps air circulation, inhibiting disease.

Although we plant an early corn, our main crop is, and always has been, the best (and oldest) variety, 'Golden Bantam', not as sweet as the impressive new hybrids, but with a true corn flavor that's unsurpassed.

We eat it fresh, of course, and we can as much as possible, because it's the only canned corn that really tastes like corn.

Vegetables should be shifted around the garden from year to year to avoid concentrations of pests and diseases, and we do that to some extent, but it isn't so necessary in beds with made soil because it is added to every year and thoroughly mixed. Our tomatoes have been in the fenced bed for ten years.

Our single zucchini is planted in a tire close to the path to the barn, so we pass it three times each day and always check it. We won't claim we never discover squash that has eluded us and grown to elephantine proportions, but by the timely vigilance its place by the side of the path forces on us, we don't get more than one or two such monstrosities per season. We pick them when they're four to six inches long to fry with bacon and eggs for breakfast.

The pea row is a plastic-lined raised bed one foot wide by forty feet long, with plastic netting stretched between several posts. Its location

—

Figure 18.
Lettuce bed.

is also strategically designed. We watch the pods as we pass every day, and very few grow to overmaturity. One-third of the row is planted in May ('Alderman' or 'Tall Telephone'), one-third to the same type two weeks later, one-sixth to green soup peas, and one-sixth to a brown Dutch variety, also for soup, which have striking mauve flowers.

We have always been big salad eaters, and although we cannot now recall how many looseleaf types were in our first garden (we have never planted iceberg types), there were several, and over the years we added more, plus butterheads. For the last forty years, we have always planted at least fifteen types of looseleaf lettuces and six to eight butterheads each season (Figure 18). The first looseleaf planting is in mid-May, the second three weeks later, and the third in early August. There are two butterhead plantings: the first started in May in the greenhouse, set out in early June, and the second started the same way the first week of July and set out by month's end. So we have fresh lettuce without bitterness from June well into October or November. A variety of greens such as arugula and cress as well as dill, parsleys (curly and Italian), sweet marjoram, and radishes ('Champion') are always planted nearby so when Jo Ann goes out the kitchen door to pick fresh lettuce, she returns with a full colander of delicious salad ingredients.

As with all our vegetables, we try new varieties every year, and by planting different types—two broccolis, four cabbages, and so forth—we increase the chances of success. If it's a dry summer, for instance, some will do better than others.

We shall not recommend vegetable varieties because our situation here is so special and because such preferences are largely a matter of taste, but a brief discussion of why we grow what we do may be illuminating. The question of tomato varieties, for instance, sheds light on changing tastes and their ramifications. For as long as we can remember, people have complained that store tomatoes are tasteless, and the same complaint was later made about modern garden varieties. Plant breeders were aiming for other qualities—earliness, hardiness, disease resistance, and the like—but in recent years, varieties with an added "flavor gene" have appeared, and they are certainly an improvement. The real problem is that tastes have changed over the last forty years or so. When we were young (and Jigs, who as a teenager picked tomatoes on a farm in New Jersey, remembers this clearly), true tomato flavor was quite *acidic*, and the 'Rutgers' variety, which we can't grow here, remains our favorite. In recent years, 'Beefsteak' types—large, meaty, and *sweet*—have become the standard, so we would find any modern variety, flavor genes or not, disappointing. We make do with 'Viva Italia', a fairly tasty 'Roma' type, resistant to disease so it stores well in our cold cellar, slowly ripening as late as the end of January. 'Bloody Butcher', an old variety, is tasty and ripens very early, but it's not much larger than a golf ball. 'Brandywine', another old variety with pretty good taste, is large and ripens after 'Bloody Butcher'.

Even the earliest tomatoes here will still have plenty of green fruit on the vines when frost comes, and if there hasn't been too much rain to encourage fungus troubles, they'll store well to ripen over months. In long-season areas, you could deliberately plant a late variety to insure a bountiful supply of green fruit. We don't postpone harvest until just before the first frost, because even temperatures in the mid-30s will damage tomatoes, not obviously, but the damage will show up later. When night temperatures drop below 40°F and look like they'll stay there, the end of September or beginning of October here, we harvest every single tomato, no matter how tiny. Don't delude yourself and think you can ride out a few frosts by covering the vines; the fruit will be damaged. In a good year we'll have sixty gallons of fruit, ripe, ripening, and green, to spread on trays and flats in the greenhouse. The tiny ones, none larger than an inch in diameter, are made into dill pickles (see recipe in "Kitchen Garden Sampler," page 61) at once. The rest are sorted over two or three times a week, a matter of fifteen or twenty minutes. The wholly rotten tomatoes go to chickens and turkeys, ripe ones go for eating, overripes and those with bad spots (cut out) for tomato juice or whatever else we want to make. When the temperature drops below freezing, the greenhouse no longer offers enough protection, so we move the flats down cellar and continue sorting as before. By January, all the large fruit is gone, and the little ones look pretty miserable, but by carefully excising bad spots, we've had fresh tomatoes, the last ones pale green, pinkish here and there, into February.

For green snap beans, any 'Blue Lake' variety is tasty and prolific. We have tried many peas, but our favorite remains 'Tall Telephone' (also called 'Alderman'), grown on netting to five or six feet, a seventy-five-day pea that gives us several wonderful meals over a month. Pick the overmature peas, dry them on a pan on the back of the woodstove, and use them to make Hopping Johnny in winter (see recipe section, page 62). We grow slicing cucumbers, any of the old standards like 'Marketmore', and gynoecious hybrid pickles, such as 'Salty' or 'Spartan Dawn'. We have no favorite cauliflower or broccoli, but we do avoid the old standard 'Calabrese' broccoli, which is tasteless and woody. Any of the 'Jade Cross' Brussels sprout varieties are good, tall and loaded with sprouts, but be sure to cut off the growing tops around Labor Day or you won't get any sprouts. 'Chieftain Savoy', an old cabbage variety now hard to find, is far and away the best Savoy cabbage, much better than newer varieties, large, sweet, and tender. We like it best of all our cabbages, but it won't store for long. For storage, we plant 'Albion' (green) and 'Rona Red', new varieties that store very well. We use them, cut fine, mainly for winter salads. All carrot varieties tend to be hard and tasteless, except when very small. The only one we have found that retains carrot taste in storage is 'Tendersweet', a large, coarse 'Imperator' type. Our favorite and most reliable, long-standing butterhead lettuces are the old varieties 'Tom Thumb', 'Four Seasons', and 'Little Gem', a baby romaine, but 'Sangria' and 'Sierra', new varieties, are good, too. We always plant old standard looseleaf lettuce, 'Black-Seeded Simpson', 'Salad Bowl' (red and green), 'Prizehead', 'Oak Leaf', 'Waldmann's Green', along with newer reds like 'Ruby', 'Red Sails', and 'Brunia', and every year we try several new ones. You can hardly go wrong with any loose-leaf lettuce, and a variety of colors and textures makes a much more interesting and tasty salad than one type alone. We have sampled many radishes, but the one we depend on is 'Champion', a prizewinning variety from the 1950s, big, tasty, and long-standing. We plant yellow and white 'Ebenezer' onion sets, planting the whites very close so they can be thinned for scallions. The best scallions, however, are the sprouts from Egyptian onions, a perennial we grow in the Harvest Bed, but they're only available in April and May here.

Always keep in mind that seed is the basis of every vegetable garden, so buy from a first-rate seed house. Burpee and Stokes are excellent, and now there are many good smaller specialty houses. Don't buy seed at the last minute in a hardware store, and don't be cheap; the most expensive seed is still a bargain. Finally, try some new varieties every year along with your old standards. You never know when you'll discover something better.

Kitchen Garden Sampler of Recipes

Over the forty years that we have been raising our own food—enough to feed us year-round—we have acquired favorite ways of preparing, preserving, or storing vegetables. When we lived in northern Vermont where the short season was compensated by early warming soil and rapid growth, there was never any shortage of bushels of parsley (three types) to make enormous batches of V8 juice featuring gallons of ripe tomatoes. It was there, where production was effortless, or seemed so by comparison with our struggles in Cape Breton, that we built up a solid repertoire of delicious homemade food products based on simple preservation techniques. Our success in these endeavors was driven in great part by our need to feed our own four growing children as well as the half-dozen teenage boys who lived with us as part of our farm/school tutoring program.

At harvest time, our kitchen was a veritable food factory (Figure 19), turning out ninety quarts of canned string beans, forty of corn, jar after jar of tomato products—juices, whole tomatoes, spicy catsup—and all kinds of sweet pickles. In the cellar, we stored sauerkraut and dill pickles in great crocks, carrots and potatoes and beets in large tubs. We packed sacks with dried peas and beans for winter soups and braided onions to hang from the farm kitchen rafters. We took all this knowledge of

Figure 19.
Kitchen stove at preserving time.

food handling with us when we moved to this worn-out farm to pursue what is mistakenly called the simple life. It's fortunate that we had acquired the skills of self-reliance beforehand, for in this new situation where even zucchini can't be taken for granted, these skills were refined to a high art. No matter how poor the season, we have always managed to make a lot out of a little, to make use of whatever grows and turn it to account. Having learned how to can vegetables, for instance, we have the ability to transform virtually any raw product into one with a long shelf life, and although we now have a small freezer, we prefer the flavor and keeping abilities of canned products, which if properly stored in a cool, dark place will last for years, their flavor undiminished. For best success, it helps to know which are the best varieties for canning, drying, or using fresh.

Corn

In the summers in the 1930s, when Jigs was growing up in an industrial city in New Jersey, his father would come home from work and then drive five miles into the country to Benkendorf's Farm (now covered with a highway and apartment houses), where Mr. Benkendorf would go out in the field to pick a dozen ears of 'Golden Bantam' corn for him, and when he got home, his mother would have the water boiling. Despite the many new hybrid varieties, sweeter and with longer shelf life, we still prefer 'Golden Bantam', one of the oldest (1902) open-pollinated varieties, because it is unsurpassed for its corn taste, the only corn we know that preserves that taste when canned, which is important to us. Well down in the fall, after we've slaughtered a steer, a meal of steak and canned corn, tasting as if it just came off the cob, can't be beat.

Canned Corn

Husk freshly picked corn; remove silk and wash the ears. Cut the corn from the cob (we use sharp knives or a corn cutter especially designed for the job and available where canning supplies are sold). Pack corn loosely into scalded canning jars, add 1 teaspoon salt to each quart, and cover corn with boiling water, leaving 1-inch head space. Adjust lids and follow directions for canning that come with your pressure canner.

We process quarts for 1 hour and 20 minutes at 10 pounds pressure; pints are processed for 55 minutes at 10 pounds pressure. Store sealed jars in a cool, dark place. To use corn: Add a little water to the pot if necessary, cover, then bring the corn to a boil and simmer for 10 minutes. If there's any left over (doubtful), use for corn chowder.

Dill Pickles

We learned about the dill crock from *The Wonderful World of Cooking* by E. H. Heth (Simon & Schuster, 1956). Nowadays we use a 2-gallon crock, but when the children were with us we used much larger sizes.

Place a layer of fresh dill sprigs in the bottom of the crock, add 3 or 4 peeled garlic cloves and a handful of black peppercorns (or pickling spices). Add a layer of pickling cucumbers, then a layer of dill, then cucumbers, and so on to within a couple of inches of the top. Fill crock with a brine made of 1 cup salt dissolved in 10 cups cold water with ¼ cup cider vinegar. Cover with grape leaves. Weight down with a ceramic plate. Leave it on the kitchen counter and skim off the white fermentation skin every day or so. Sample pickles after a week. Eat them right from the crock—they'll ripen day by day—then refrigerate them to halt the fermentation process. It's best to make small batches as you need them. For crisp winter dills, follow the directions below.

Canned Dill Pickles

For 10 pounds fresh green cucumbers. Wash and pack them in scalded jars (widemouthed mayonnaise jars work well), leaving them whole if possible. To each jar add 1 peeled garlic clove, 5 peppercorns, a large sprig of dill, and a small pinch of hot pepper (optional). Boil together 3 quarts water, 1 cup salt, 4 cups cider vinegar, and fill jars at once. Seal jars tight.

Canned Dill Tomatoes

Just before frost, when we strip the vines of tomatoes, we save all the tiny green ones and can them just as we do cucumber pickles. An unusual and delicious pickle.

Peas

In early fall, before the cold rains, we pull all the pea vines and sort the semidried pods by types. The overripe 'Aldermans' supply the ingredients for Hopping Johnny: The peas are soaked overnight, simmered for several hours with a piece of ham bone, then rice is added to its rich liquor and cooked until all the liquid is absorbed and the rice is tender. The green and brown Dutch soup kinds are cooked into hearty winter soups. The method for making soup from either of these peas is the same, except that the Dutch beans require longer cooking and the resulting soup is meaty flavored.

Green Pea/Dutch Brown Pea Soup

Soak peas overnight in water. A rule of thumb is to use 10 cups water to 4 cups peas. (If you forget to presoak them, you can use the quick method: Bring peas to a boil, boil for 2 minutes, let them sit for an hour, then resume cooking.) The next day, add a ham bone and a scant tablespoon of salt, then simmer until the peas are soft. Add water or saved water from cooking vegetables, as needed, stirring the soup often to make sure it doesn't get scorched on the bottom. If you don't have a bone to use, substitute a tablespoon of bacon fat or olive oil. Add chopped fresh or dried herbs an hour before the soup is finished cooking. General herbs and seasonings include curled and Italian parsley, summer savory, celery leaves, lovage, onion and garlic salt, fresh ground pepper, all to taste. Remember that it takes double the amount if fresh rather than dried herbs are used. We use dried herbs in the winter, about a teaspoon of each and the same amount of spices (easy on the garlic).

Spring Salad

We follow the old country tradition of living by the seasons, of eating fresh vegetables in the summer and preserved vegetables the rest of the year. By May, when our stored cabbages give out, we yearn for something fresh. It's too early for lettuce from the garden but not for spring dande-lions, which are rich in vitamin A and iron. For us, their main virtue is their fresh taste. By knowing just where to find them (in deep, rich soil where they are somewhat blanched and sweetened) and how to harvest them by cutting the crown from the root to leave the head intact, it doesn't take long at all to collect and prepare a salad of wild greens, with young sorrel leaves, tasty lovage sprouts, and new chives. On the rare occasion we have store-bought lettuce on hand—preferably an iceberg type and romaine, both of which last a long time in the fridge—we add that to the mix. We always have our homemade cottage cheese and the ingredients for a simple dressing of olive oil and herb vinegar to dress the salad. The flavor of fresh greens straight from the spring earth is more delicious, zestful, and refreshing than those from any fancy salad bar.

But as soon as the garden starts producing enough lettuce to thin, we begin creating serious main-course summer salad.

Summer Salad

Choose a variety of lettuces for texture and color, for instance, crunchy leaf lettuces combined with the smooth, buttery hearts of butterheads. Pull these young, as thinnings, or cut off the largest leaves in best condition.

For butterheads, cut the head below the crown when it feels firm and before it shows any signs of elongating (the first sign of bolting). We like the limey green, flushed burgundy hearts of the heirloom 'Four Seasons' (1885) and the tennis-ball baby type 'Tom Thumb'—literally all crisped delicious heart—another heirloom butterhead (1804) and one that Thomas Jefferson grew.

Pull the hearts apart, add the leaf lettuce (remove part of the lower white stem end if it's bitter), and wash all in several changes of cold water. Place leaves and hearts in a salad shaker and spin until dry (We find the Zyliss shaker with a pull string works best).

After the lettuce is dried, break up the leaves and hearts into desired sizes; we leave all but the large leaves whole since they keep better this way, so any leftover salad can be served again the following day. Put the prepared lettuce in a large wooden bowl and toss in finely cut fresh basil, salad burnet, sweet marjoram, and dill sprigs to taste. Add a handful of freshly plucked color-coordinated nasturtium flowers—sweet and peppery—but be sure to inspect these for insects first.

Serve this salad with an olive oil–vinegar dressing: ¼ cup vinegar (we like dill or purple basil vinegar) to ½ cup oil, a pressed garlic clove, and fresh ground pepper to taste. Include a crusty loaf of Italian bread and butter, side dishes of cottage cheese, sliced tomatoes, and cucumbers—a simple yet satisfying meal on a hot summer day.

Tomatoes

The glory of our vegetable garden is ripe tomatoes. As they begin to turn, we watch them eagerly every day, anxious not to miss a single one that's ready to pick. We take great care all season to prune, stake, and water them in a dry spell (otherwise they're subject to blossom end rot). Finally, by late summer the harvest begins in earnest and soon there are far too many to keep around, even eating them three times a day as we do, so we begin to process them in a variety of ways. Although we will use any ripe tomatoes, one of the best for preserving is the old-fashioned Amish variety 'Brandywine' (1885), a vigorous plant that produces hefty, luscious fruits with a tomatoey (acid) flavor.

Catsup

Homemade catsup has no resemblance to the commercial variety. It is spicy and tangy rather than sweet. We use it as the basis for Oyster Sauce with horseradish and for making a tasty meat loaf.

10 pounds ripe tomatoes

4 onions

2 sweet red peppers

1 clove garlic

¾ cup brown sugar

2-inch stick of cinnamon

1 teaspoon black peppercorns

1 teaspoon whole cloves

1 teaspoon whole allspice

1 teaspoon celery seed

2 cups cider vinegar

1 tablespoon salt

1 teaspoon paprika

¼ teaspoon cayenne

Peel and chop tomatoes, onions, and peppers, and put the ingredients into a widemouthed 2-gallon stainless steel pot (it cooks evenly). Add garlic that has been pushed through a garlic press. Cover the mixture and bring it to a boil, remove the cover, and cook until the mixture is soft, then put it through a food mill (the forty-five-year-old one we use is hand-powered and works fine). Pour the mixture back into the pot and simmer until it is reduced by half, or about 30 minutes. Add the whole spices tied up in cheesecloth (make a little bag) and cook the mixture slowly until very thick, stirring frequently with a wooden spoon to prevent scorching at the bottom. Remove the spice bag and pour the hot mixture into scalded jars and seal. Makes about 4 pints.

Garden Special

The smudged back pages devoted to canning in our treasured 1951 Fannie Farmer cookbook attest to our faithfulness to the old order, the days when putting up one's own food was taken seriously. It was there that we found this gem of a recipe (deleted from later editions), one we have followed for decades whenever we have the garden ingredients on hand. Garden Special is the basis for a wonderful Italian vegetable or minestrone soup, to which you can add whatever is on hand: a beef bone, shell beans, carrots, potatoes, a bit of leftover rice.

6 sweet peppers, green or red

1 quart diced onions

1 quart diced celery

1 quart water

4 quarts ripe tomatoes, peeled and quartered

3 tablespoons salt

2 scant tablespoons sugar

1 teaspoon pepper

Prepare all ingredients before measuring. Cook peppers, onions, and celery (the leaves as well as stalks) with water or tomato juice for 20 minutes. Add water, tomatoes, and seasonings, bring to a boil, then ladle into scalded quart or pint canning jars and process in a boiling water bath for 40 minutes (quarts) or 30 minutes (pints). Note: Once we discovered the steam canner (look for it where canning supplies are sold), we never used the old boiling water bath method again, which requires a great deal of water to cover the jars and fuel to maintain the boiling point. The steam canner method is speedy and uses just two quarts of water to maintain steam. If you use a steam canner, maintain steam for the same amount of time required for the boiling water bath.

Tomato Juice

If we had to choose just one way of preserving our surplus ripe tomatoes, this would be it. Home-canned tomato juice is a luxury item, one that brings a touch of elegance to any meal. It is also a fast, painless way to process a lot of ripe tomatoes.

Use a widemouthed 2-gallon stainless steel pot. Add washed, trimmed, but unpeeled ripe tomatoes, cut up into quarters or halves, depending on size. Don't fill the pot more than two-thirds full; add a good handful of coarsely chopped Italian parsley. Cover, bring to a boil, and simmer, stirring often to prevent sticking. When the tomatoes are soft, put the mixture through a food mill. Pour the hot juice into scalded quart or pint jars, adding 1 teaspoon of salt for quarts or ½ teaspoon for pints. Seal at once, then process in a boiling water bath or steam canner for 10 minutes.

Zucchini

No need for zucchini jokes here. A single plant of 'Greyzini', a sleek, crisp, dark-skinned type grown in a large truck tire, suffices for summer breakfasts. We pick zucchini at the tender baby stage, not more than six inches long and an inch or so around. We check the plant every day on our way back to the house after morning chores in the barn when we pass through the pasture gate to the far end of the tire garden. We keep up with the babies all summer, using one or two every morning.

Fried Baby Zucchini

Fried zucchini is part of the summer breakfast ensemble, which includes eggs, bacon, cottage cheese, and tomatoes.

In a cast iron frying pan, heat a tablespoon of olive oil until hot, add the zucchini sliced very thin, taking care not to crowd the slices in the pan; there should be only a single layer. Sprinkle them lightly with salt and fresh-ground pepper. Cover the pan, and when the slices are beginning to brown on one side, flip them over and cook them quickly until they are brown on the other side, adding a little chopped basil just before they are done. Serve at once with a saucer of freshly picked nasturtium flowers for those who like such embellishments (Jo Ann, not Jigs!).

CHAPTER FOUR

An Old-Fashioned Fruit Garden

~

ONE OF THE FEATURES THAT ATTRACTED Jigs to the farm when he first saw it was the number of old apple trees—all standards—around the house and along the lane just below the house. Ranging in age from thirty to one hundred years, some were huge, the largest we have ever seen, and all were scraggly thickets of dead limbs and unpruned, riotous growth. A neighbor whose house stood in a field with nary a flower or bush or tree in sight advised us to cut them down: "Nasty old things, dropping a mess of no-good fruit underfoot, makes the place look old-fashioned."

We kept our own counsel, and began pruning. By the spring of 1972, we had rejuvenated fourteen around the house and an equal number scattered around the farm. Nine we would use and maintain: the three along the lane (winter and late fall apples), two fall apples behind the house, three early fall apples on the east side, and one 'Russet', a winter apple, near the *Rosa gallica* hedge. These were undoubtedly purchased from the plant peddler who carried fruit trees and bushes, as well as ornamentals, from farm to farm around the island until 1940.

We eat the apples and use them in all the customary ways: jelly, sauce, baked goods, dried apples, cider. The late fall and winter apples are picked in October and stored on the front porch in four-gallon buckets, where they entice customers who come in for something else, so we sell some that way, give some to our friends, and at the time of the first hard frost, we carry the buckets down cellar for winter use.

Do not imagine that exhausts the uses of apples here. Beginning in September, we pick up the drops every day from all the trees—not just the ones we prune—to feed the pigs, and after the cows are stabled in October, we feed them a gallon of apples apiece at noon. We leave some of the apples on the trees along the lane so we can watch grosbeaks and crossbills picking at them in November and December. The drops from the inedible (so to speak) trees out back and beyond the Rose and Harvest Beds are relished by deer in January, when they scrape away the snow to get at them.

Just a few years ago that bank was an unsightly thicket of wild raspberries, thistles, burdocks, and goldenrod, densely backed by several bushy wild apple trees crowded with spiky limbs almost from the ground up. After cutting down the worst specimens, we closely pruned the two remaining, and now they are essential parts of the vista of the bank, tall, slender, and graceful, pulling up the whole bank, as it were, making a design in space that would be absent without them, nothing more than a bank of flowers tied to the earth. It is a little more difficult to define the effect on the larger landscape of several wild apple trees scattered here and there over the fields. The closest we can come to it is to say that they domesticate the far vistas of the farm with their familiar contorted forms; wild they may be, but no apple tree is so wild

Figure 19.
One of our winter apples.

that it does not remind us of home, of the dooryard and orchard. We have not landscaped these pastures and meadows, but the wild apple trees, shading the cows on hot summer noons, bearing their orange leaves to the last in November long after other trees are stripped, shaking crooked limbs against the gray skies of winter, modestly but steadfastly assert a humble beauty, a quietly pastoral background that greatly enhances the more intensely cultivated area around the house and makes the whole farm an aesthetic unity. So these gnarled trees, which a local man advised us to fell—"Scraggly old things, dropping a mess of no-good fruit all over the place, make the place look old-fashioned"—have proved to be one of our finest assets (Figure 19).

Of the five dwarf and semidwarf apples planted on the edges of the cultivated land around the house, only two survive, the 'Cortland' beyond the blackberries and the 'MacIntosh' beyond the west end of the red currants. The others succumbed in the last few years to European fruit canker, a disease that has recently appeared in Nova Scotia.

We planted four plums, four pears, and one crabapple along the lane, but they all died out except for one pear. This poorly drained soil is difficult for such trees, probably not as strong as standards, and we should have assumed they were short lived and should just have planted more trees every few years. We planted lilacs where the trees were. The cherries, sour and sweet, did well for a while, but only one sour tree remains. It was stupid to plant them near the barnyard; the cows and horses, periodically breaking down the fences, loved the poor trees to death. They should have been planted near the house.

Elderberries have been an unqualified success. They like a lot of phosphates, so we pour soapy wastewater on them regularly, manure them in the fall, and give each bush two handfuls of 0-20-20 in spring. We cut them down every few years when they get too tall and woody. Birds have spread their seeds far and wide, and now we have bushes along the lane and a beautiful big one right against the front of the barn. We use the fruit for jam, jelly, sauce, and tea. Despite the depredations of birds, we have so many bushes that we always have enough for ourselves. Even without their fruit we would value them for the way they clothe the bank, replacing what was a barren view of the house site from the lane with a distant suggestion of the leafy bowers awaiting the visitor.

Blackberries are another success, but they are rampant and must be controlled by mowing around the edges. Blueberries, after a slow start because the cows like to lean over the fence to munch on the foliage (we moved the fence twice!), now provide us with more fruit from a dozen plants than any other bush fruits, twenty-five gallons from mid-August into October. As with the blackberries, we eat them fresh, and we also make them into jam, juice, and canned fruit for winter. They get a full bushel of manure per bush in fall, and two handfuls of 6-12-12 in spring. Their foliage, shades of muted red, is a beautiful addition to the fall landscape.

We planted five plants each of red currants, black currants, and gooseberries in rows right behind each other, six feet apart each way, and there are two red currants above that planting, in a row with mint beds, as well as a hedge of six gooseberries behind the lovage bed, on the way to the smokehouse. They are all pruned in fall, but we give special attention to black currants, vigorous growers setting out runners everywhere. We heap compost around each plant in spring, add a handful of 6-12-12, and cover with newspaper or rags with sawdust on top to keep down weeds. We make jams and jellies from all three, and black currants are also very good dried, eaten like raisins or made into a tea with candied orange peel. They make a wonderful juice and a pretty fair red wine.

There was one ancient rhubarb plant here—a huge, coarse green type, not very good—but we dug up the massive root, made several divisions, and planted them at the top of the slope above the first row of currants. We don't harvest the stems but let the flowering stalks grow up (five or six feet) to form a handsome accent of creamy plumes lasting six weeks or so, behind the mint beds. From Vermont, we brought roots of our favorite rhubarb, a large, vigorous red-green variety, and in 1972 we bought roots of a pure red variety. They were all planted around the edges above the currants, in a double row beside the smokehouse, and at the top of the bank where the row of specimen roses is now. No matter how much we mulched them, weeds were always a problem. For the first few years, with about fifty plants, we produced enough for marmalade, juice, and wine, but as Jo Ann's jam business expanded, we decided to try a raised bed. We made one sixty feet long and three feet wide edged with logs, across the laneway from the vegetable beds, and despite the deep roots of rhubarb, we lined it with plastic but heaped it up with compost to more than one foot. As Figure 9 (see page 26) attests, the bed has been a great success.

Our strawberries thrived in the mid-1970s, but the soil and weed problems finally forced us to find a place for them in our raised vegetable beds, and now they're at the end of the tomato bed. For the same reasons, we made another raised bed, sixty feet long and one foot wide, behind the rhubarb, for raspberries. We eat these fruits with thick cream from our Jersey cows or make them into jam.

Although these removals certainly worked and solved our problems, we were a little sorry that we couldn't keep these fruits in scattered plantings, interspersed with other things, providing a variegated landscape to please the eye with different shapes, different flowers, and different fruits and foliage. In any place with decent soil, such scattered plantings can be maintained. We still have that landscape, but now some elements are gone, shifted to a single location, where we must be satisfied with their obviously improved health and growth.

Fruit Garden Sampler of Recipes

When Jo Ann was growing up in a Massachusetts suburb in the 1930s and 1940s, most of the fruit the family ate came straight from the brand new supermarket around the corner, and it was canned in a heavy, sweet syrup. Her most vivid memories of those years is of an entirely different experience, however: picking and eating wild raspberries along a dusty back road of rural Maine where she often spent summers as a camper. Seeing herself from a distance of more than fifty years, her hair is in pigtails, she wears a regulation green cap, a white cotton short-sleeved shirt and regulation camp shorts—green with white stripes on the sides—bobby socks, brown-and-white saddle shoes, a sweater tied around her waist. One sweaty hand clutches a brown paper-bag lunch (two peanut butter and jelly sandwiches and a large red apple), while the other reaches out greedily to pluck the irresistibly plump, sun-drenched fruits growing in profusion along the roadsides. What a revelation to a child of the suburbs who thought all fruit originated in the local Stop & Shop!

She could not have known in those long-ago summers by Little Sebago Lake that one day she and Jigs would live in the backlands of Cape Breton Island in Nova Scotia on an old-fashioned, self-reliant farm where she would master the art of turning fresh fruit into jams, jellies, sauces, fruit butters, leathers, and juices, while Jigs, who led the way in fruit preserving in the early years, still makes the wine.

APPLES

The number of apple products we make attests to the apple's hardiness and endurance over many years. In mid-June the ground around our trees is quickly covered with white blossoms. By fall, our porch is full of buckets of apples to turn into sundry products, to eat, to feed to livestock, to sell or give to friends and neighbors. Many of the old varieties we found growing on the farm are still recognizable types: 'Wolf River' for dried apples, 'Duchess' for early applesauce, 'Golden Russet' for winter eating.

Apple Cider

Jigs learned about cider in his college days, when he used to help a farmer make hay, and afterward the man would draw a big pitcher of pale gold cider from a barrel in the cellar and they would sit on a bench under an apple tree in the gloaming and talk about the hay and the weather and cows, drinking the cider, and Jigs would say, "Boy, this is good!" and have another glass. But cider is more potent than it seems, and his bike used to wobble strangely on his way home.

When we lived in Vermont, we used to haul a three-quarter-ton truck full of bags of apples to Jim Kempton's old red mill in South Northfield, Vermont, where we'd spend the day grinding and pressing the apples into four barrels of juice that we'd take home, roll into our huge cellar (twelve feet from floor to ceiling) and up onto their sides in racks. Drilling a one-quarter-inch hole through each bung, we'd insert a plastic tube and put the other end into a glass of water, so CO_2 could escape but air couldn't enter. One barrel was for vinegar. The other three were tapped in turn, a wooden spigot inserted, and we were ready to drink what was at first apple juice—great with Jigs's buttermilk doughnuts— gradually fermenting to become cider. A year later, we'd be drinking the last barrel, the cider then a clear dry wine with a faint but unmistakable apple flavor. Any sound apples would do, the sweeter the better. 'Baldwins' were traditional in New England but 'Russets' are best.

Dried Apples

Peel and core large apples. Slice thinly across the core so you wind up with circles with a hole in the middle. You may string them on sticks, not touching, and suspend them over the woodstove, or thread them on strings, or spread them on cookie sheets placed in a gas-stove oven with the pilot light on, or put them on screens in the sun with cheesecloth over and under them. When they are quite dry and leathery, store loosely in jars. A very nice snack.

Apple Ginger

This is a very old recipe that we have never seen duplicated. Apple Ginger is a translucent, amber, jellylike preserve with tiny, suspended pieces of crystallized ginger throughout. It is extraordinarily versatile—spread on toast, muffins, or biscuits like an ordinary jam or jelly, used as a condiment with pork dishes, as a glaze for roast chicken, or as an out-of-this-world topping for the best vanilla ice cream. If you are using homegrown apples, make this early in the season while they are still hard and firm.

3 pounds green apples (for pectin)
mixed with red for color
Sugar
½ pound crystallized ginger
(a little less if you want a less potent flavor)

Pare and core apples; cut apples into small pieces and put aside. Place parings and cores only in a widemouthed 2-gallon stainless steel pot. Cover with water and simmer, covered, until the apples are soft, stirring occasionally. Strain. Measure juice and pour it back into the rinsed pot. Stir in 1 cup sugar for every 1½ cups juice. Stir in cut-up apples and 4 more cups sugar. Stir in crystallized ginger. Simmer, uncovered, until thick, stirring as necessary. Remove Apple Ginger from heat. Pour into scalded jelly jars and seal at once.

Apple Leather

Not one bit of apple (or any fruit or vegetable for that matter) ever need go to waste once you have mastered the art of making leathers. In the fall, Jo Ann can turn bushels of fruit into a delicious, natural confection. Any fruit can be used—soft or hard fruits, leftovers, odd bits and pieces at the end of the season. This is a good way to use fruit too good to discard but unsuitable for using in jams or jellies. While all sorts of combinations are possible—raspberry and strawberry; red currant and gooseberry; apple and cranberry—our favorite remains plain apple leather. The result is a pliable reddish-brown, somewhat glossy sheet, the color and texture of real leather, with an intensely sweet flavor, the essence of apple.

Cut up any amount of apples. No need to skin or core, but trim out any bad spots. Place them in a 2-gallon stainless steel pot, add a little water to prevent scorching, then cover, bring to a boil, stirring often. Uncover and simmer until the apples are soft. Put the mixture through a food mill. Spread the pulp thinly on cookie sheets lined with one layer of heavy plastic freezer wrap. Set pans in the sun, or in a just-warm oven (not over 150°F), or on top of a woodstove. Turn fruit when it can be lifted off the plastic without falling apart; it should be barely sticky to the touch and still pliable. Remove plastic and dry the other side of the leather. Roll up finished leather in fresh plastic and store in jars or well-covered containers. To use: Unroll and cut off pieces with kitchen scissors. If dried properly, leathers will keep indefinitely.

Apple Sweetmeats

After Jo Ann created this chunky applesauce adapted from Ella Shannon Bowles and Dorothy S. Towle's *Secrets of New England Cooking*, there was no going back to conventional applesauce. Use a large, hard apple with some red coloring.

3 cups sugar

1 quart water

5 pounds unpeeled apple slices

Cinnamon

In a 2-gallon stainless steel pot, combine sugar and water, stirring to dissolve sugar. Bring to a boil, drop in apples, bring to the boiling point, and simmer until the apples are just soft. Remove pot from heat, add cinnamon to taste. Ladle sweetmeats into scalded canning jars, leaving $\frac{1}{2}$ -inch headspace. Tighten lids and process jars in a boiling water bath or steam canner for 10 minutes.

BLACK CURRANTS

In *Fruits for the Home Garden*, the great American horticulturalist U. P. Hedrick lamented the absence of black currants from American gardens: "The black currant, so greatly prized in all other northern countries, is hardly known on this side of the Atlantic." This is not surprising, considering that during the 1920s black currants were banned from cultivation across the United States because, as a carrier for white pine blister-rust fungus, they posed a threat to commercially valuable white pine plantations (the fungus does little damage to the black currant itself). With the development of fungus-resistant white pine cultivars, as well as the decline of the white pine lumber industry, black currants are once more being grown in the United States.

We knew nothing about them when we ordered six bushes of the rust-resistant cultivar 'Consort' shortly after we'd moved to the farm. We grew them mainly because Jigs had always been interested in them, and they did grow into beautiful, arching shrubs covered with little greenish-white blooms at the same time as the tall wild shadberry tree in the rough pasture below them. But we were not prepared for the enormous harvest. Without a freezer then and with no recipes that dealt specifically with black currants, Jo Ann adapted and invented her own black currant repertoire.

Dried Black Currants

Layer ripe black currants in a large preserving pot, adding 1 cup of sugar for every 3 cups of berries, and let sit overnight. In the morning, bring the resulting fruit and juice to a boil. Reduce the heat, and stirring occasionally to make sure the berries don't stick to the bottom of the pot, simmer gently for 15 minutes. Strain the berries, reserving the juice (to be used in next recipe). Spread the berries on brown paper-lined pans and set them in a sunny spot to dry, stirring the berries—now quasi-raisins—so they don't stick together. Change the paper after the first day. Drying may take several days, depending on conditions. Use these dried currants as you would raisins: to eat out of hand, to add to bread and cake dough, or to flavor tea. Store in a covered container in a cool, dark place, where they will keep indefinitely.

Black Currant Juice

Bring the strained and reserved currant juice, now a thick syrup, to a boil and cook for 5 minutes. Pour into scalded canning jars and seal at once or freeze in plastic containers. To serve as juice, dilute the syrup using 3 parts water to 1 part juice (we usually make up 1 gallon of juice at a time by mixing 1 quart of syrup with 3 quarts water). This is a great breakfast juice high in vitamin C (the British call it Ribena) or the base for sorbet.

Black Currant Sorbet

This is a beautiful rosy pink color, elegant to the eye and delightfully cooling on a hot summer day. For a special dessert, serve in parfait glasses, alternating layers with pieces of angel food cake, top with whipped cream, then embellish each glass with a striped, mauve-pink 'Zebrina' mallow flower. For such specialized frozen-fruit dishes, we use a small electric ice-cream maker rather than our 6-quart vintage hand-powered White Mountain Freezer.

2 cups black currant juice

1 cup water

2 cups sugar

Premix juice, water, and sugar, then freeze according to manufacturer's directions for an electric ice-cream/frozen yogurt maker. Ours uses 9 cups of crushed ice and table salt.

Black Currant–Orange Tea

This is our favorite non-caffeine beverage. Fill a covered quart container with a mix of dried black currants and candied orange peel cut into small pieces. For one cup tea: Place 1–2 teaspoons of the mixture into a teacup, pour boiling water over, and let steep—covered with a saucer to keep hot—until it is well colored (about tea color). No sweetener is needed.

RED CURRANTS

Like black currants, red currants are attractive arching shrubs, most beautiful when they are adorned with clusters of small, translucent red berries. These, too, are rich in pectin and vitamin C, but too tart to eat out of hand. When combined with sugar—not enough to mask their flavor—red currants make superb jellies, jams, and pancake sauce.

Bar-le-Duc Red Currant Jelly

This is neither a true jelly nor the authentic Bar-le-Duc, named after a city in France. In the original version, the seeds of each berry are removed before being made into a concoction that is a cross between a jam and a jelly. In our version, the seeds are left in, but as in the real thing, whole berries are suspended in jellied juice. Use on toast or as a condiment with meat.

1 quart red currants without stems
(mainly ripe, with some underripe)
⅓ cup water
2 cups sugar

In a 2-gallon widemouthed preserving pot, combine red currants and water. Cover and simmer until berries are just tender but still whole.

Stir in sugar. Stirring gently, cook at a rolling boil, uncovered, until a small amount of the mixture sheets off a spoon. Remove jelly from heat, let boiling subside, and skim off foam. Then pour the jelly into hot, sterilized jelly jars and seal at once. Makes 1½–2 pints.

BLUEBERRIES

Our highbush blueberry hedge is ornamental throughout the growing season, from the first little white bell-flower clusters to scarlet foliage in the fall. But nothing is more beautiful than the bushes in full fruit, so heavily laden with enormous berries (don't believe that cultivated blueberries aren't tasty) that the branches bend toward the ground.

Blueberry Frozen Yogurt

Blueberry Frozen Yogurt has a delicious tangy flavor. We use our homemade yogurt and it works fine.

1 cup fresh or frozen blueberries

1 cup sugar

1 quart plain yogurt

Place blueberries and sugar in a blender and process at medium speed until smooth (flecks of blue are o.k.). Freeze in an electric ice-cream/frozen yogurt maker according to the manufacturer's directions.

Blueberry Preserves

After we have satisfied ourselves with fresh blueberries and sour cream, blueberry muffins, and blueberry jams, Jo Ann makes this delicious thick sauce. We mix this with Apple Sweetmeats for winter or spring lunch.

Blueberries

Sugar

In a large preserving pot, combine blueberries and sugar, using ¼ to ½ cup sugar to each quart of blueberries. Bring to a boil, stirring frequently to prevent sticking. Remove preserves from heat. Ladle fruit into scalded canning jars, leaving ½-inch headspace, tighten lids, and process jars for 10 minutes in a boiling water bath or steam canner.

Elderberries

The native elderberry is an easily grown, attractive shrub with long, arching green-leaved stems that give it a vaselike shape. By midsummer, when the gooseberries begin to ripen, elderberries produce quantities of sweetly fragrant, saucer-shaped creamy umbels referred to as elder blow. From the "blow" we make *Elderflower Pancakes:* Substitute a cup of freshly picked florets for a cup of flour in your favorite pancake recipe and discover how light pancakes can be (it helps to use buttermilk for the liquid). For *Elderflower-Mint Tea* (an old cold remedy): Steep a teaspoon or two of dried flowers and mint in 1 cup boiling water. If for a cold, be sure to add lots of lemon and honey.

Elderberry Jelly

This is one of our favorite jellies, adapted from a recipe called Venison Jelly that used wild grapes. It's delicious with cream cheese or as a condiment with beef or venison. Since the fruit is low in pectin, use high-pectin crabapples to ensure a firm set.

6 pounds crabapples

4 quarts ripe elderberries

1 quart apple cider vinegar

1 quart water

¼ cup stick cinnamon

¼ cup whole cloves

Sugar

Put whole crabapples in a large preserving pot with the elderberries, vinegar, water, and spices. Simmer, covered, until the fruit is soft, stirring as needed. Mash fruit. Strain mixture through a jelly bag (we use doubled cheesecloth, suspended so the liquid drains into a pot underneath). Let drip for several hours or overnight. Measure juice and cook 4 cups at a time in a 2-gallon widemouthed stainless steel pot, uncovered. Stir in 1 cup sugar for each 1 cup juice and bring mixture to a rapid boil. Continue boiling for about 10 minutes or until a small amount of liquid sheets off a metal spoon. Pour into scalded jelly jars and seal at once. Makes about 4½ pints.

RHUBARB

Rhubarb is the first fruit (actually vegetable) of the growing season, and we eagerly anticipate pulling—never cutting—the first thick, juicy stems for stewing. Once production is in top form, we pick stems every few days to eat cooked and processed in a variety of ways.

Rhubarb Juice

Make this at the end of the rhubarb season when stalks become too tough and stringy for any other purpose.

5 pounds rhubarb, mixed green and red types

2 lemons

2 oranges

3 quarts water

3 cups sugar

Cut rhubarb into 1-inch pieces, cut up oranges and lemons, skin and all, and place fruit in a large preserving pot with 3 quarts water. Cover and simmer until fruit is soft. Strain through a cheesecloth jelly bag and let drip for several hours or overnight. Bring juice to a boil, covered, stir in sugar, then bring mixture to a boil again and cook for 5 minutes. Remove juice from heat, pour into scalded canning jars, leaving $1/2$-inch headspace. Tighten lids and process for 10 minutes in a boiling water bath or steam canner.

Summer Punch

This is wonderful on a hot summer day.

2 cups cold tea

$3/4$ cup rhubarb juice

$1/4$ cup lemon balm/mint juice

(extracted from a handful each of the fresh herb, prepared by steeping as for regular tea in a quart teapot)

1½ tablespoons fresh lemon juice

Combine in a pitcher, then pour over ice cubes in individual tall glasses. Add a sprig of fresh peppermint to each glass.

Rhubarb Marmalade

Jigs first made this when we were searching for ways to preserve a large rhubarb patch. The treasured recipe is adapted from the first edition (1896) of the *Boston Cooking-School Cook Book* by Fannie Merritt Farmer: ". . . all that has life requires nourishment." We love this incomparable marmalade on our homemade English muffins.

8 juicy oranges
5 pounds rhubarb, a mix of green and red, cut into ½-inch pieces
4 pounds sugar

Make thin cuts in orange skin, in quarters, and remove peel; set peel aside. Divide oranges into sections, remove seeds, cut sections into small pieces, and place them in a 2-gallon widemouthed stainless steel pot with the cut-up rhubarb; cover and boil for 30 minutes, being sure to stir mixture from the bottom to prevent scorching. Stir in sugar and prepared peel (see below), and simmer for about 2 hours or until mixture thickens. Pour into jelly jars, tighten lids, and process for 5 minutes in a boiling water bath or steam canner.

To prepare peel: Boil quartered skins in cold water to cover until they are tender. Drain, cool, then scrape off white pith; cut the remaining skins into very small pieces.

STRAWBERRIES

It might seem unnecessary to describe how to prepare strawberries and cream, but in our experience modern cooks don't always know how to handle fruit to bring out its best flavor.

A Dish of Strawberries

We are aficionados of this classic dish and have put a lot of thought and care (though not much work) into its preparation. You can, of course, buy different kinds of cream—sweet, whipping, sour—but if you're lucky enough to own a Jersey cream cow, you can make your own first-rate products, especially Devonshire, or clotted, cream.

Strawberries should be dead ripe and at room temperature. Hull and cut up into bite-size pieces. Sprinkle with a little sugar, cover, and let stand at room temperature for an hour to draw out juices. For those who feel comfortable violating the genre, a little ripe kiwi fruit adds appeal (mainly color and texture). Top with cream.

The World's Best Strawberry Jam

Discovering the secret of making this jam without commercial pectin and with a minimum of sugar propelled Jo Ann into a small-scale jam and jelly business specializing in high-quality products that rely on the fruit's natural pectin. Use a mixture of ripe and underripe fruit, and cook it in small batches. This is a chunky jam with a great strawberry flavor.

4 cups prepared strawberries

$2\frac{1}{4}$ cups sugar

Figure 20A.
Preserving strawberries.

In a 2-gallon widemouthed stainless steel pot, cover and heat berries, mashing them (not overzealously) as they heat. Stir in sugar, bring mixture to a rolling boil, turn the heat down a little, and continue cooking for about 15 minutes or until the mixture thickens and begins to cling to the bottom of the pot (don't overcook!). Remove jam from the heat and let it subside. Stir, skimming the froth if desired (only for cosmetic reasons), then pour into scalded jelly jars and seal at once (Figures 20A and 20B).

FRUIT WINES

We've made lots of different wines over the years, but our favorites, the only ones we make today, are rhubarb and black currant. The first is sweet, the second makes a moderately dry red wine that we drink with our Friday evening Sabbath meal.

—

Figure 20B.
Stored preserves.

Rhubarb Wine

Wash 10 pounds of rhubarb stalks (end-of-season tough ones are o.k.) and cut into 1-inch pieces. Slice 2 lemons into small pieces. Dump into a crock, add 2 gallons of boiling water. Cover and let stand for 3 days. Strain through cheesecloth into another crock and stir in 4 pounds of white sugar. Add 2 tablespoons baker's or wine yeast. Cover and let stand at room temperature until vigorous fermentation subsides. Siphon into gallon glass jugs, leaving sediment behind. Plug jugs with cotton. Repeat in a month. When all fermentation ceases (no more bubbles at the surface), siphon into bottles and cap or cork. This is a great summer wine served over ice.

Black Currant Wine

Wash 6 pounds of ripe currants and crush with a masher in a crock. Add 7 quarts water, stir thoroughly, cover. The next day, strain into another crock, add 5 pounds white sugar, stir well to dissolve. Add 2 tablespoons yeast, cover, let stand at room temperature until vigorous fermentation subsides. Siphon into gallon glass jugs, leaving sediment behind, plug with cotton, and let stand away from direct sunlight. Repeat the siphon process in a month. Finally, siphon into bottles when all bubbling ceases.

If we're short on currants, we heat them in water, mash frequently, strain off the juice, and submit the pulp to the same treatment again, even a third time. Then we measure all the juice, and for every gallon, we use 3 pounds of sugar and 1 tablespoon yeast. You may vary the sugar a bit—a half-pound either way—depending on your taste. This is a good cooking wine, too. ⬬

CHAPTER FIVE

The Flowering Herb Garden

~

THE FIRST SUMMER ON THE FARM, folks came by in their pickups just to see what "the rich Americans" were up to. They parked in the driveway, we invited them in to tea (the custom), they left. Angus, however, only had to walk up the road from just below our mailbox where he lived on a relative's rundown farm. Known for never having done a lick of work in his life (he lived by his wits), he seemed fascinated by our labors, especially Jo Ann's—a woman single-mindedly at work among rocks and debris under an old apple tree who claimed she was making a flower garden.

By this time, Angus was used to our ways and as long as he knew we'd invite him in for tea and bread and molasses, anything we did was fine with him. Now, when the garden is in full bloom in late June, alive with butterflies sipping nectar from hundreds of colorful flowers, we remember that day in early summer when the farm looked so different, when Angus, long dead these many years, made himself comfortable on a big, round rock, surveyed the bleak landscape around him, and shook his head in wonder at our activities.

However improbable it looked, this was an excellent site for a flower garden. South facing, it occupies a prominent piece of ground close to the house and almost directly opposite the top of the lane, from whence the visitor's gaze first encompasses the farm panorama—house, barn, fields, and orchards. Once we cleared most of the rocks except those too large to haul away, we discovered that the earth beneath was deep, dark, and humusy, the best soil on the entire farm, softened by the rock pile and years of decayed vegetation. The area was roughly circular in shape (the equivalent of about 500 square feet) with an old apple tree toward the back that provided an otherwise sunny site with shady growing conditions, too (Figure 21). Thus, the range of plants that could

Figure 21.
The evolving Flowering Herb Garden.

be grown here encompassed all types, from those needing full sun to those that prefer partial shade in varying degrees.

The problem was we had no idea what to grow or what was suitable to the site and climate. But more than that, we had no idea how to go about it—we lacked the knowledge necessary to successfully raise a variety of plants from seed or to grow them from root (our previous experience had been confined largely to growing vegetables and a few herbs), and we knew nothing about what it takes to maintain perennial plants in healthy condition from one growing season to the next. Nor did we know anything important about soil, because in our previous experiences, things just grew when you planted them in the loamy, Vermont ground. Jo Ann had a vague idea of a flowery scene, of tall, swaying delphiniums, lilies, perhaps a rose, but that's as far as our plan went, a garden in the mind's eye. The sort of practical information we needed—not readily available in those days—was (and still is) largely confined to ideal conditions. Without practical know-how or anyone to teach us, we were destined to learn by trial and error.

When the land was cleared of rocks and debris, we sowed annuals. They germinated well on ground that had lain fallow for many years, and soon cosmos, poppies, and bachelor's button waved gaily in the wind and cheered us on as we rebuilt the barn, cut posts and rails for fences, cleared spruce from old pastures. We sowed seed for perennials, too, but little was seen of them that summer.

The following spring, after our first experience of fearsome maritime winds and ice (rather than snow) underfoot, we surveyed our new flower garden. The only plants that had survived were some of Jigs's curious herbs that Jo Ann had parked there temporarily until she found a suitable place to grow them. All our previous experience with herbs had led us to believe there were two types: the culinary ones such as parsleys, marjoram, thyme, and basil, and others that were literary, the sort Jigs, former English teacher, had grown in Vermont for their literary associations, plants with lovely names like elecampane, pennyroyal, and angelica. We had always planted the culinary herbs in rows in the vegetable garden, a practice we expected to continue in Cape Breton (until we discovered germination in clay soil was poor and erratic and different techniques were needed for doing what we had always taken for granted). The literary types had enjoyed benign neglect in our Vermont home. Although we had enjoyed seeing bright calendulas by the kitchen door, had admired the six-foot stately angelica (we learned to candy its young stems for a digestive, like after-dinner mints), our interest was not greatly aroused. We had not yet developed a sensitivity to the landscape of our daily lives, perhaps because we had never lived long enough in one place.

But now in their new formidable home on cold clay ground, where nothing else had survived, the literary herbs assumed a new importance as possible candidates for our dream garden of all flowers. All of them, we noticed, did produce rather pretty blooms, varied in color and form, with what for us was the added bonus of aroma and attraction to bees, butterflies, and hummingbirds. We became aficionados of these Old World herbs (for that's what they were), from parts of Europe where they grew in heavy, moist soil and a cool climate similar to ours. Plants such as lungwort, chives, blue comfrey (*Symphytum caucasicum*), sweet cicely, and sweet rocket (*Hesperis matronalis*) proved so satisfying for their toughness and beauty that we have used them freely throughout the landscape.

But there were other problems associated with our choice of ornamentals, or rather with the plants that chose to stay with us. They were by nature vigorous, especially given their preferred habitat. Some not only thrived, they threatened to overtake the entire planting. We were on the right track, but we still had much to learn. Tansy, for instance, produces attractive yellow button flowers in late summer over finely cut, dark green aromatic leaves, a handsome plant if you have a football field to grow it in. The three pretty seedlings Jo Ann fondly planted in a corner of this garden soon had to be uprooted and the whole area searched for bits of root that might live to creep on and on.

Gradually we learned to cope with the phenomenon of vigor once we understood there are degrees, and that some plants are easier to accommodate than others. We managed by reducing some plants every year (blue comfrey, Roman wormwood), or restraining them in some way (sweet woodruff and Geranium 'Johnson's Blue' are grown inside heavy iron rims), or banishing them altogether, like tansy. An early planting of double soapwort (*Saponaria officinalis* 'Rosea Plena'), valued for its late summer bloom and sweet evening scent, should have been removed, but after trying unsuccessfully for several years to kill it (Roundup did not touch it), we accepted its presence and learned to chop out extra roots every spring. Beware what you put in the ground, for it may stick around even without your permission.

The ability of our Old World herby types to survive is astonishing. Blue comfrey, a plant that will grow in sun or shade if the soil is moist, a mass of blue trumpets for almost a month beginning in June, and a great attractor for hummingbirds, was once charged and reduced to a pulpy heap by our resident bull who had gotten loose (Figure 22). It

Figure 22.
Bull charging blue comfrey.

was crushed under broken limbs from the old apple tree during a fall storm, and in a planting at the end of our lane, it was rolled over by the enormous wheels of a pulp truck. It has always returned refreshed from these episodes, its beauty and vigor undimmed.

Aside from learning how to deal with the vigor of plants that were only too happy at the site, there was the odd shape of the garden itself. Fortunately, we were so ignorant about basic garden design that we didn't realize an island bed (as it is known), would be more difficult to fill success-fully than a standard border, where something—a wall, fence, or shrubs—affords a convenient way to rank plants by height (not rigidly, of course), with taller types generally in the back and shorter ones up front.

In a island bed cut into the grass, where the planting can be seen from all sides, the general rule is to place taller types in the center, with plants of decreasing height toward its edges. Our irregular circle with its apple tree off to one side didn't conform to the standard, but since we weren't aware of the convention, we arranged the plants according to what appeared most aesthetically effective. We should say, we moved the plants around until we liked where they were. The "move-its" afflicts most serious gardeners and should not be a source of shame. It's nice if you can get it right the first time, but few of us can manage to do this with every planting. There are bound to be mistakes of judgment since gardeners are dealing with many different types of plants whose growth varies according to growing conditions. Some plants will grow taller and wider than expected, for instance, and in this case, may be in the wrong place.

The most innovative step, prescribed by the practical need to raise the planting above the level of shaggy grass (this was when Jigs cut the lawn only occasionally with a horse-drawn mower rather than a small power mower as he does now), was to edge the entire circle with lungwort (*Pulmonaria officinalis*). (See Figure 23, on page 100.) A low plant with spotted leaves and clusters of little pink and blue trumpets, it is easily grown in moist soil in either sun or shade. Called "hundreds-and-thousands" for very good reason, it spreads fast by rhizomatous roots, so we soon established a thick hedge that effectively created a living frame for the garden during the whole season, first with its mass of flowers in the spring, followed by its attractive spotted leaves. Weeds, we found, had little chance to enter the garden.

Over the course of thirty years many plants—herbs and flowers— have come and gone at this site because they weren't reliably hardy (*Agastache*, now grown as an annual) or drainage was poor (hyssop, clary sage, lavender). We gradually included more flowers among the herbs— daylilies, astilbe—as well as hostas and hardy roses (we were thrilled to

Figure 23.
Lungwort hedge in spring.

discover that many thrive in heavy soil). A few annuals—all herby types—proved successful at the fringes of the circle, among them nicotianas, calendulas, borage, nasturtium, violas, and painted sage or annual clary (*Salvia viridis*). Once planted, annual poppies (*Papaver somniferum*) have sown themselves from year to year and are always delightful when they appear, as if by magic, in shades of raspberry, watermelon, peach, and mauve.

After several years, we enlarged the Flowering Herb Garden without digging by laying down a large sheet of plastic over the new area in the fall to kill weeds and soften the sod; rain-soaked phone books held the plastic in place against wind. The following spring, after the plastic was removed, the new area was thickly covered with composted barn manure and planted with annuals (the soil wasn't ready for deeper-rooted perennials). A winding path from back to front of the circle was laid out with plastic grain bags, then the bags were covered with sawdust—an instant no-dig path. The need to enlarge the garden and add a path to tend it led to a new way of regarding the circular space, now broken up into two curving borders running from shade to sun that fit together like pieces of a puzzle. Irregularities created bays to feature tall, striking accents near the outer edges of the circle—the handsome white-flowered 'Henry Hudson' rose, three feet tall and three feet wide, with a mound of Geranium 'Johnson's Blue' at its feet. This taught us the value of accents in the surrounding landscape, where a single plant or a simple combination can create stunning effects at a distance. In many ways, this first ornamental garden was our teacher, showing us effective ways to grow plants in a variety of situations.

As we developed this garden, its surroundings came under scrutiny. Two nearby plantings, another island planting we call the Tulip Bed (formerly the site of an old coal shed) for tulips, phlox, lilies, and peonies, and a dooryard garden enhanced the general area, forming a continuous attractive link between house and barn along a path that winds behind the two island beds through the old apple orchard, then passes between the back of the vegetable tire garden and the top of the wildflower bank through a gate into the barn pasture. Our daily trips to the barn assumed a new and different dimension as we became aware of each new bloom, each fresh scent and aroma.

By late spring clumps of emerging herbs and flowers in assorted greens from dark to lime (daylilies) or crimson (peonies) interspersed with vivid red and yellow tulips (from twenty-five-year-old plantings) fill the Flowering Herb Garden and adjacent Tulip Bed, both now outlined by an undulating mass of azure-blue lungwort—eighteen inches wide and one foot high—one roughly circular in form, the other rectangular. The effect is spectacular, especially since these plantings and the naturalized daffodils along the lane contribute the only spring color in an all-green landscape.

Early bloom in the Flowering Herb Garden is special for the perfect harmony, as if by design, of its pastel-dominated color scheme in the soft pinks, lilac, and rosy mauve of bistort, columbines, and sweet rocket, the whites of sweet woodruff, sweet cicely, and white chives, the mixed blues of mountain bluet, 'Johnson's Blue' geranium, and Jacob's ladder, the light chartreuse of lady's mantle, and the sky blue forget-me-nots that thread their way throughout the garden in sun and shade (Figure 24). We say "as if by design," for we cannot take credit for knowing in advance that what we planted would create such a pleasing picture. Many of the plants of this season are pastels, so almost any combination will produce appealing results.

By mid-June the air surrounding the Flowering Herb Garden is sweet with thousands of apple blossoms falling like snow on the ground, mingling with the honeyed aroma of spring herbs in bloom. Soon the garden is alive with yellow swallowtail and little orange butterflies, with bees, with a variety of flying insects and hummingbirds, all gathering nectar from a former rock pile! This first flower garden taught us important lessons about creating a successful perennial garden, one that offers bloom mixed with attractive foliage throughout the season. Through trial and error, we found that the most satisfying arrangement of plants—whether in an island bed, a traditional border, or whatever the design—is multistoried, with taller plants a backdrop for shorter types, but irregularly planted so that tall accents appear among shorter ones, where each plant is seen to advantage as part of a complementary and varied group in a fluid and flowing layered tapestry of varied forms, textures, and colors. A planting consisting solely of mounded forms of the same height with similar foliage would be boring, but mounded forms

—

Figure 24.
Early bloom in the Flowering Herb Garden
(front to back): lungwort, white chives, Geranium *'Johnson's Blue',*
bistort, sweet rocket, Oriental poppy.

combined with contrasting types—arching or straight—of differing height and girth, create more interest in each plant and in the picture as a whole. This knowledge has proved invaluable in all our landscaping.

While we did not design with color in mind—our need was to match plants to habitat—we observed the mediating influence of neutral pastels, whites, greens, silver, and grays among plants of vivid and clashing colors—bright reds, fuchsia, purples, orange. We saw, for instance, that flamboyant red-orange Oriental poppies when rising through a drift of soft pink bistort and a sea of lilac sweet rocket are not out of place, even when rich pink and rose Russell lupines are added to the mix. These early lessons in color, like those in design, made us conscious of combinations elsewhere in the landscape. Later, with more experience, we would experiment with the bright reds, oranges, yellows, and purples of late summer and fall, but we remembered the lessons the plants themselves had taught us about moderating effects. By depending on herbs for much of our bloom, we fell into a ready-made palette of harmonious colors and, where needed for a change, pleasing contrasts. Too bland a diet can be boring.

As it matured, the Flowering Herb Garden became easier to maintain (a good thing as the gardener ages). In early spring we renew the sawdust path and prune the three shrub roses just to maintain shape and remove dead and crossed branches. By early June, we cut the undulating borders of lungwort back to the ground with a brush hook to encourage the regrowth of fresh, spotted foliage, and we pull out the drifts of blowsy forget-me-nots throughout the garden (it resows readily).

It is very important to cut back each plant after it has bloomed to induce fresh foliage, not only because plants have a better chance of reblooming but because foliage forms in themselves are an important asset in the overall planting. Sweet cicely may only bloom for two weeks in late spring, but if cut back before the white umbels produce seeds, the plant is quickly transformed into an attractive mound of ferny foliage all summer. In time of drought, it is especially important to cut back plants immediately after flowering so they reserve energy for maintaining growth. To avoid staking and to keep plants within bounds, some, like white mugwort (*Artemisia lactiflora*), are cut back in early summer to reduce height and create a bushier, self-sustaining plant (white mugwort is "dwarfed" to three and one-half to four feet from five feet). Finally, cutting back plants after they have bloomed gives neighboring plants the extra room they need to spread out and take center stage. Some late bloomers like garlic chives and sedum are left in their natural state for their attractive seed and flower heads, while others are trimmed after blooming but left with "arms" or stems to catch snow for winter protection.

In winter, we cover the area with a thick protective mulch of horse manure, then with a sawdust or wood chip cover. In the spring after plants are growing again, this is worked into the soil with a light dusting of fertilizer, usually 6-12-12 to add phosphates and potash for good root and bud formation. Plants are divided and moved or new plants added in the spring or fall, depending on their bloom time: Spring bloomers are moved or divided in the fall, late bloomers in the spring, when a half-cup of bonemeal is added to the planting hole. As for weeds, there are virtually none, since the herbaceous border shades them out.

The pretty garden we see today has been a long time in the making. It should be clear from this account that our style is not to install an instantly perfect ornamental garden—is it ever really possible?—but to let it evolve naturally, dictated by the shape of the land and the possibilities it suggests, by the soil and site, and by our needs and desires as they develop and change over time. In this way we have acquired the sort of broad knowledge that comes from direct, intimate experience with every detail of garden making, from failures as well as triumphs. For us, this is the most satisfying way to garden.

Over time as the area has developed, the Flowering Herb Garden has become much more than a single feature, the garden of all flowers we had first envisioned. It has become an integral part of the layered tapestry of the farm panorama as it is seen against a background of varied shapes, forms, textures, and colors from other gardens, buildings, trees, lawns, pastures, barn, and hayfield beyond.

Sampler of Early Season Herbs & Flowers

Creating gardens that carry on beautifully from spring through fall is a continuing and absorbing challenge, the work of a lifetime. We have observed that however successful we are in our efforts, each garden has its special moment, determined by the community of plants that flourish in a specific habitat at certain times of the growing season. That time in the Flowering Herb Garden is during the relatively cool temperatures of spring through early summer when it is dominated by light woodland and meadow plants, many of them scented and in the pastel range, that thrive in the garden's deep, humusy soil. During this season several (marked with an asterisk) will grow equally well in sun or shade *as long as the soil is evenly moist.* Think about how you may grow these herbs and flowers in your own landscape, bearing in mind their extended uses in cottage garden settings and for naturalizing (most of the herbs here are cottage garden favorites). Except where noted, these are all perennials hardy to Zone 4.

Late Spring to Early Summer (late May to June here)

Alchemilla mollis, **lady's mantle,** 12–18 in. The genus name "alchemilla" means "little magical one" and may refer to the beneficial properties once associated with drops of water that gather in the folds of the plant's pleated leaves. Flowers are tiny, held in chartreuse-colored sprays that last for more than a month; we cut clusters to use in dried bouquets and pressed-flower cards (in the language of flowers, lady's mantle means "comfort"). We grow lady's mantle here in dappled shade as a medium-tall hedge to line a path. Elsewhere, it spills over rocks in sun or spreads out under trees as a naturalized ground cover.

Allium moly, **golden garlic,** 8–12 in., sun. Once regarded as a good-luck charm, this floral talisman of prosperity sends up yellow star flowers in loose clusters through a lacy mound of Roman wormwood (*Artemisia pontica*) near the entrance to the garden. After it blooms, the plant dies back and we forget it was ever there until late June the following season. Plant bulbs close together in clumps for best effect, and where space permits, allow it to naturalize.

Allium schoenoprasum, **chives,** 12 in., sun. We grow the white-flowered variant here and the familiar mauve in the Harvest Bed (and naturalize both together in a wet meadow). The white flowers, a little dull in color, are most beautiful in swelling bud against Geranium 'Johnson's Blue'. In rich soil, chives need dividing every two or three years; leaves and flowers can be used for flavoring the same as mauve chives.

Aquilegia vulgaris, **columbine,** 2½ ft. All columbines in this garden are descended from hand-me-down roots or seeds of old-fashioned "granny's bonnet," ranging from single to double types atop slender stems in colors ranging from burgundy, purples, and pinks to white; lobed basal foliage grows up from a firmly anchored taproot, so only move columbine in the seedling stage. Each bloom is composed of five petal-like sepals set on top of five true petals, each one ending in an elongated spur with a nectar cup at its base (hummingbirds are frequent visitors). Columbines grow in dappled shade at the back of the apple tree with dicentras, Jacob's ladder, primulas, and forget-me-not.

Artemisia pontica, **Roman wormwood,** 18 in., sun. This silvery-gray herb used to flavor vermouth forms a low, lacy mound of growth that increases by energetic underground runners. An indispensable silver note among the bright colors of Russell lupines, salvias, and daylilies, it needs to be reduced each spring by pulling out extra roots (not difficult) and clipping back stems so new growth forms a neat mound; thick plantings become floppy in the middle.

Centaurea montana, **mountain bluet,** 2½ ft. Originating in mountainous regions of Europe, this is a tough plant protected from drought and windy conditions by silvery hairs that cover its foliage; flowers, intensely blue in color, resemble an oversize, spidery bachelor's button. We grow mountain bluet as a short hedge to lead from dappled shade to sun. In rich soil it quickly becomes overgrown and should be divided at least every two years to maintain its form.

Dicentra **sp., wild bleeding heart,** 12 in. We are very fond of these native plants for their elegant, ferny foliage and long-lasting, dusky pink pouchlike flowers that bloom in dangling racemes from spring through summer if given partial shade and moist soil. *D. eximia*, fringed bleeding heart, and *D. formosa*, Western bleeding heart, are nearly identical except that Western bleeding heart's foliage has a grayish cast. We use both as contained ground covers in a garden setting: Fringed bleeding heart blooms in a great swath under the apple tree between white sweet woodruff and blue Jacob's ladder, while Western bleeding heart fills in beneath the golden currant shrub. Elsewhere, we use either to mark the edge of a hosta planting that merges into the semiwild; their roots are brittle, so handle with care.

*Doronicum caucasicum, leopard's bane, 3 ft. Unusual for its bright yellow daisy flowers—two inches across—in a sea of pastels, leopard's bane makes a splash in early summer when it blooms in a wide swath with sweet cicely. Ground-hugging leaves deteriorate by midsummer, when the plant is hidden by other growth. Divide after bloom to ensure longevity (in our experience, leopard's bane is short-lived).

Filipendula vulgaris 'Flore Pleno', dropwort, 3 ft., sun. Although native to dry pastures, dropwort flourishes at this site. Plants produce underground drop-shaped roots once used to treat kidney and lung ailments. We consider it indispensable for its ferny foliage and exquisite rose-tinted buds, shaped like tiny antique pearls. These are held high above the foliage on wand-like stems. Dropwort is one of those plants whose flowers are more attractive in bud than in flower (these are fluffy white with protruding stamens). As soon as they are spent—after about two weeks—we cut back stems to revitalize the handsome mound of foliage, an asset all season. Dropwort's pretty bud display echoes the nearby mass of rose-flushed buds on the wide crown of 'Henry Hudson' rose.

*Gallium odoratum, sweet woodruff, 6 in. A delightful woodland plant, sweet woodruff creates a mound of shiny, dark green, pointed leaves in whorls, embellished in late spring by masses of starry white flowers. Scent is most noticeable when the drying leaves release coumarin—a sweet perfume—the same phenomenon we notice in new-mown hay. Grown at the base of the apple tree in a heavy iron rim set in the ground, it is confined to a decorative circular accent between wild bleeding heart and pansies. On the bank, we allow it to grow unchecked in full sun beneath the hardy white rugosa rose 'Blanc Double de Coubert'. Leaves and flower sprigs are used to flavor jellies, and in May Wine to welcome spring.

Geranium **'Johnson's Blue'**, 12 in. A mounded ground cover with lobed leaves and a mass of light blue flowers in early June. Plants sprawl over a wide area, even climbing through the nearby 'Henry Hudson' rose, but extra roots are easy to pull out. It is a striking companion for white chives, pink bistort, and all the pastels of early summer.

Hemerocallis, **daylily,** 12 in.–2½ ft. Two daylilies are most welcome in mid- to late June for their bright color, perfume, and prolific bloom. The old-fashioned lemon lily (*H. lilioasphodelus*) bears a profusion of sweetly scented yellow trumpets over a mound of grassy foliage, while 'Stella de Oro' bears egg-yolk yellow flowers that continue to open right into fall. Gardeners may grumble about its uncompromising brightness, but we find it cheerful (especially when it is still blooming in November!). In this garden, we grow it by the entranceway, backed by a frill of silvery gray Roman wormwood that tones it down a bit. We grow lemon lily alongside the path as it winds its way from front to back so we will breathe in the flowers' perfume when we walk by. Beware: True lemon lily is hard to find; nursery plants may be impostors. Look for smallish, perfumed flowers and narrow foliage.

Hesperis matronalis, **sweet (or dame's) rocket,** 3 ft. A long-blooming biennial with coarse leaves (edible like mustard greens in early growth) and loose clusters of phlox-like flowers, its most outstanding characteristic is its floating evening scent, sweet with a clove note. If trimmed after first bloom in late spring, sweet rocket will produce flowers most of the summer. We grow sweet rocket also in a cottage garden dooryard planting to enjoy its scent and let it expand at will in naturalized plantings.

Lunaria annua, **silver dollar or honesty,** 3 ft. We like silver dollar (also biennial), valued mainly for its decorative pods, for its late spring pink-purple bloom in loose, phlox-like heads among sweet cicely, Solomon's seal, and wild bleeding heart (although it will gladly grow elsewhere, too, we confine it to partial shade); by late summer, its rough leaves and tall, awkward growth are covered by other plants. To harvest for dried flowers: Cut back stalks with dried pods, remove outer covering on both sides of the pod as well as the seeds within; you are now left with transparent moons or "silver dollars" for dried arrangements.

Lupinus **'Dwarf Russell Hybrids',** 3 ft., sun. We grew these from pass-along seeds, so we weren't sure what to expect. Only one color germinated, producing tightly packed stalks of bicolored flowers, pink and rose. In early June, tiers of bloom create a dramatic accent near the front of the island bed, backed by white-flowering 'Henry Hudson'. We cut back stalks for continuous (but less prolific) bloom during the summer and to keep lupine's distinctive palm-shaped foliage in trim. Propagate by seed sown in winter to germinate in spring, by division, or by stem or root cuttings. Move only in its early stages of growth (it has a long, fleshy taproot).

Myosotis sylvatica, **forget-me-not,** 16 in. We grew this from seed over twenty-five years ago, and descendants continue to self-sow in all our gardens. The dominant color is sky blue, but white and pink variants are not uncommon. A profusion of small, five-petaled flowers with a bright yellow center grow on uncoiling spikes, assuring a long season of bloom beginning in mid-spring and continuing through early summer. Although charming for the airy drifts that weave throughout the garden, an overabundance of plants signals neglect. Be sure to pull out spent plants; don't worry, they self-seed prolifically.

Myrrhis odorata, **sweet cicely,** 3 ft., partial shade. Growing from a deep taproot, sweet cicely produces an attractive mound of light green ferny foliage with an anise flavor (chop young leaves into stewed rhubarb to cut the sugar needed); oils from its seeds were once used for furniture polish. By late May, saucer-size umbels of white scented flowers bloom atop rising stems. Bloom time is short (two weeks). Soon after spent stalks are cut back, foliage returns refreshed. We are sometimes tempted to delay this procedure, entranced by the beauty of showy seed clusters—shiny dark brown and delicious, like licorice candy—but such negligence results in an army of seedlings the following spring.

Papaver orientale, **Oriental poppy,** 3 ft., sun. We grow only the flamboyant vermilion version—six-inch-wide flowers with frill-like black stamens—whose swelling buds we watch daily. Mid-June bloom bears company with pastel sweet rocket and bistort, a combination that works well. The presence of astilbe and daylilies nearby promises a smooth transition to fill in the wide gap left when just a single plant is cut back. If you want to move this poppy, wait until it is dormant (early spring or fall); its roots are fleshy, deep, and persistent.

*Polemonium caeruleum, **Jacob's ladder,** 18 in. Leaves, arranged like rungs of a ladder on either side of arching stems, reflect its common

name. A cottage garden favorite considered old-fashioned at the turn of the twentieth century, it was once used to treat fevers, nervous complaints, and epilepsy, based on the plant's astringent properties. Its pretty, blue-cupped flowers with prominent golden stamens are of more interest now. These begin to open in late spring with yellow cowslips in the shade of the apple tree.

***Polygonatum multiflorum*, Solomon's seal,** 3 ft., partial shade. In late spring, small ivory bells—chartreuse-rimmed and waxy—dangle from long, arching stems, blooming over several weeks as flowers open from bottom to top of the stem. The ribbed, slightly puckered leaves are striking all season, even in late fall when they slowly turn from green to golden buff. The starchy roots have been used for flour and for medicine; new shoots used to be eaten as a spring vegetable.

****Polygonum bistorta* 'Superbum',** **bistort,** $2^{1}/_{2}$–3 ft. (Figure 25). When this is in full bloom in early June, it stands out among all the other flowers. It is an improved form of the meadow wildflower, with stiff, upright stems growing up from a wide mound of tongue-shaped foliage, topped by

Figure 25.
Swallowtail butterfly on bistort.

masses of fluffy pink, hawthorn-scented pokers (of great interest to swallowtail butterflies). Its dark, twisted roots (a characteristic preserved in the epithet "bistorta," or twice-twisted) were used for tanning leather; its new shoots were once used to flavor Bistort Pudding, a spring restorative. We use bistort extensively throughout the landscape for shade plantings and for naturalizing.

Primula veris, **cowslip,** 8 in. A flower beloved of cottage gardens, with an extraordinary number of medicinal and culinary uses from conserves, cough medicines, ointments, to cowslip wine—legendary for its narcotic effect—this sweetly scented meadow plant is synonymous with spring. Clusters of five to twelve nodding, bright yellow flowers grow up from a basal rosette of crinkled, tapering leaves. We grow the red variant, too, in a well-shaded colony with pansies, Jacob's ladder, and forget-me-not. To maintain vigor, divide plants every three years after blooming, and be sure to water them well if conditions are dry and hot (death to cowslips). Extras can be established in light woodland.

Pulmonaria officinalis, **lungwort,** 6–18 in. One of the most important plants in our landscape, it forms a stunning hedge of azure blue bells around the Flowering Herb Garden and adjacent Tulip Bed. Flowers are at their height by May, when hummingbirds and bees find it a source of early nectar. When cut back a month later, the hedge is transformed into a fresh spotted-foliage frame for the plants within. Its wealth of folk names—such as William and Mary, Jack and Jill, Soldiers and Sailors—suggest flowers that turn from pink in bud to blue in flower, a characteristic of the borage family. Lungwort, a favorite cottage garden plant, was thought to have healing properties to treat diseased lungs, based on the appearance of its lung-shaped, spotted leaves. *For hedging:*

Space rhizomatous roots 6 inches apart, water well, and mulch to keep the soil cool and moist; an 18-inch-wide hedge is most effective in bloom. Cut it down to the ground when flowers are spent (we use a long-handled sickle); new foliage will grow back within a week.

***Rosa* 'Henry Hudson'.** Described in "Roses" (Chapter Seven), this is our favorite garden rose for its ability to fit into a small planting and remain a distinctive feature all season: in early summer with a prolific display of small, pointed, rose-flushed buds followed by scented white flowers; in fall with a canopy of rosy-bronze foliage; and in the depths of winter with a naked crown, wide and twiggy. As with herbs, spent flowers should be deadheaded.

***Salvia* spp.,** 18–24 in., sun. We grow two salvias here: *S.* 'May Night', a cultivar of *S.* x *superba* (a spontaneous garden hybrid) and *S. verticillata* 'Purple Rain', a cultivar of whorled clary. 'May Night' is a compact plant, just under 2 feet, with heavily packed dark violet-blue flower spikes, held above musk-scented pebbly leaves (a sign of drought resistance). Blooming for more than a month, it is a distinctive foil for silver-gray Roman wormwood, both yellow daylilies, and a clump of nearby purple velvet pansies (a happy accident). Spikes are trimmed back after flowering to encourage fresh production; by midsummer the plant is cut back (not severely) for later rebloom. 'Purple Rain', also drought resistant, creates a low mound of velvety leaves topped for most of the summer by down-covered flower spikes of a dusky lavender hue (these dry dark purple for potpourri); it combines well over its long season with daylilies, monarda, and sundrops. The wild origins of these salvias suggest their use for soothing eyewash in the same way as clary sage (*S. sclarea*).

*Symphytum caucasicum, blue comfrey, 3–4 ft. A showy member of the borage family, blue comfrey has a commanding presence in late spring and early summer among pinks, whites, and other blues, with its tall form and prolific mass of dangling blue bells (in common with lungwort and borage, its buds are pink). Used since ancient times to heal bruises and broken bones, every part of the plant is beneficial: Hummingbirds and bees are drawn to its nectar, our chicken flock gobbles up stalks and spent flowers, and when thrown on the compost heap, whole plants decompose rapidly, releasing valuable nutrients. In rich soil and confined circumstances, plants need to be divided every spring. A good subject for naturalizing.

*Viola sp., 6–8 in. Wild pansies (*Viola tricolor*) and garden pansies (*V.* x *wittrockiana*), short-lived perennials, thrive in the conditions here. The wild sort, better known as Johnny-jump-up, lives up to its name, self-seeding in cool, moist pockets along the garden path and at the back of the apple tree among primulas, Jacob's ladder, and columbine. We started with a golden-eyed all-purple type that eventually produced desirable variants, among them a cream and violet "face" delicately lined with black whiskers, which obligingly grows through the shaded base of clustered bellflower (*Campanula glomerata*) nearly all summer, even through heat. Such types are noted and propagated by stem cuttings (seeds are variable). Wild pansy's older name, heartsease, preserves its use as a heart stimulant. We also maintain colonies of its showier cousin, the garden pansy, in shades of yellow, cream, raspberry, burgundy, and blue at the base of the apple tree where they can be seen as we pass by every day. Cut back both pansies just before they are entirely spent so they rebloom in late summer and fall.

DIRECTIONS FOR CANDIED PETALS
& PRESSED FLORAL CARDS

We like to candy viola petals for cake decorations and press especially pretty faces for floral notes on stiff cards; in the language of flowers, "pansy," from the French *pensée*, means "a thought" (usually a sad one).

Candied Petals

Lay fresh unblemished petals on doubled sheets of waxed paper. Brush front surface with egg white beaten with a little water, then sprinkle the surface with sugar; repeat on the back surface. Place petals on clean waxed paper and turn daily until they are dry to the touch. We like to use them as soon as possible, but they can be stored in paper-lined boxes for a few weeks.

Pressed Floral Cards

Faces with some dark petals show up best when dried. Spread them flat on a thick layer of newspaper; cover them with another layer, then with heavy weights—encyclopedias work well. After a few days, change paper, add weights, and leave until wholly dry. Carefully pick off flowers and store them in a marked envelope until ready to use. Lightly dab the card with glue where you want the pansy to be, then gently press it in; add other flowers like roses for love, lady's mantle for comfort, mint for wisdom, horehound for health, and rosemary for remembrance; with a fine pen identify each pressed flower or leaf and its meaning, weaving your writing to fit around the plants, then seal the card by covering it firmly with plastic wrap. ●

CHAPTER SIX

The Harvest Bed

—

IT SOON BECAME CLEAR that the Flowering Herb Garden could not provide enough herbs for Jo Ann's growing herb business, Jo Ann's Kitchen & Garden. She needed a separate bed to grow blocks of lovage, lemon balm, chives, dill, calendulas, and chamomile for serious harvesting. It was fine to be able to run out and snip fresh chives from a bunch in the island bed for breakfast extravaganzas of homemade cottage cheese and fresh garden tomatoes, but we now needed much more than that—a reliable source of herbs in quantity for a range of herb products.

Since we needed a sunny site to grow these herbs, our choice was limited to flat ground on the west side of the house that had once been a strawberry bed but now grew nothing but grass where calves were tethered. This area was near a poultry house for the temporary shelter of pullets, meat birds, and turkeys too old for an incubator but too young to be moved directly into their unheated summer quarters (the poultry house was equipped with a heat lamp). The unlikely juxtaposition of the humble poultry house and what became known as the Harvest Bed proved to be a fruitful association that generated the development of the entire west side of the house. But nothing was further from our minds one fine Mother's Day more than twelve years ago when we laid out a raised bed sixty feet long by four feet wide on sod ground using the same technique that had proved so successful for growing vegetables: We placed plastic grain bags over the sod, then enclosed the area with spruce logs, leaving a six-inch edging of plastic beyond the logs, which we later covered with wood shavings to discourage weeds from creeping into the bed. The enclosure was filled with rough compost (not completely broken down), stomped into place, and allowed to settle for a week or so. Finally, we topped the entire bed with several inches of aged, composted manure, a rich, dark, friable mixture. The completed depth of the bed was eight inches.

Because the Harvest Bed was lined with plastic, we concentrated on growing annual herbs or shallow-rooted perennials like chives and lemon balm. Deep rooted lovage—the main flavoring ingredient in Jo Ann's famous Herb Salt and other mixes—was planted just beyond the end of the bed in unimproved sod ground by making a slit in the sod with a sharp spade, then shoving in the root and roughly closing the slit by stamping on it (we were perfecting our no-dig methods!). The surrounding area was heavily mulched with a thick layer of compost from the poultry house, then topped with rotted sawdust, all of which eventually broke down to become crumbly, rich soil. The lovage has thrived here, producing two heavy crops of leafy stalks a season. Aside from its practical value, lovage is a tall, handsome green accent in early summer, a background for mauve and white flowering chives and yellow-flowered Achillea 'Moonshine' in the Harvest Bed itself.

For a couple of years after this bed was established, the turkeys, having graduated from the heated poultry house and now being housed in summer quarters, were allowed to freely roam the pastures during the day—plenty for them to eat there, Jigs observed. Jo Ann, as usual, was anxious about free-roaming animals (the more restraints the better for them), but Jigs reasoned, why should they want to eat petunias when they had acres of lush forage? Enjoyable as it was to observe them going about together, sailing up the knoll to the farmhouse from their summer quarters below, chirping as they went, when they had dined on Jo Ann's petunias once too often they were confined to a large yard we added to the front of the poultry house. The fence, seven feet tall (turkeys can fly) and made from uneven, weathered slab boards, now stood between one side of the yard and the Harvest Bed, so it belonged as much to the herbs as to the turkeys. It provided an appealing rustic structure that complemented the log-enclosed raised bed, gave plants protection from wind (an ever-present factor), and offered us the chance to grow tall plants like hollyhocks and sunflowers. Even the leaning poles supporting the fence on the Harvest Bed side, we discovered, could be attractively clothed in runner beans—the traditional scarlet, the heirloom bicolor 'Painted Lady', and white-flowered Dutch pole beans.

The Harvest Bed was assuming another dimension altogether, becoming more like a traditional border with a cottage garden flavor. The notion of a strictly utilitarian planting of blocks of herbs for harvesting faded as soon as the first hollyhocks sent up their stalks to thirteen feet, adorned all the way up with wide-open, flushed pink, dark-eyed trumpets. By the simplest means—the only ones available to us—this new planting was transforming a neglected area, integrating the disparate elements of poultry house and yard into a harmonious working and living environment.

Once we had acknowledged the force of beauty in the soaring hollyhocks and determined that the Harvest Bed existed for more than production, it became an important aesthetic component of our lives— what we saw first thing in the morning from our bedroom window, during the day as we went about our work, and at twilight on the way to shut in the poultry. If it could be managed, why not make this garden beautiful as well as practical? We remained true to our original aim of providing herbs for harvesting, even though most of these were now planted as grouped accents, rather than in blocks. Chives are just as easy to harvest when grown in groups of three repeated along the border. This way, when they are cut back, other plants fill the spot, so there is a constant flow of flowers and foliage rather than a noticeable emptiness.

With so much space available, wonderful soil, excellent drainage, and a sunny exposure, we were encouraged to explore a wide range of herbs that had been impossible to grow at the Flowering Herb Garden site with its heavy, moist growing conditions. The criteria we used for choosing suitable plants were that, besides being beautiful, they should be useful for flavoring, scent, seed production, crafts, bees, hummingbirds, or butterflies. Certain plants like lovage (though grown in an "annex," we regarded it as an integral part of the Harvest Bed), chives, lemon balm, dill, sage, calendulas, and chamomile were indispensable. But soon others fell into that category as the list of products in Jo Ann's business expanded to include potpourri, vinegars, skin fresheners, and dried posies. And workshops conducted at the farm or elsewhere demanded a range of artemisias for wreath making.

As we added more perennials, we had to adapt the plastic-lined bed to grow plants with more demanding roots, such as echinacea, rue, Achillea 'Moonshine', Russian sage, lavender, and the artemisias. For these we slashed a hole through the plastic before planting them, so their roots would have room to spread, and this has worked well, although if we had foreseen the direction of the Harvest Bed, we might have used a thick layer of newspaper instead of plastic. Just as we had learned to deal with invasive perennials in the Flowering Herb Garden, now we found ways to grow similar types we could not do without: Fernleaf tansy, with arching, lacy leaves, a bracing scent, and creeping roots (on a par with regular tansy) is grown in an old iron tub next to garlic chives; at the foot of the tub, we confine lemon-scented costmary, a tall rangy plant especially aggressive in rich soil, to a mat of ground-hugging foliage—perfectly flat, pinked at its edges—by cutting it back and harvesting the leaves several times during the growing season for simmering potpourri, skin freshener, and assorted crafts (it makes a wonderful aromatic bookmark, as suggested in one of its common names, Bible Leaf). Artemisia 'Silver King', which could easily colonize the whole bed if left on its own, is maintained as a wide, distinctive swath against the fence in the middle of the border. When it threatens to move ahead in any direction, its wandering roots are ruthlessly (and easily) pulled out like weeds.

The general design of the Harvest Bed follows the classic border, with plants of descending height from back to front, but as we had learned from the Flowering Herb Garden experience, variations on this scheme create a more satisfying arrangement than strict adherence to soldierly ranked plants. Since we decided to regard the Harvest Bed as an ornamental garden of useful plants, we grouped them for best effect in terms of forms, textures, and, especially, color. Whereas the Herb Garden is dominated by Old World herbs in the pastel range, this planting offered the chance to explore the more exuberant colors of many annuals, among them Calendula 'Touch of Red', rich pink and purple painted sage or annual clary (*Salvia viridis*), red and green amaranthus, tangerine and yellow marigolds (we're especially fond of the citrus-scented signet types, *Tagetes tenuifolia*). This turn in our gardening efforts was applauded by Jigs, who had always chafed at the understated colors of the "posh weeds" in the Flowering Herb Garden. "The first thing I require in flowers," he has stated more than once, "is color." This principle has had a very positive influence throughout the landscape, but nowhere is it more evident than in the Harvest Bed.

There's something to gather from this garden all season, beginning in April as soon as the snow melts when we cut young shoots—eaten like scallions—from the base of Egyptian onions (*Allium* x *proliferum*), a small, productive patch of which is maintained at the rear of the bed. Nothing tastes so good as fresh greens after a winter of stored vegetables. The curlicues of bulblets that form later at the top of the plant produce a striking effect weaving through scarlet bee balm. By May there are young sorrel leaves to pick, as well as the reddish tips of emerging lovage and thick, young chive spears, all added to spring dandelion salad. As the soil warms and the sun strengthens, plants shoot up fast and soon (too soon, we think, with the press of spring work), and the chives and lovage are ready to harvest (Figure 26, on page 124). First, the chives are cut back (the succulent leaves are cut up fine, dried, and stored until needed), and flower stalks are separated, bunched, and hung to dry away from light (the flowers, like the leaves, are added to Jo Ann's Herb Salt mixture). By early June, it's time to cut the lovage, the most time-consuming and important of all the herbs we raise for harvest. We produce about four gallons of dark green, dried and flaked herbs each year to meet our needs. The strong-tasting, celery-flavored leaves with a touch of anise are delicious when used as a general flavoring (sparingly, if fresh) or as a salt substitute.

Figure 26.
Harvesting chives in early summer.

As the summer advances, plants are trimmed for their foliage (costmary, thyme, parsley, sage), for dried flowers and petals (Achillea 'Moonshine', chamomile, painted sage, calendulas, double feverfew, lavender), for pods (poppies, nigella), seeds (coriander and many others), wreaths and household uses (artemisias). We cut fresh flowers and foliage all summer for bouquets for the heart of our house, the farm kitchen, with its woodstove and long, wooden trestle table—and our two guest log cabins. From early May to late October, the Harvest Bed is truly a source of herbs for use and delight. It's a joy to lead guests down the garden path, to stop with them to sniff, to touch the plants, to pick aromatic sprigs for them to take, to observe the activities of bees and butterflies, intent on gathering nectar among the flowers.

The effect of this garden in full bloom, with its bright yellows and oranges, pinks, reds, blues, and purples among green and gray foliage, raised above a carpet of green grass and backed by the tall rustic fence, is far greater than one might have expected. After all, these are common plants for the most part, arranged in a straightforward way, as in any traditional border. But here, the border is *jammed* with plants. By late summer, a low hedge of short 'Fiesta' calendulas at the front of the bed—primrose yellow and orange—leads to a low corner accent of spreading compact oregano (nutmeg-scented, crowned with tiny pink flowers), followed by upright mounds of citrus-scented tangerine marigolds (*Tagetes tenuifolia* 'Little Giant'), and behind these are lush bunches of emerald green parsley ('Bravura'), wands of light pink cilantro with lacy green foliage, and rising sprays of bronze fennel. Repeated splashes of pink and purple painted sage toward the middle of the bed grow adjacent to groups of glowing, deep orange 'Touch of Red' calendulas (Figure 27),

Figure 27.
Calendula 'Touch of Red' with painted sage.

interspersed with sky blue Nigella 'Miss Jekyll'. A wide planting of borage carries blue to the back of the bed, where the silvery white sprays of Artemisia 'Silver King' invest all the surrounding colors with a deeper intensity: the blue-green foliage of rue, tall tiers of purple-blue Agastache 'Liquorice Blue' (see Agastache, page 131), soft orange Mexican sunflowers (Tithonia 'Goldfinger'), and monardas in three colors, red, pink, and rose-purple. Against the fence, our favorite garden sunflower, 'Autumn Beauty', lifts its multicolored heads to the sun, but the dark-eyed pink hollyhocks rise above all. You can stand at the top of the Harvest Bed and see to the very end, where creamy white sprays of white mugwort (*Artemisia lactiflora*) and gray wormwood (Figure 28) shelter tall pink-purple Echinacea 'Magnus'—a large-flowered type in which the ray petals are nearly horizontal—more orange Mexican sunflower (a most underrated annual and a butterfly favorite), white-starred garlic chives (*Allium tuberosum*), and 'Music Box', a cheery dwarf sunflower, in bronzy-red and yellows. With such an abundance of plants jostling for space, the ones up front spill over the logs, softening their straight edges.

—

Figure 28.
Silvery wormwood with purple coneflower and garlic chives.

Visitors are always startled by the Harvest Bed with its vibrant display of color, especially because it's unexpected (Figure 29). This is a "secret" garden in the sense that it is hidden from the front of the house, so it has a greater impact when you round the corner and come upon it—all laid out brilliantly against the fence, under the blue sky in the summer sun. The cramming of plants within a narrow and well-defined framework and the rustic fence has a lot to do with the garden's visual impact, as does the pastoral setting, the "bones" of the surrounding trees and shrubbery. To the west, just beyond the lovage, apple trees and a large hawthorn stand at the edge of a deep ravine, and to the south at the top of the knoll is a bank of elderberries. Then there is the appeal of the poultry house and yard with live poultry within, an

interesting living feature of the garden itself. What makes the garden work, what makes this scene seem so right, is that it naturally flows from the life of the farm. It was created to fill a need, not to put our stamp artificially upon the ground. We did not set out to "landscape" the area in the professional way (a professional might have advised us to camouflage or hide the poultry house!). Rather, our needs, our resources, and the growing conditions dictated (and limited) our choices. The use of rough-and-ready building materials (logs and fence) complemented the existing poultry house and the general homey, unpretentious farm setting. This garden, like the Flowering Herb Garden, was a great teacher, showing us a way to make the most of what we had, suggesting new and satisfying ways to express our developing aesthetic vision.

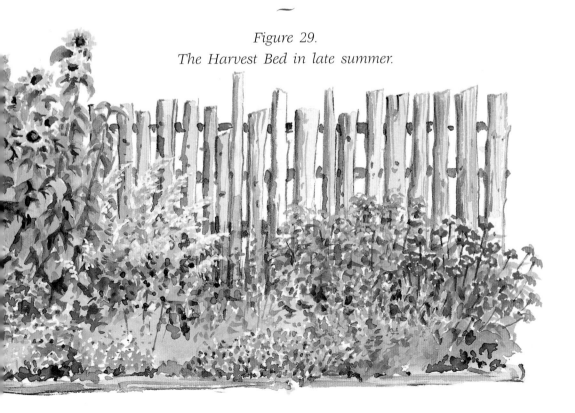

Figure 29.
The Harvest Bed in late summer.

Maintenance of this planting follows along the lines of the Flowering Herb Garden except that a thick top-dressing of composted barn manure (the soil for our raised beds) is added in the late fall or early winter after several killing frosts, instead of the horse manure mulch we add to the Flowering Herb Garden. This is because the plants in this bed are growing on plastic, and it is important to maintain the soil level. Fall cleanup includes cutting back old stalks (since most of the plants are harvested in some way during the summer, this is minimal), pulling up spent annuals, cleaning up debris to prevent insect and disease infestations, and clearing out weeds (there are few here since the planting is so crowded).

The Harvest Bed far exceeded our original intent in ways we could not have imagined. Our expanding interests would soon be reflected in new plantings on that piece of once bare ground.

Sampler of Mid- to Late-Season Herbs & Flowers

Just as the Flowering Herb Garden is at its height of lushness in early summer, the Harvest Bed reaches its peak by midsummer and carries on until late fall. This is when the planting is dominated by colorful annuals, mediated by a framework of silvery artemisias and hardy perennials (to Zone 4), some of them woody and shrublike in form. Here the emphasis is on scented and nectar-rich plants that attract hummingbirds, bees, and butterflies, as well as on plants that can be harvested all summer to create useful products. Latin plant names with the epithet *officinalis* mean the plant was available from the apothecary, or as we would say, from the drugstore.

If you enjoy growing herbs for use as well as beauty, explore this group of annuals and perennials in an open, sunny site where soil is friable and well drained.

ANNUALS

Agastache **'Liquorice Blue', anise hyssop,** 2 ft. Start plants indoors ten to twelve weeks before the last expected frost. This seed strain, which flowers the first season, is valuable where *Agastache foeniculum* is not a reliably hardy perennial. By late summer, plants bloom in tiers of tubular blue flowers very attractive to bees, butterflies, and hummingbirds. A narrow, compact plant, Agastache can be tucked into small places for contrast with silvery foliage or bright colors (red, orange, yellows). We use the anise-scented leaves for tea and potpourri. The name of this seed strain may vary. Look for blue-flowered types that flower the first season.

Anethum graveolens, **dill,** 3–4 ft. Sow seeds directly in the ground beginning in late spring. We like to grow the tall 'Mammoth' here as a decorative filler near the back of the border, where successive sowings in late spring create accents of bright yellow umbels beginning in midsummer. We pick young leaves for salad and add flower and seed heads to the dill crock; steeped seeds make a good digestive tea.

Artemisia annua, **sweet Annie,** 6 ft. Ten to twelve weeks before the last frost, prechill seeds for two weeks in the fridge, then sow indoors. In the ground by early summer, sweet Annie is a tiny seedling of finely cut leaves, but by late summer it is a towering plant shaped like a tree, wide at its base, tapering to a point at its top, citrus scented with a hint of camphor. This is when small, round yellow flowers appear against a background of filmy green foliage. As the plant matures, stems become brittle and the flowers turn reddish, then brown. Cut back plants for wreaths before frost and when the stems are still pliable.

Borago officinalis, **borage,** to 3 ft. Sow seeds directly in the soil in late spring. A rough-stemmed, rough-leaved plant, borage is saved from obscurity by beautiful blue star flowers borne in nodding clusters to protect their nectar from rain. Borage's rich source of food for bees is reflected in its other common name, bee bread. We like to candy the flowers for cake decorations. Beware of overbearing self-sown plants that will need trimming back during the summer.

Calendula officinalis, **pot marigold,** 2 ft. Sow seeds directly in the soil when it has warmed, by late spring or early summer. We have never met a calendula type we didn't like for its simple charm and ease of culture. The unimproved species bears smallish pale orange or yellow daisies to one and one-half inches wide, some with brown centers, on stems that grow from pale green, sticky leaves; flowers in improved strains range from two to three inches wide. All calendula types self-sow and gain impact in wide swaths or drifts of bloom. One of our favorites is 'Touch of Red', where the back of every petal is tinged with red, giving flowers a warm, antique glow. 'Fiesta' is a large-flowered dwarf type that seldom needs deadheading and makes a good edging plant. Calendula petals used to be sold in barrels to flavor soups and stews. We dry petals to add flavor and color to our Herb Salt and Herb Blend mixes (see page 142).

Coriandrum sativum, **cilantro/coriander,** to 2½ ft. Sow seeds directly in the soil in late spring. Although we have never cultivated a taste for cilantro's oddly flavored leaves, we have become attached to the production of pale pink flower umbels on wandlike stems that weave themselves through the front and middle of the border all summer if seeds are sown successively for three weeks from late spring to early summer. We harvest the distinctive round, striped seeds for spicing meat dishes and, when crushed, for scenting potpourri.

Helianthus annuus, **sunflower,** 2–6 ft. Sow seeds directly in the soil when soil warms, and water until they germinate. We plant the large-flowered kind in the vegetable garden, but here we grow garden types bred for the production of multistemmed colorful flowers in yellow, bronze, red, and bicolors, all good for cutting. Our favorites, all singles, are 'Autumn Beauty', to six feet, and the dwarf 'Music Box'.

Nigella damascena, **love-in-a-mist,** 18 in. Sow seeds directly in the soil in late spring. All our plants are descendants of 'Miss Jekyll', sown years ago. This delicate plant is most effective when allowed to self-sow in drifts of sky blue flowers followed by striped, balloon-like pods. Both flowers and pods are enveloped in a "mist" of airy leaves. If you want to use the dried pods for winter bouquets, cut single stems before the pod opens at the top to release its many jet-black seeds.

Phaseolus coccineus, **scarlet runner bean,** climber, 6–8 ft. We plant the large mottled beans when the soil has warmed (when we plant string beans and corn) and give them a wooden pole to climb up to the top of the turkey yard fence. At the same time, we plant seeds of white runner beans and the coral/white bicolor antique 'Painted Lady' to run up the same pole for mixed colorful bloom by midsummer. We pick the pods before frost, shell the beans, and dry them out on screens before storing them in a covered crock. We soak the beans overnight, then add them to thick vegetable soup (minestrone). All the runner bean varieties taste the same when cooked.

Salvia officinalis, cooking sage, to $2\frac{1}{2}$ ft. Start plants indoors ten to twelve weeks before the last frost. The pebbly apple-green leaves of first-year plants are the ones we harvest during the summer and dry to use in pork sausage and teas (with dried chamomile flowers), and to flavor a variety of cheeses, hard and semisoft, that we make with Jersey cow milk. Highly regarded as a digestive, sage is an herb we treasure as much for its looks as its uses. The second year, plants produce lovely spikes of dark purple flowers on stems that grow increasingly woody. By raising seedlings every season, you can enjoy both leaves for flavoring and second-year flower spikes for beauty.

Salvia viridis, annual clary/painted sage, 18 in. Start plants indoors eight to ten weeks before the last frost. It is the top bracts of this plant, rather than the insignificant flowers tucked in leaf axils, that give it distinction. Veined with green and infused with purple, pink, or white, annual clary is very showy when grown in a group since a single plant can be lost among other growth (they will accomplish this themselves, since like nigella and calendula, they self-sow prolifically). To dry for winter bouquets, cut stems when the top color is still fresh, bunch in groups of twelve stems, and hang them upside down out of direct light until they are thoroughly dry. The soaked seeds of annual clary have the same herbal properties to clear objects from eyes ("clear eye") as true clary (*Salvia sclarea*).

Tagetes tenuifolia, signet marigold, 6–12 in. Start plants indoors eight to ten weeks before the last frost. Low plants that grow into a perfect mound, signet marigolds are distinguished from other marigolds by their strong citrusy aroma and the production of many small, five-petaled single flowers, bright yellow or orange, sometimes blotched with purple-brown. We value these for their low rounded form, their masses of bloom, and the warm scent that is released by brushing. Plants are brittle and should be handled with care; soil should not be overly rich. We steep flowers in vinegar for homemade skin freshener (see page 143).

***Tithonia rotundifolia* 'Goldfinger', Mexican sunflower,** 24–30 in. Start plants indoors six to eight weeks before the last frost. After a friend gave us a few seedlings, we have never been without this undervalued annual. It owes its singular beauty to large daisy flowers in late summer— soft orange in color—its velvety green foliage, and in the improved form, 'Goldfinger', of compact habit. All these virtues make it a prime mixer in any planting. Very attractive to butterflies.

PERENNIALS

***Achillea* 'Moonshine',** 2 ft. A compact, slowly spreading plant that combines silvery foliage with wide, lemon-yellow flower umbels nearly all summer if flower stalks are regularly pruned. We keep plants in trim by cutting fresh flowers to dry for winter bouquets and wreaths.

***Alcea rosea,* hollyhock,** 6 ft. or more. A biennial that establishes basal foliage and a long taproot its first year, then sends up flowering stems the second year (plants need staking). Cut back stalks in the fall to encourage offspring at the plant's base. Propagate favorite colors by replanting a piece of the mother plant, but avoid seedlings from plants that vary in flower color. To deal with rust disease, see Chapter Eleven under "Disease and Insect Control." All parts of the plant have the soothing properties associated with mallows to treat skin problems and coughs; flowers of the black hollyhock have been used to color wine. We dry flowers to add to herbal teas (they lend a smoothness to the brew) and to potpourri.

***Allium* x *proliferum*, Egyptian onion,** 2 ft. Clumps of bulblets, produced at the top of the plant by midsummer, bend down to the ground where they replant themselves, thus the common name "walking onion." To start a patch, plant individual cloves about six inches apart and keep plants weeded well. We pull young shoots for early scallions (very sweet) in the spring. You can also use the bulblets for flavoring.

***Allium schoenoprasum*, chives,** 1 ft. This is one of the most useful and prettiest of herbs. The first spears are always the thickest and tastiest. We chop them fine and add them to homemade cottage cheese and cream cheese. Later, we use the flowers for seasoning, too, after pulling them apart. After we harvest all the leaves and flowers for our Herb Salt and Herb Blend (see page 142), we mulch the cut-back plants with compost so they will produce more useful growth (and bloom). Under these conditions, plants should be thinned out every two or three years (we naturalize extras in a bog).

***Allium tuberosum*, garlic chives,** 2–3 ft. This underrated plant for its use and beauty is a boon to the garden in late summer, when the handsome clump of flat leaves is topped by a canopy of white-starred umbels. We use the leaves to make garlic-flavored salad vinegar with dill and mint. Although the flowers are too strongly scented for bouquets, the seed heads are attractive when dried.

***Anthemis tinctoria*, dyer's chamomile/golden marguerite,** 2 ft. Plants produce masses of two-inch-wide golden daisies nearly all summer if plants are pruned regularly to keep them more or less upright. Otherwise they will sprawl, and while this lax habit has a certain appeal, it wears out the plant. Dyer's chamomile is a short-lived perennial that needs to be propagated by stem cuttings in the spring. You can make a brilliant yellow dye from the flowers, but we've never tried it.

Artemisia absinthum, **wormwood,** 3 ft. We have grown wormwood for over forty years, wherever we live, for its useful properties as a moth deterrent and cure-all for digestive disorders (only a small amount should be used because it is potentially poisonous). Shrublike plants have ornamental value for their deeply divided silvery-gray leaves, velvety in texture; the taste of wormwood is exceedingly bitter, and even its aroma can cause headaches. We handle the plant as little as possible, just for spring pruning of woody stems to renew growth, and before flowering, to dry as a medicinal. Wormwood is most famous as the main flavoring ingredient in absinthe. 'Lambrook Silver', a more compact, ornamental form from eighteen to thirty-two inches tall, has luxuriant silvery foliage; an unnamed Chinese species of Artemisia we grew from seed produces a magnificent tall screen of filmy green foliage (silver on reverse).

Artemisia lactiflora, **white mugwort,** 4 ft. A close cousin of wormwood, this is grown mainly for its creamy-white flowering stems in late summer, scented like hawthorn. It's a plant of bushlike propor-tions to five feet with green leaves (silver on reverse), and we control its growth by cutting it back one-third or even halfway in midsummer. If soil is kept on the lean side, it will not need staking. To harvest for wreaths, we cut flowering stems in fresh bloom.

Artemisia **'Silver King',** 5 ft. When we read disparaging accounts of this favorite silvery plant, we take them with a grain of salt. Once you have accepted a plant for its invaluable qualities, you find ways to live with its vigor. Yes, 'Silver King', a cultivar of western mugwort

(*A. ludoviciana*), will colonize as large an area with its creeping roots as you permit, but if you are vigilant and reduce plantings every season without fail, they can be kept in check. Foliage is deeply cut and so silvery as to appear almost white. A wide background swath illuminates the entire bed, and like all silvers, it deepens, by contrast, those bright colors around it at the same time that it blends them harmoniously together. 'Valerie Finnis' is a more refined and elegant cultivar with broader leaves. To harvest for wreaths, cut stems just after the small creamy flowers have opened.

Chrysanthemum balsamita, costmary/Bible Leaf, $2\frac{1}{2}$ ft. This is an herb whose beauty resides solely in its long tapering green leaves (to twelve inches), whose edges look like they were trimmed with pinking shears. Occasionally mature plants—gawky in appearance—produce flowering stems of small button flowers. Costmary's lemon-scented leaves are packed with essential oils, are very attractive to slugs, and are hard to dry, but we can't live without them. To stimulate the production of fresh, unchewed leaves, we harvest foliage regularly to use in simmering potpourri and skin freshener (see page 143); we also like to press perfect leaves to include in letters. Costmary was used by the early colonists in preparations to ease childbirth, hence its common name "sweet Mary."

Echinacea purpurea 'Magnus', purple coneflower, $2\frac{1}{2}$–3 ft. We like to grow the showier cultivar here and the wildflower on the bank. 'Magnus' has large flowers with horizontal, flaring pink-purplish petals and the usual bronze central cone. An attractor for butterflies in late summer, it is a great companion for all silvery plants. In recent years, purple coneflower and other species have become well known in preparations purported to help boost flagging immune systems.

Levisticum officinale, **lovage,** 5–6 feet. One of the most useful plants we grow, like an oversize celery with dark green divided leaves, its flavor is intensely celery-like with a dash of angelica. In spring we relish the reddish-green shoots as an early green chopped into dandelion salad or cottage cheese. Before plants send up large hollow stems that bear umbels of tiny yellowish flowers, we cut back plants almost to the ground so we can dry the lush foliage to use in our Herb Salt and Herb Blend mixes (see page 142).

Monarda **sp.,** 3 ft. Years ago we sowed seeds of 'Panorama Mix', a seed strain of hybrid monardas ranging in color from violet and purple to shades of warm pink, and these are the ones we grow in the Harvest Bed. Hybrids created by crossing native species, among them scarlet *Monarda didyma*—a plant of damp and shady habitats—and violet *M. fistulosa*—a plant that prefers dry and sunny habitats—are better suited to ordinary garden conditions. These produce showy, tubular flowers in whorls from color-tinged bracts, and aromas ranging from sweet to sharp and spicy that are released when plants are lightly brushed. Depending on the length of the flower tube, each color type attracts either bees or hummingbirds, or both. Leaves can be dried for teas or used to flavor soups and meat dishes (like bay leaf), flowers can be dried to add to winter bouquets (Figure 30) or potpourri.

Origanum vulgare **'Compactum Nanum',** 6 in. This undervalued variant of wild marjoram creates a low, perfectly rounded form of spice-scented foliage (like nutmeg) topped by tiny pink flowers in late summer. It has proved consistently hardy and only needs to be divided every other season. We save trimmings to add to potpourri.

Origanum vulgare **subsp.** *vulgare* **'Showy Oregano',** 18–24 in. We first grew this dwarf, more compact and showier form of wild marjoram

Figure 30.
Harvest Bed bouquet.

when we sowed seeds of what was labeled 'Greek Oregano'. We were delighted with the results, not for flavoring but as a flowery mounded accent at the front of the Harvest Bed. Plants need to be thinned every year, but it's worth the effort. The masses of nectar-rich pink florets with purplish-tinged bracts are covered with bees most of the summer.

Perovskia atriplicifolia, **Russian sage,** 3–5 feet. This plant is neither Russian nor a sage, but it is very desirable for landscaping (we're not sure if it's an herb). A shrublike plant, it has a billowy, airy grace and silvery cast, whorls of lavender flowers by late summer, and a compelling spicy aroma with a camphoraceous note. To keep it returning every year, its roots need perfect drainage, and its woody stems need spring pruning to stimulate new growth (wait until you see a hint of silver sprouting from bare stems).

Rumex acetosa, **garden sorrel,** $2\frac{1}{2}$ ft. When this herb's reddish-tipped leaves push through cold soil in the early spring at the same time as lovage and chives, we hail the new growing season (and our first salads). Puckered leaves are sour in flavor, so only a small handful is needed for flavoring (unless you are a devotee of sorrel soup—we're not). By early summer, seed stalks bear greenish flower panicles that turn to reddish-brown, similar in appearance to dock, to which it is related; these have some value when dried for winter bouquets. Renew plantings by division every few years.

Ruta graveolens, **rue,** 3 ft. We value rue for its mounded, shrubby appearance, one that gives substance to a planting dominated by annuals. Its lacy, glaucous foliage is protected from drought by the powder that dusts its leaves (giving them a bluish appearance). By midsummer, plants are topped by yellow flower clusters that bring swallowtail butterflies. Even after the flowers are gone, the desiccated seed heads remain attractive into the winter months (flowers and seed heads dry well for winter bouquets). Rue's reputation for warding off evil is derived from its pungent-acrid scent. Under certain conditions, the action of sunlight on the oils in the plant's leaves can cause a skin rash and the intensity of oil increases in older plants, so wear gloves if you have sensitive skin. In our many years of growing rue, we have never been bothered, but beware.

Tanacetum parthenium, **feverfew,** 2 ft. A charming daisy flower with a wide, flattish yellow center and stubby white rays, single feverfew and its double-flowered cousin, 'Flore Pleno' (white pompons) has a long history of medicinal use to treat fevers and headaches. Every part of the plant, even its seeds, exudes a strong medicinal aroma. We value feverfew as a mixer among annuals and perennials, and the double form as a dried flower. This is a short-lived perennial that becomes woody with age and produces fewer flowers or dies off, so be sure to make cuttings in the spring by replanting a piece of basal growth with a heel of old stem.

Tanacetum vulgare **'Crispum', fernleaf tansy,** 3–4 ft. Despite its aggressive ways, we like tansy for its fresh, cleansing scent and finely cut leaves. While we curb our desires by growing regular tansy in naturalized stands away from cultivated plants, we can't resist the handsome variant 'Crispum', with arching, heavily textured, emerald green leaves like miniature hat plumes, so we found a way to include it in the Harvest Bed by growing it in an old, leaky tub. Unlike regular tansy, 'Crispum' rarely produces yellow button flowers, but its foliage is in demand for fresh bouquets, especially with roses. Heavily mulched, it only needs watering in drought periods. Traditionally, tansy has a long history of use as a medicinal and dye plant.

DIRECTIONS FOR HERB SALT/SALT-FREE HERB BLEND; SKIN FRESHENER; BEGINNER'S ARTEMISIA WREATH BASE

All-Purpose Herb Salt/Salt-Free Herb Blend

For every cup of table salt, mix in the following amounts of dried, flaked herbs (we press dried leaves through a colander): 1 cup lovage or celery leaves; ½ cup parsley; ½ cup chives, cut fine; a small handful each of dried calendula and chive petals. Mix in 1 tablespoon good dark-red paprika, 1½ teaspoons onion powder, 1 teaspoon pulverized dill, ¾ teaspoon ground black pepper, ¾ teaspoon powdered garlic. Mix all ingredients well, then store in jars away from light. For a salt-free blend, omit salt and spices. Use these mixes instead of salt to flavor soups, stews, rice, salads, meat, fish dishes, and even popcorn.

Skin Freshener

Place the following in a widemouthed jar with a nonreactive cover: 1 part each the foliage of costmary, mint, and southernwood (Artemisia abrotanum) sprays; these will need to be trimmed with clippers since they're woody. Add a large handful of signet marigolds, foliage and flowers. Pour cider vinegar to cover the herbs, then place the jar, covered, in a sunny spot for about two weeks; strain the mixture through two thicknesses of cheesecloth and pour it into small, narrow-necked jars, diluting it by half with water, then cover with a nonreactive cover (if in doubt, first cover the jar opening with plastic wrap). To use this on hot, muggy days to refresh your spirits, dab it behind your ears and on your neck and wrists—it's like applying an ice pack (Jo Ann used to keep a bottle close by when she worked in the hayfield). Store in a cupboard away from light.

Beginner's Artemisia Wreath Base

Jo Ann designed this simplified technique for teaching classes of beginners who thought they had no talent for such crafts (she started with herself). Within an hour, each student can produce an elegant wreath base. Assemble the following materials:

1. Clothes hanger
2. Artemisia of choice

3. Green floral tape

4. Roll of 28-gauge flexible wire

5. Kitchen scissors

6. Small spray bottle

Cover clothes hanger, including top hook, with floral tape, holding it at an angle and stretching it gently. Cut off sprays of three- to four-inch leafy stems from the dried herbage, first spraying them lightly with water so they don't shatter when you work with them. Holding the leafy stems in the shape of a fan, keep adding to the bunch until the fan is full, then trim the stems so they're even. Cut a twelve-inch piece of wire, wrap about four inches of it tightly at the base of the fan so it is forced to spread out evenly, place the fan so it's centered on the base, then wrap the rest of the wire to attach the fan tightly to the base. When the next fan is attached, it is laid on top of the stems of the first one and so on, until the whole base is thickly and tightly covered with artemisia. No glue gun is needed to embellish the wreath with dried flowers; these can be inserted snugly into the base with their stems. The beauty of these simple wreaths is in the artemisias themselves, in their range of silver, gray, cream, and amber colors. For interesting effects (and if you're short of material), mix types together. ●

CHAPTER SEVEN

Roses

—

THE FIRST SPRING ON THE FARM, we planted six roots of the Virginia or common rose (*Rosa virginiana*), dug from the thickets that grow alongside the dirt roads here. We had built a fifteen-foot extension onto the front porch and we thought a hedge would look nice there. The choice was accidentally brilliant. "Accidentally" since we had chosen the Virginia rose not for its characteristics (about which we knew nothing), but because it was there and we had little cash to spend on landscaping; "brilliant" because it was the finest rose for our needs.

This underrated native has been one of the most successful of our plantings. Although bone ignorant about roses—the wide variety of types, the pitfalls of growing them, the ones suited to our purposes—we had "chosen" a terrific all-season hedge. Growing naturally to six feet, the Virginia rose's leaves are dark green and glossy; its flowers, in the classic wild design, are five-petaled and loosely arranged around fluffy golden stamens. Varying in color from light to dark pink, the roses freely waft their scent in midsummer. Like most wild roses, they are once-blooming,

Figure 31.
Jigs on porch with Virginia rose in the fall.

but by early fall so many clusters of dark-red round fruits or hips abound that the bushes appear to rebloom. Leaves gradually turn from green to rosy-bronze and vivid scarlet, and like the hips, they remain well into winter. In thirty years, the Virginia rose hedge has given us nothing but pleasure (Figure 31), requiring only shearing back every spring to confine its height to five feet (taller than that obstructs the view).

Despite this initial success, we did not draw any conclusions about roses, either about their suitability for our growing conditions or for general landscaping. We had other things on our mind: how to grow enough food from one season to the next to feed our family of six. We were not immune to creating beauty in our lives, as our efforts in the Harvest Bed attest, but we weren't going out of our way to explore the possibilities among roses. Like many gardeners, we felt that growing roses was fraught with difficulties, a subject best left to specialists or those with lots of time and money on their hands.

Five years after planting the Virginia rose hedge, circumstances encouraged us to take the plunge and plant roses in front of our handsome, newly built log cabin (1973) for paying summer guests. Building the cabin was a family project of which we were proud. We had gone deep into the woods to select suitable trees for cabin logs, had cut them down with crosscut saws, had skidded them down a steep hill with a horse, and with the team had hauled them across difficult terrain to the site. There we peeled, then cut them into lengths, and built up the cabin, log by log. The area in front of its spacious front porch called for a planting. But of what? In our mind's eye we saw roses.

In 1976, succumbing to advertisements for superhardy roses, we planted three: 'Therese Bugnet' and 'Sir Thomas Lipton', both shrub types, and 'Blaze', a climber. The first two were hardy enough but did not thrive, the last succumbed after one season. 'Therese Bugnet', a justly praised, vigorous hybrid with rugosa parentage in its lines, is vase-shaped, bearing clusters of moderately fragrant soft-pink double roses on distinctive red stems; a first great flush of bloom is followed by moderate flowering all summer. When we moved suckers to a different site, they thrived, but we failed to note why. The famous 'Sir Thomas Lipton' is a double white, fragrant rose reputed to bloom all summer, but it languished and was eventually removed. We successfully grew one other rose about this time, the deep yellow Persian (*Rosa foetida* 'Persiana'). We had planted it in front of the house, but when we added the greenhouse and had to move it, it died. That was when we learned about grafted roses. In replanting this rose, we had neglected to bury the graft (where the top rose and understock are joined) deep enough, with the result that it was damaged by exposure to severe winter conditions, so the top part—the Persian rose—died, leaving the vigorous, wild understock—the thorny dog rose (*Rosa canina*)—to take over.

These experiences cooled our brief romance with roses. From the early to the late 1980s we added only two more roses to our landscape: a wild rugosa, *Rosa rugosa* 'Rubra Plena' (Figure 32)—large, loosely double crimson flowers with strong clove scent—and the ancient Apothecary's rose, *Rosa gallica* 'Officinalis'—semidouble rose-red flowers with showy golden stamens—both from neighbor's shoots. These we planted in our rough-and-ready fashion (we made no exceptions, even for roses): Rather than dig the recommended depth and width for roses—two feet deep by eighteen inches wide, impossible in our hard sod ground without a backhoe—we dug a hole just large enough to accommodate the roots, then heavily mulched the surrounding area. As the nutrient-rich compost mulch broke down, it released nutrients to the roots beneath and eventually turned hard sod into friable earth. This feeding of nutrients from the top down rather than directly to the roots in the traditional manner is a slower way to grow roses, but the point is, roses can thereby be grown successfully in unfavorable conditions; it just takes longer (add

Figure 32.
Victor relaxes beside the informal rugosa hedge.

on about two growing seasons to the traditional three years for a rose to attain its mature size). Both plantings are now fine informal hedges (we don't trim them): The five-foot rugosa hedge defines the top of the driveway along one side; the Apothecary, three feet tall and wide, established on a slope opposite the driveway, connects the Flowering Herb Garden to the path that leads to the barn. The flowers' combined aromas float over the landscape during the month of July and into August.

By the late 1980s, we were selling perennial herbs and flowers as well as roses propagated from our modest collection. Our customers liked these, but they wanted more. They wanted roses that were hardy without winter protection and were low-maintenance, disease- and insect-free, scented, and everblooming. In other words, they wanted the perfect rose, the one that has continued to elude rose breeders. We had some experience with roses, but we knew we had a lot to learn, so we set out to discover how close we could come to fulfilling our customers' expectations. We would use our experiments as the basis for future workshops and plant sales. The types we decided to explore belong to the same group of tough roses we were already growing; these are shrub roses, so called because of their stature and substantial hardwood growth.

The first step was to establish a bed for evaluating garden types that grew to three feet for mixed plantings among perennials and annuals. The obvious choice of site—sunny with good air circulation to discourage disease—was adjacent to the Harvest Bed on the west side of the house where there was plenty of room before the land sharply slopes down toward the pasture and pond below. The only other planting there was a long-established rough hedge of elderberries near the top of the knoll.

In deference to their deep roots, we spread a thick layer of newspaper, rather than plastic, over sod ground, covering an area exactly parallel to the long, narrow Harvest Bed (sixty feet long by four feet wide), enclosed it with recycled electricity poles when our old ones were replaced by the power company, and filled it with rough and finished compost. We made sure the grass path between the beds was wide enough to operate a small power mower or for two people to walk. The plan was to leave enough room among them to try out a variety of companion plants: annuals and perennials, flowers, herbs, and ground covers. The roses, ten altogether, were staggered down the bed in a zigzag pattern, so no single one would overshadow the others.

The no-dig raised bed was an unqualified success for growing roses, and in three seasons they looked like they had been there forever. No wonder we were able to achieve in just a few years what had been beyond our ability two decades earlier. The beautiful roses adorning our new log cabin, the ones we had seen in our mind's eye in 1976, had failed because we had ignored the basic requirements of virtually all roses: sun; well-drained, enriched soil; and uncrowded growing conditions. The cabin had been built at the edge of woodland on marshy ground unsuitable for any other purpose, and none of our raised bed tricks could alter that fact. We had not then absorbed the primary lesson of successful gardening: match plants to habitat, not the other way around.

But although we had carefully chosen roses for their stated height (often at variance with how they actually grew), we had neglected to consider their form, a most important aspect of shrub roses. While vigorous rugosas like 'Dart's Dash' and 'Frau Dagmar Hartopp' do grow upward to three feet, they also spread three feet wide or more, making them difficult to accommodate in a small or medium-size bed or border; these, we learned, are better for hedges or accents. 'Jens Munk', on the other hand, grew to over four feet in the raised bed (advertised as three and one-half), but its arching stems allowed room for companion plants. Planted in the center of the bed (a happy accident), it is a focal point all season, its branches laden with semidouble, fragrant pink flowers—an appealing and underrated modern rose (1974) with old rose charm.

Soon we started adding plant companions. As a substitute for lavender, which is often combined with roses but is difficult to grow here, we planted southernwood, a shrubby, aromatic artemisia with soft gray-green, finely cut foliage. "Poor man's lavender" will grow in virtually any ground, is immune to drought, and can be confined to two and one-half feet by hard pruning in spring. Since gray and silver plants are classic rose companions (and drought resistant), we pursued this theme with lamb's ears at the front of the bed and with the biennial rose campion (*Lychnis coronaria*), throughout. Its first-year silvery rosettes, lovely in themselves, produce silvery stems the second year, topped by the generous production of small, deep magenta or pure white flowers.

The silver theme was carried aloft in a planter fashioned from a scrap of attractive cast-iron openwork (an old woodstove cover). After it was turned upside down to resemble a basket, it was nailed atop a three-foot fence post, then the basket was lined with moss, topped with soil, and planted with beach wormwood (*Artemisia stelleriana*) or with false licorice (*Helichrysum petiolare*), both trailing types, the former with ghostly white, deeply cut, felted foliage, the latter a mass of stiff silvery stems covered with silvery round leaves. The exposed soil surface of the planter was thickly mulched with small rocks to retain moisture, thus reducing the need for daily watering.

We focused on three other colors for the Rose Bed: blues, pinks, and white, with purple accents and dashes of lime and gold. Among annuals, we have planted white sweet alyssum (*Lobularia maritima*); pansies of all sorts (these live on in the shade of taller roses year after year with only a midsummer cutback); open-pollinated petunias—white vining and the small-flowered magenta wild sort (*Petunia integrifolia*)—both lax and spreading like ground covers; Chinese forget-me-not (Cynoglossum 'Firmament'), with tight clusters of tiny blue flowers; dwarf viper's bugloss (Echium 'Brilliant'), with uncoiling stems crowded with pink, lilac, blue, or white flowers; Texas bluebonnet (*Lupinus texensis*); baby's breath; dwarf lime nicotiana; tall-stemmed Calendula 'Pacific Beauty' (gold and apricot); painted sage—pink and white; and a range of ruffled, pastel, and red Shirley poppies. For late summer bloom, we planted Lavatera 'Mont Blanc' and the seldom grown 'Ruby Regis', a striking deep rose, as well as the magnificent *Malope trifida*, or Spanish mallow, an oversize lavatera with similar, but showier flowers, each with a chartreuse eye (also seldom grown).

Among perennial rose companions, we have grown pink monarda, various salvias ('East Friesland' and 'May Night'), veronicas, pure white musk mallow (*Malva moschata*), and pinks (especially the glaucous-leaved, fragrant Dianthus 'Ballad Blend'). Herbs, besides southernwood, include catmint (Nepeta 'Dropmore Blue')—a graceful trailing form at the edge of the bed's wooden barriers—and single and double white feverfew. A few ground covers such as white violets (*Viola odorata*), Lamium 'Beacon Silver', and Roman wormwood (*Artemisia pontica*)—a frilly silver mound that, like the others, must be controlled in a garden bed. These are attractive beneath low, wide roses like 'Dart's Dash' and 'Frau Dagmar Hartopp'. The Rose Bed, like the Harvest Bed opposite it, is jammed with plants, a colorful tapestry of form and color, of foliage and flowers in complementary layers, a suggestion of how roses may be grown in a flower bed or border.

Several years after the Rose Bed was established, we had an illuminating experience, one that put all our garden-making efforts in perspective. When viewed from certain angles, the path between the Harvest Bed and Rose Bed disappears and the two beds appear to merge into one wide border, an astonishing sight.

Imagine the scene: We emerge from a quick swim (and wash) in our pond after a heavy two hours in the heat, sweaty and itchy from putting in a load of hay with the horses. We quickly dress, pick up our boots and socks and walk through the pasture to the knoll above, ascend the wooden stairs by the elderberry hedge and when we reach the very top, just before we turn right toward the house, we pause, transfixed by

Figure 33.
Harvest and Rose Bed in full bloom.

the wide, colorful border ahead and on our left. No barriers are evident
from this perspective, except for the one in front of the Rose Bed, and
it is mostly obscured by an abundance of flowers and foliage—petunias,
echium, and southernwood—trailing over its side onto the green carpet
of grass (Figure 33). Did we create this new garden or did it spring up,
as if by magic, while we were working in the field?

In the background, dark-eyed pink hollyhocks rise above the top of
the weathered slabs; brown-centered sunflowers, bronze and yellow, are
beginning to open here and there, scarlet runner beans—lengthening
pods and colorful flowers—are tall, bushy accents clinging to the fence

(through which we can just see white turkeys), soft orange Tithonia spreads wide behind bright pink and purple painted sage, mounds of tangerine marigolds, green origanums, and drifts of bright calendulas are seen as background for what appears to be the front of the bed (it's actually the Rose Bed) of flowing mauve, silvers, grays, and blues, of vivid pink monarda shimmering with bees, straight spikes of white painted sage, tall golden and apricot calendulas, with roses—red, pink, and white—rising above them, opulent 'Jens Munk' in the middle of the bed, red velvet 'Survivor' rose on a trellis at the very end.

The illusory border not only emphasized our emerging garden style— a preference for mixed plantings of herbs, flowers, and roses, a repetition of sweeps of color, mediating pastels, silvers, and gold, close plantings with no bare ground, an air of informality tightly defined by barriers (and therefore appearing more abundant)—but just as important, it emphasized the interdependence of every element in our landscape. The Rose Bed complements the Harvest Bed, and these in turn depend on the presence of the turkey fence and yard as well as the surrounding land itself—the green grass, the steep slope to the pasture below, the surrounding woodland—for their greatest effect, for a sense of harmony and balance. What we had seen by chance—a trick of the eye—inspired us to maintain the choice as an aesthetic ideal.

The need to test more vigorous roses to six feet led to the further development of the west side of the house, already unrecognizable from its humble beginnings. The only area here where there was room to establish the informal hedge we envisioned was at the top of the knoll above the elderberries and blackberries. Here we dug holes to accom-modate roots as we had for earlier hedge plantings, in hard, sod ground, then heavily mulched a large circle around each rose: newspaper, compost, old hay or straw on top. At first unsightly, the mulch broke down after two seasons into soil that was soft enough to weed. Although the resulting hedge was far from uniform in appearance, we liked its diversity of shapes, some roses straight and tall, others wide and arching. We took the bold step of altering sprawling growth that interfered with mowing or was unattractive. The double cinnamon rose (*Rosa cinnamomea* 'Plena'), for instance, has long, weak stems that blow in the wind, causing the bush to lean. We liked the rose well enough— double pink flowers, small and fragrant—but not its ungainly shape, so we trimmed out extra growth, twined the remaining stems tightly around a fence post (a foot shorter than the bush), and wound old panty hose legs around them to hold them in place, thus creating a small pillar rose (Figure 34). Traditionally, a pillar rose is one of tall, upright habit that is secured to a post to create vertical bloom. We used a similar technique on the dog rose (*Rosa canina*) planted at the end of the hedge with phenomenal results. A no-account, thorny rose was transformed into a handsome and neat vertical accent of bright green foliage all season, an impressive tower of summer bloom—each flower composed of five clear pink petals, white at their base, surrounding numerous golden stamens—followed by abundant sprays of dark-red oval hips all fall, and well into winter. All of these vigorous roses are kept within bounds by hard spring pruning and summer mowing.

Now the area was bound on one side by an informal hedge, on the other by the turkey fence, with two long, straight beds between them. The grass was confined to two paths, one between the Harvest and Rose Beds, the other between the Rose Bed and the Rose Bank, as we now called it (see Figure 7, on page 24). The visual pleasure we derived from this straightforward design made us appreciate the ancient love of garden geometry. The long, rectangular, straight-edged beds create a sense of order and boundaries within which there is freedom to create graceful plantings of abundant variety; the paths gave us a convenient way to enjoy the plants' aromas and beauty at close range, especially at twilight on the way to shut in the poultry, when silvers, whites, and pale yellows are luminous.

But we were not finished here. We needed a place to grow a few climbing roses, and the side of the fence facing the house, at right angles to the Harvest Bed, was the logical choice. Here we established an old multiflora hybrid—"vigorous" is too tame to describe its nature—that we call Veronica's Rambler after the elderly gardener who gave us a root. Growing on long stems to ten feet and bearing masses of cone-shaped

Figure 34.
Pillar dog rose.

heads, each composed of numerous small, cupped, tea-scented flowers ranging from dark to light pink as they mature, it erupts in midsummer, wholly dominating the fence and the entire surrounding area, drawing visitors like a magnet. Its strong, stout stems insert themselves into the narrow spaces between the fence boards, obviating the need for any other support. 'Dorothy Perkins' and 'Excelsa' (sometimes called Red Dorothy Perkins) flower just after Veronica's Rambler, the one with tight pink flower clusters, the other with red, but both are weak stemmed and require tying up to the fence (as we learned, they do better on an arbor). With a thriving *Clematis* x *jackmanii* by the turkey fence gate (a place where a Golden Comet pullet can be found every afternoon, perched among its large purple flowers), and a mix of perennials— 'Johnson's Blue' geranium, phlox, and rudbeckia—we declared the area complete (Figure 35).

The living and working landscape around the house, log cabin, vegetable garden, Herb and Harvest Beds, Rose Bed and Bank soon expanded to include rose accents beyond the hedges we have already described. Unlike a hedge, an accent is a single plant of any sort that not only enhances the area where it grows but stands out as a distinctive feature that can be seen from a distance and that can transform an otherwise dull area. On a steep slope between the Apothecary rose hedge and the shop—soon to be naturalized with wild flowers—we planted a single rose, the famous rugosa 'Blanc Double de Coubert', considered to be the most beautiful of all white roses. A mature bush reaches six feet, its spreading stems are clothed in handsome dark green foliage, its ravishing flowers, exquisite in long buds, are intensely fragrant and pure white, loosely clustered but not blowsy, tailored just enough to preserve their shape for several days. 'Blanc' produces roses all season, but not as generously as during its first flush in early July.

Just beyond the slope, where the path to the barn crosses through a red wooden gate to the barn pasture, we planted *Rosa* 'Henry Kelsey', a Canadian-bred rose in the Explorer series, and a fine distant accent (See Figure 36, on page 161). With trailing stems, bushes are said to reach nine feet, but we tied the stems horizontally to the pasture rail fence, where they are stimulated to produce more blooms than if left to grow

Figure 35.
Golden Comet pullet on top of the turkey fence
with Clematis *x* jackmanii.

upright. Flowers are deep red, semidouble with showy golden stamens, and borne in heavy clusters all season (with a pause in August); fragrance is light. 'Henry Kelsey' not only creates a pretty picture draped over the fence, but it is the end of a vista along the path between the slope and the vegetable garden, marking the transition from house and gardens to the heart of the farm—the barn, pastures, and hay field beyond.

But what about the perfect rose, the one our customers were looking for? How have our roses stacked up against the desired characteristics of hardiness, low maintenance, freedom from disease and pests, scent, and nonstop blooming? Since there are many more possible candidates than the forty-two roses we have grown over the last thirty years, our conclusions are merely suggestive.

1. Hardiness. The roses we selected to grow were chosen mainly from species or wild types, Old Garden Roses (Albas, Gallicas, Damasks), rugosas and their hybrids, the Canadian Explorer series (bred for cold climates), and the Canadian prairie-bred Morden series (bred for resistance to cold, wind, and drought). We avoided David Austin roses, desirable as they are, because most are marginally hardy here at best. While dieback occurs regularly in a few roses—'Champlain', 'Alexander MacKenzie', 'The Fairy'—all our roses have proved to be ironclad hardy with no winter protection.

2. Low Maintenance. Shrub roses require pruning only to trim to the desired shape and eliminate dead, old, or crossed branches. Ours receive an annual top-dressing of compost and a handful to one-half cup of fertilizer, depending on the size of the rose. As part of our fall routine, each rose—or bed of roses—receives another top-dressing of horse manure or compost (a passive form of winter protection). We occasion-

Figure 36.
Rosa *'Henry Kelsey' on pasture fence.*

ally water roses during drought periods (at least those roses easily reached from the house) with a bucket of wastewater recycled from the kitchen, but other than that, all depend on rainfall (with regular watering, most would produce more flowers).

3. Disease- and insect-free. Shrub roses are tough, and although some are afflicted with disease from time to time (powdery mildew, black spot) and insects (white fly and aphids), in our experience these attacks are not serious enough to hurt them. If hardy shrub roses are planted in favorable conditions and routinely enriched, as described above, they bounce back in healthy trim. Spraying against insects or disease is a matter of choice. For serious infestations of white fly, we have sprayed with Malathion when none of the "organic" methods worked; however, we prefer to focus on cultural practices where these can be effective. When we moved lemon balm—a white fly attractor—from the Harvest Bed and grew it elsewhere as an annual (thus denying insects winter quarters), our problems with white fly diminished considerably. 'Henry Kelsey' is susceptible to black spot (a fungus that appears as black spots on foliage), but this is an affliction of short duration in late summer during hot, humid weather and the rose is vigorous enough to produce replacement leaves by late summer. The only rose that has never been bothered by either disease or insects is the wild rugosa, *Rosa rugosa* 'Rubra Plena'.

4. Scent. Since we ourselves prefer fragrant roses, we sought such types, but hardiness was considered more important (we'd rather have a scentless rose than none at all). Fortunately, the hardiest types (rugosas and their hybrids) are the most fragrant. Those with the most intense, floating scent are *R. rugosa* 'Rubra Plena' and 'Blanc Double de Coubert'.

5. Everblooming. This is tricky. Some roses described as everblooming are actually repeat bloomers; that is, they bloom in flushes. The time between flushes may vary—shorter in some types, longer in others—but usually there is a noticeable pause while the rose seems to be taking a deep breath, drawing on its reserves to produce more buds. While it may be literally true that a rose like 'Therese Bugnet' is never without bloom, it cannot be called truly everblooming in the sense of the even production of flowers all season, as in the Hybrid Teas. But even if 'Champlain' is our only truly everblooming rose, the shrub roses, as a group, bloom in turn from June through November.

Our experiment to find The Perfect (Superhardy) Rose may have failed according to these standards, but it also showed us the folly of such a concept, for as we have learned, each rose possesses virtues that give it a desirable character all its own. We admire a variety of rugosas for their intense fragrance, handsome deep green leaves, and generally tough constitutions; antique roses for their often glaucous leaves (Albas), lush flowers, and heavenly scent; Mordens for their tailored flowers (like Hybrid Teas), bright colors, smooth, thornless stems, and resistance to drought; Grootendoorsts for their small, but prolific, fringed flowers into November, and the distinct mounded shape of the shrub; Veronica's Rambler for its incomparable show of flowers and stout supporting stems. We cherish 'John Davis' for its tight-centered, clear pink flowers— yes, the majority of hardy roses are pink, but there is infinite variety among them, from the shell pink 'Morden Blush' to the deep magenta of the fabulous quartered blooms of 'Charles de Mills'. And not least, we love 'Henry Hudson' for its mass of pointed, flushed pink buds, fragrant white flowers (these must be deadheaded, an admitted flaw), its accommodation to a garden setting, and its pleasing form at all seasons, even in the winter, when its compact, twiggy head, dusted with snow, holds itself up like a cupped palm.

If the old apple trees, the barn, the farmhouse, fields, and surrounding woods were the beginning bones of our landscape, then roses are its finishing touch, the connecting link to the entire farm panorama of house, gardens, barn, and pastures. Conquering fear of the unknown, we have become rose aficionados, convinced by our experiences that roses have too much to offer to be ignored. They are, as someone once observed, a gift of the angels. That we have succeeded in growing them in such unpromising circumstances and with such limited resources should be encouraging to others. We say, go forth and grow roses, the ones best suited to your own soil and climate, give them sun, room to grow, and well-drained soil, and they will be a source of great pleasure for you, as they are for us

Sampler of Favorite Hardy Roses
(and the Absolute Truth About Them)

We do not have the last word on roses. There are gardeners who have devoted a lifetime to growing many more than we have, yet we can say we have explored one facet of the subject, hardy roses, and about these we are committed to conveying a balanced view—we note attributes as well as failings—to help guide the uninitiated. Most hardy roses are thorny in varying degree, so we only note thorns if they are a prominent feature.

The roses described here, all hardy to Zone 4, fall into several categories: species or wild, unimproved types; antique or Old Garden Roses (OGRs); early rugosa hybrids; Explorer Roses—named after explorers of Canada—a series begun at the Ottawa Experimental Farm in Canada in 1961 using *Rosa rugosa* and *R. kordesii* in their parentage (the former is vigorous, with white or purplish-pink scented flowers; the latter introduces true red flowers and a climbing habit), with the goal of producing extreme hardiness, repeat bloom, and resistance to disease; Parkland Roses—with "Morden" in their names—were developed at the Agriculture Canada Research Station in Morden, Manitoba, beginning in the early 1960s, for prairie and similar conditions using the wild prairie rose, *Rosa arkansana,* in its program to produce long-blooming, disease-resistant roses (with light fragrance or none) that quickly recover from winter dieback; and climbers and ramblers. As already noted, all of these roses are hardy to Zone 4 with little or no winter cover. By choosing wisely you can have roses in bloom from late spring to late summer.

Because we think it very important to dispel the notion that, unlike Hybrid Tea roses, hardy roses are large shrubs suitable only for specimen or hedge planting, we include here annuals and perennials we have successfully combined with hardy roses in a confined garden situation; consider also Harvest Bed and Flowering Herb Garden annuals and perennials such as annual clary, love-in-a-mist, feverfew, monardas, bistort, lupines, Geranium 'Johnson's Blue', and pansies, as well as favorite plants whose form, whether low and spreading, slender, or bushy, complements your garden roses. As with the rose selection itself, we hope readers will use these recommendations as the beginning of their own explorations.

'Agnes', 5 ft. x 5 ft. (*R. rugosa* x *R. foetida* 'Persiana'), 1922. In our experience 'Agnes' is prone to foliage disease and blooms once (claims to the contrary), but for those who crave a hardy yellow rose of distinction, this is it. Early blooming flowers have a fruity fragrance, are exquisitely shaped and flushed with apricot, turning light yellow as they mature. Plants are propagated by grafting.

'Blanc Double de Coubert', 5 ft. x 5 ft. (hybrid rugosa), 1892. This classic rugosa is justly famed for the beauty of its pure white, powerfully scented, double flowers. Extremely vigorous, with dark green leaves that set off both flowers and elongated buds, 'Blanc Double de Coubert' makes a terrific distant accent and a fine hedge. An early flush of bloom with consistent repeating to frost and a high canopy of golden foliage in the fall give this rose a long season of interest.

'Champlain', 3 ft. (Explorer: *R. kordesii* hybrid), 1982. While winter dieback prevents this rose from attaining its full size, its clusters of small red velvet roses from early summer to frost (truly everblooming) and its slender, open form highly recommend it as a garden rose. It is especially shown to advantage with white-flowered companions like double feverfew; remember that, as with all companion plantings, roses do best when not overcrowded.

'Charles de Mills', 4 ft. x 4 ft. (OGR, *Gallica* hybrid), date unknown. Sumptuously quartered blooms (a quantity of petals are crammed into four sections), almost five inches wide and scented, nearly maroon in color maturing to lighter purple, 'Charles de Mills' is a striking rose whose color alone gives it distinction among so many pinks (with which it nicely combines); once-blooming in midsummer. We have found that stems have difficulty supporting the weight of their blooms, so offer some support or confine growth by reducing the number of stems when pruning in the spring.

'Dart's Dash', 3 ft. x 4 ft. (hybrid rugosa), date unknown. One of several hybrid rugosas similar to the wild type, this is distinguished by its relatively low, wide form and double pink-purplish flowers (well scented) that repeat bloom from early summer to frost; large red hips and golden-bronze foliage in the fall.

'Dorothy Perkins', climber (*R. wichuraiana* x Hybrid Perpetual 'Mme Gabriel Luizet'), 1901. Although it declined in popularity because of its susceptibility to powdery mildew, where it survives as a family heirloom or an easily propagated pass-along plant, it is cherished for its extraordinary hardiness and its ability to clothe an arbor with profuse, once-blooming clusters of small pink flowers in midsummer; stems are very lax and must be supported to grow upright. This is a good choice for seaside or maritime climates, where 'Dorothy Perkins' seems to be immune to powdery mildew. No noticeable scent.

'Excelsa', climber (parentage unknown), 1908. Also called Red Dorothy Perkins for its similarity in appearance, this one is more striking, with profuse clusters of small velvety-red flowers. These two climbers pair well on an arbor where they bloom together; there is a White Dorothy Perkins that could be added for spectacular bloom. None of these have noticeable scent.

'Frau Dagmar Hartopp'/'Frau Dagmar Hastrup', 3 ft. x 4 ft. (rugosa hybrid), 1914 (See Figure 37, on page 168). Wider than its height, this singular rugosa bears well-scented, loose single blooms of a shimmering pink from early summer to fall. These are quickly followed by the formation of large red hips that turn very dark as they mature. A fall canopy of crimson foliage combined with spectacular hip display gives 'Frau Dagmar Hartopp' a long season of interest. Best as a single specimen/accent or hedge.

'Grootendoorst Supreme', 4 ft. x 3 ft. (sport of 'F. J. Grootendoorst': *R. rugosa rubra* x Polyantha 'Mme Norbert Levasseur'), 1936. The Grootendoorsts have been disparaged by rose authorities as "soulless," presumably because they lack scent. For those who crave hardy, long-blooming roses, however, the Grootendoorsts' ability to survive harsh winter conditions and return each season bearing bouquet-like sprays of small roses in early summer, with repeat blooming well into late fall, make them highly recommended. The flower sprays of 'Grootendoorst

Supreme', of a deeper color than 'F. J. Grootendoorst', are deep crimson and resemble miniature fringed carnations; thorny. We grow this one in a hedge of mixed roses.

'Hansa', 6 ft. x 6 ft. (rugosa hybrid), 1923. Very similar to the wild form except for the larger size of its blooms (with a similar clove scent) and attractive vaselike shape; a prolific first flush in early summer is followed by repeat bloom all season. A good accent or hedge rose.

'Harrison's Yellow', 6½ ft. x 11 ft. (*R. pimpinellifolia* x *R. foetida*), 1839. A once-blooming, semidouble, sulfur-yellow rose spectacular in late spring, it could be trained as a climber or pillar rose. While we have had no problems, it may be susceptible to black spot. We do know

Figure 37.
The spectacular rose hips on 'Frau Dagmar Hartopp'.

Figure 38.
Rosa *'Henry Hudson' buds and flower..*

that it suckers vigorously, which is why nineteenth-century American pioneers moving from east to west so easily pulled up shoots to plant across the land. Its history is preserved in its other common name, Yellow Rose of Texas.

'Henry Hudson', 2½ ft. x 3 ft. (Explorer: *R. rugosa* 'Schneezwerg' seedling), 1976 (Figure 38). One of the most successful modern hardy roses for its compact, dense form (most apparent in winter) that enhances any garden planting, the stunning beauty of its profuse bud display—small, pointed, and flushed pink—against dark green leaves, and its consistently generous repeat bloom from early summer to frost. Open flowers are semidouble, white, and fragrant, but (its only flaw) spent blooms resembling dirty rags must be deadheaded. If this is done routinely after each flush of bloom, it won't seem onerous and is a small price to pay for a nearly perfect rose; long-lasting fall foliage is rosy gold.

'Henry Kelsey', 10 ft. (Explorer: *R. kordesii* hybrid), 1976. If you've ever pined for a superhardy red climbing rose, this is it. With profuse (unscented), long-lasting, double-flowered clusters, enhanced by golden stamens in early summer and later repeat bloom, 'Henry Kelsey' shows to great advantage when its thorny stems are pegged down horizontally on a rail fence (this stimulates bloom). Black spot appears in August, but when temperatures cool, damaged leaves are quickly replaced.

'Jens Munk', 5 ft. x 5 ft. (Explorer: *R. rugosa* 'Schneezwerg' x 'Frau Dagmar Hartopp'), 1974. One of our favorite roses for its relaxed Old World look, achieved by the profuse bloom of semidouble clear pink flowers for most of the summer on arching branches; spicy fragrance is light. By heavy pruning of vigorous stem growth in the spring, we manage to grow this charming rose as a long-season accent in confined garden conditions; rose-and-golden fall foliage.

'John Davis', 6 ft. (Explorer: *R. kordesii* hybrid), 1986. An exquisitely formed pink rose with a tight center that gives it a long-lasting quality; scent is light. Flowers bloom in midsummer and repeat until frost. If its long trailing stems are tied to a post, 'John Davis' makes a magnificent pillar rose paired with purple-flowered *Clematis* x *jackmanii*.

'Leda', 3 ft. x 3 ft. (OGR, Painted Damask), before 1827. The most distinctive feature of this antique rose is its small, ruffled, sweetly scented white flowers, edged or "painted" rose. Although it only blooms once in early summer, flowering lasts a month. We have never found it to repeat bloom, as is sometimes claimed.

'Morden Blush', 1½–2 ft. (Parkland hybrid), 1988. This garden rose has the longest flowering of the Parkland series, from early summer to frost. More beautiful in bud and early bloom, its tight-centered, shell-pink flowers (great for corsages) open flat and in hot weather turn white. Very light fragrance.

'Morden Centennial', 4 ft. (Parkland hybrid), 1980. A superior rose with large, well-formed, medium-pink, double flowers (lightly scented) that repeat bloom from early summer to frost; it helps to remove spent blooms. Slender plants fit well in a garden setting.

'Pink Grootendoorst', 4 ft. x 3 ft. (same as 'Grootendoorst Supreme'), 1923. The flower sprays of 'Pink Grootendoorst' are nearly shell pink in color; stems are thorny. While vigorous, this Grootendoorst, with hard spring trimming of stems, can be grown as a showy, long-season accent in a generous flower border.

***Rosa canina,* dog rose,** 8 ft. x 6 ft. (species). Introduced from Europe by the early American colonists, the dog rose is extremely vigorous (and thorny) and is widely used as understock for grafting roses. Few gardeners can claim complete ignorance of this rose since when grafted roses winter-kill, the dog rose usually makes its unwanted appearance as the surviving understock. We turned it to advantage by tying its spreading stems to a post to create an upright or pillar form. Early blooming flowers are single and clear pink with white at their base, sweetly scented; small, oval, bright-red hips (high in vitamin C) form prolific clusters in the fall against bright, nearly evergreen foliage.

R. *cinnamomea* 'Plena', Cinnamon Rose, 4 ft. (OGR), before 1597. Once popular as a hedge, this once-blooming rose has small, double, raspberry-pink flowers, sweetly scented, in clusters, nice to dry whole for potpourri. Cinnamon refers to the rose's reddish-colored stems. Although its flowering period in early summer is brief, fall foliage is dark crimson and long lasting.

R. *foetida* 'Persiana', Persian Yellow, 5 ft. (OGR), 1837. Very important in breeding for its deep yellow color, Persian Yellow is magnificent in full bloom in early summer; scent is fruity. Flowers are very double, blooming in two flushes that quickly follow one another. This rose is always grafted, so plant (and move) with care.

R. *gallica* 'Officinalis', Apothecary's Rose, 3 ft. x 3 ft. (OGR), before 1600. This rose, introduced to Europe from Damascus in the thirteenth century, was brought to America by the colonists as an indispensable medicinal for its astringent properties. In early summer its once-blooming, ruffled rose-red flowers—semidouble and showing a frilly mass of golden stamens—are modern in appearance despite the rose's antiquity; when picked and dried for potpourri, the petals' fragrance gains in intensity. Its low, wide form makes the Apothecary's Rose useful as a hedge, but suckering will have to be controlled by regular mowing around the plant.

R. *rugosa* 'Rubra Plena', 6 ft. x 6 ft. (rugosa variant), date unknown. A flawless rose for the beauty of its lush semidouble purplish-pink flowers, powerful clove scent, healthy dark green foliage followed by large orange-red hips and crimson-and-gold foliage in the fall, and its absolute immunity to pests and diseases. Profuse early summer bloom is followed by repeat bloom all summer. This rugosa is a fine low-maintenance informal hedge and supplies the best petals for making rose petal jelly. For some reason, nurseries rarely offer it.

R. virginiana, **Virginia Rose,** 6 ft. (native species). An unjustly neglected native rose for low-maintenance landscaping and hedging, the Virginia Rose has a long season of interest despite its relatively brief bloom in midsummer. Flowers are single petaled, sweetly scented, and variably pink, from light to dark, showing off well against a background of green, glossy foliage. By fall, leaves show a colorful mixture of colors ranging from bronzy red to deep scarlet and purple, and these as well as a profusion of round red fruit clusters are long lasting. There is also a rare double-flowered form.

'Queen of Denmark'/'Königin von Dänemark', 3 ft. x 2½ ft. (OGR, Alba hybrid), 1826. A dense, compact shrub with glaucous foliage, it blooms lavishly once in midsummer with very double, quartered and cupped flowers, pure pink, and well scented. It is sometimes affected by powdery mildew in late summer.

'Therese Bugnet', 6 ft. (complex hybrid), 1950. It has the distinction of being cherished by gardeners all across North America for its outstanding characteristics of extreme hardiness, adaptability, and outstanding bloom in early summer, followed by intermittent repeat bloom to frost. Double flowers in clusters, soft pink and lightly scented, have an old-fashioned look especially when they are in full, lush bloom; stems are reddish.

Veronica's Rambler, 10–12 ft. (Multiflora rambler), date unknown. This is the ultimate pass-along rose. From a small piece given to us by an elderly gardener, it grew into a magnificent once-blooming rose whose thick (and thorny) stems support massive bloom in midsummer before 'Dorothy Perkins' and 'Excelsa'; stems are strong enough to insert themselves between the spaces of a slab fence and need no other support. Flowers are borne in cone-headed clusters composed of small pink, tea-scented flowers whose shades vary as they mature. Pushed out of fashion by everblooming types, old ramblers are still valued for their reliability and prolific flower display.

Rose Companions

ANNUALS

Calendula **'Pacific Beauty',** 18–24 in. Sow seeds outdoors when soil has warmed. An elegant variation on the cottage garden favorite, this seed strain produces long-stemmed, large, semidouble flowered daisies (some with dark centers) in colors that include cream, golden yellow, apricot, and orange.

Cynoglossum amabile **'Firmament',** Chinese forget-me-not, 18 in. Sow seeds outdoors in late spring or early summer. A dainty appearing but tough, self-seeding annual with gray-green leaves and sprays of bright blue forget-me-not type flowers, indispensable in rose bouquets. 'Blue Showers' and 'Pink Mystery' are taller forms.

Echium vulgare **'Dwarf Brilliant',** 18 in. Sow seeds outdoors in late spring or early summer. An improved form of viper's bugloss with rough basal leaves and elongating stems that uncoil all summer, packed with pink buds that open to small, funnel-shaped flowers in shades of blue and violet, occasionally white. Bees love them.

Lavatera **'Mont Blanc'** (white), L. 'Silver Cup' (pink), L. 'Regis Ruby' (cerise-pink), 21–24 in. Germination is most successful when seeds are sown outdoors before the last frost; seedlings suffer from transplanting. We like all lavateras for their strong bushy forms and large trumpet blooms in late summer, but our favorite is 'Regis Ruby' for its big state-ment: a mass of bright trumpets each four inches wide.

***Lobularia maritima* 'Snow Crystals',** sweet alyssum, 3 in. x 18 in. Start plants indoors ten to twelve weeks before the last frost; for best results, transplant seedlings in small clumps rather than as individual plants. We find the white form by far the most effective and vigorous of the sweet alyssums, valued for softening hard edges at the corners of raised beds with a frilly mound of bloom all summer and into early winter, if plants are trimmed back when they look tired. 'Snow Crystals' is a larger-flowered type. We dust with rotenone if there is evidence of cabbageworm destruc-tion (sweet alyssum belongs to the same Cruciferae family as cabbage).

Malope trifida, 3 ft. x 3 ft. Sow the same as lavateras. We discov-ered this close relative of Lavatera several years ago, and since then we have never been without it. Bushy, with showier flowers—large trumpets in glistening shades of pink with a chartreuse eye from the sepals at the flower's base—it bears exquisite elongated buds and pods. A good cut flower. This and the lavateras are stand-ins for once-blooming roses, which they resemble.

***Nicotiana* 'Dwarf Hybrids',** 10–12 in. Start plants indoors eight to ten weeks before the last frost. We have tried most of the dwarf types in rose and lime in the 'Domino', 'Nicki', and 'Merlin' series. In an open sunny site all bloom longer under the protective shade of a vigorous rose like 'Jens Munk'.

***Papaver rhoeas* 'Shirley',** 30 in. Sow seeds in the ground in late spring. These lovely variants of the wild corn poppy have an ethereal grace with their ruffled, nearly translucent, often rimmed flowers, single or doubles, in shades of pink, red, rose, salmon, and white.

Petunia **x** *hybrida.* Start plants indoors ten to twelve weeks before the last frost. We have tried many petunias over the years, and all combine well with roses in an open, sunny site, especially at the edges of a bed or border. Our favorites are the smaller-flowered low, spreading ground-cover types like the multiflora 'Fantasy' series. Plants produce one and one-half inch trumpets in the classic design in shades of blush and dark pink, purple velvet (our favorite), red, and white and do not need to be pinched to promote side growth. We like, too, the lax, old-fashioned vining petunias and the small-flowered, magenta wild petunia, *Petunia integrifolia* (also of vining habit), both described in detail in the Sampler section of Chapter Nine, "The Contained Garden."

PERENNIALS

Allium sphaerocephalum, **drumstick allium,** 2–3 ft. An under-valued allium that willingly fills small spaces around garden roses when its wandlike stems rise up in midsummer to bear striking purple-headed blooms that last for weeks (these dry well in their early stages).

Artemisia abrotanum, **southernwood,** 3 ft. x 3 ft. A never-fail herb that takes hold in virtually any soil (except wet) in a sunny site, this old-fashioned shrubby plant bears feathery gray-green leaves with a strong scent of lemon and camphor. In its natural state it sprawls (not unattractively), but in confined space you can control its growth to a neat mound by clipping stems back to six inches in the spring.

A. schmidtiana **'Silver Mound',** 10 in. x 18 in. We like to grow this perfectly mounded plant in the corner of our raised bed, where it spreads over its barriers and creates a striking presence of silky, silvery leaves. To prevent plants from collapsing in the middle, divide them regularly in the spring when soil has warmed, and keep soil lean.

***Clematis* x *jackmanii*, Jackmani clematis**, climber. A companion vertical accent for climbing roses, this first hybrid clematis (1858) offers long-blooming large purple flowers beginning in midsummer. Provide shade at its feet (we grow clumps of purple violets) and sun at its head, friable soil, support (chicken wire against a fence works well), and you should succeed with this and similar types.

***Dianthus* sp., pinks,** 12–15 in. We are always looking for hardy pinks. Two that we like to grow with roses are the vivid scarlet 'Ideal' (*D. chinensis* x *D. barbatus*), a compact type that can take the heat, produces masses of showy (but scentless) bloom, and 'Ballad Blend' (an improved form of *D. plumarius* 'Spring Beauty'). A vigorous and perfumed plant (sweet and spicy), it produces mats of handsome glaucous foliage— especially blue in the fall—and large, double, fringed flowers in early to midsummer in rose, salmon, pink, and white with darker centers. Both pinks are short lived and should be regularly propagated by pulling off side shoots with a bit of the main stem after plants have flowered.

***Helichrysum petiolare*, false licorice,** 1½ ft.–3 ft., tender perennial. We are fond of this spreading silvery plant with small, round woolly leaves on stiff stems; its aroma, released when foliage is rubbed, is deliciously anise-scented. We grow false licorice in containers in the Rose Bed and elsewhere and prize its ability to take heat and drought (we mulch containers with small rocks to conserve moisture); it combines well with flowers in the pink, rose, and purple range.

***Lychnis coronaria*, rose campion,** 2 ft., biennial. First-year plants produce silvery basal growth similar in appearance to lamb's ears, which would be reason enough to grow them. Second-year plants produce a multitude of slender stems topped by small, vivid rose flowers (striking against gray stems); variants include white flowers and the eyed type, 'Occulata'.

Nepeta x *faassenii* **'Dropmore Blue',** 10 in. x 10 in. We like this spice-scented plant for its multitude of purple-blue flower spikes in early summer over a long period. It's best to cut back plants after they have peaked to encourage later bloom. Mature plants trail gracefully over barriers at the front of the border.

Salvia **'East Friesland',** S. 'May Night', 18–24 in. These are very similar in appearance: In late spring, 'May Night' produces dark violet-blue flower spikes; by early summer, 'East Friesland', with musk-scented leaves, produces heavily packed, deep-violet flower spikes enhanced by maroon bracts. Under favorable conditions both will rebloom if cut back.

Stachys byzantina, **lamb's ears,** 12–18 in. We grow a vigorous pass-along strain with large woolly leaves that spread out to form a silvery mat at the front of the Rose Bed. In early summer, we let the woolly stems bear their fairy wands of small pinkish-purple flowers densely packed into woolly plumed heads. After we have admired them, we cut plants back to foliage to encourage fresh growth.

DIRECTIONS FOR ROSE POTPOURRI
& ROSE PETAL JELLY

Rose Potpourri

Pick petals on a sunny day after the dew has dried, choosing scented types with good color. Spread them out on cookie sheets to dry away from light; warmth from the pilot light of a gas stove works well. If small, whole flowers are picked to dry, it is vital to check for bugs like earwigs, which hide in the center of the flowers and if undetected could consume them (we speak from experience). When crispy dry, store dried petals and other colorful flowers (your choice of types and colors) in a covered container until ready to combine with other ingredients. Add 1 teaspoon essential rose oil to 3 tablespoons plant fixative (orrisroot, cellulose, or your choice) in a small covered jar; shake it now and then over the next three days so the oil and fixative are mixed and blended. Now add this, and if you like, spices (whole or crushed cinnamon and cloves) and dried orange peel to the dried flowers, mixing well. Store in a tightly covered opaque container and shake or turn upside down every day or every other day over the next six weeks. The potpourri is now ready to use. To make it last longer, display away from light, stir and cover occasionally.

Rose Petal Jelly

2 quarts dark fragrant petals (rugosas are best), loosely packed

3 cups water

1 package pectin crystals

2 tablespoons lemon juice

4 cups sugar

Pick petals on a sunny day when the dew has dried; gently pull them from fresh flowers that are fully opened. Place petals in a saucepan, cover them with the water, cover the pot, and bring the mixture to the boiling point. Remove cover and, over the next 15 minutes, occasionally bruise petals gently with the bottom of a glass. Strain the petals, reserving the liquid and discarding the blanched petals. Into a widemouthed saucepan, measure out 3 cups of the strained liquid, adding water if necessary; stir in the pectin crystals and lemon juice and bring to a rolling boil that can't be stirred down. Stir in sugar and return to a rolling boil; continue to stir and boil for 1 minute. Remove pot from heat and let mixture settle. Pour into sterilized, scalded jelly jars and seal at once. This jelly tastes like roses smell and is delicious on bran muffins or whole wheat toast with cream cheese. ●

CHAPTER EIGHT

The Art of Naturalizing

—

ONE RAW SPRING DAY in the early 1980s, we hitched the team to the wagon and proceeded to fill it to overflowing with the thick, tangled roots of yellow flag iris (*Iris pseudacorus*), which were undermining the front wall of the greenhouse. We had rescued them from a 1930's planting that languished by the back door, and planted them at this new site to create what we imagined would be an ideal low-maintenance border. But in enriched soil, yellow flag—a vigorous type—expanded at an alarming rate. What to do with the bounty? We liked the iris for its small, yellow blooms in the classic fleur-de-lis design and for its sword-like foliage, attractive all season, but we had to move it since it was obviously in the wrong place.

We knew from experience that yellow flag is a tough plant, one that even prefers wet feet, so having an abundant supply of damp spots at our disposal and loath to discard any form of munificence, we "planted" a wagonful of roots throughout the open landscape, from the edge of the woods by the little cabin to the wetland area along the lane leading to the

Figure 39.
Planting yellow flag iris.

farm (Figure 39). This was our method: Armed with pitchforks, we flung a heap of roots onto the ground, then one of us jumped off the wagon and pushed them, with the heel of a boot, into the ooze. Not all survived this rough treatment, but enough did to point the way to what would become an important feature of the landscape—naturalized plantings.

What is a naturalized planting? Is it the same as a wild garden? What is a wild flower? What is natural? These were questions that meant nothing to us then. In the beginning we acted from necessity, matching the material at hand (an abundance of vigorous roots) to a favored habitat. Why had we not used this knowledge earlier, why had we made such a fundamental error in judgment in the first place? Why hadn't we thought of growing yellow flag in conditions where its exuberant nature would not be a problem, and indeed, would be an asset?

Although we were aware of growing cultivated plants in semiwild conditions with minimum interference (a broad definition of naturalizing), our single experience was with daffodils, which we planted in rough pasture near the top of the lane in the late 1970s. We followed the prescribed manner: one hundred bulbs, White Flower Farm's famous "The Works," were thrown around in small handfuls on both sides of the

Figure 40.
Heeling in.

road, then they were shoved into slits in the heavy clay ground where they had fallen—a method that assures a natural, informal look (Figure 40). The only attention they have ever received has been a handful of bonemeal around each clump after flowering (with hundreds, finally thousands of blooms, we gave up deadheading them). The planting has been an unqualified success, increasing its spread every year, offering a spectacular monthlong spring display of blooms in every size and shape, single, double, bunch-flowered, and perfumed, ruffled, fluted, and rimmed, in glistening white and lovely shades of yellow, orange, even apricot-pink, all the more colorful against a background of still-bare gardens, hills, fields, and trees (see Figure 2, on page 16).

There's nothing wrong with this method; in fact it is the best way to create wide sweeps of bloom in a natural setting. Daffodils, and other bulbs, work well because they store their own food underground and are impervious to drought. What we didn't realize was that there are many other tough plants, equally able to grow with little or no attention, and there are other ways to go about naturalizing them, but there was little information on the subject then (and now). Lack of information, however, was not the only reason we had not pursued this method with other plants like yellow flag iris. The truth is we conceived of gardening as a form of effacing the wild, not adding to it.

With the farm already encircled by woods and encroaching marshland, establishing plantings in the wild—except as well-defined gardens—was farthest from our minds. Didn't we spend most of our waking hours figuring out strategies to overcome nature, to deal with the serious problems of soil and climate that daunted our efforts to raise food for ourselves and for our livestock? In the fall, we plowed the hay field; in winter, even on the most blustery days, we spread manure on the frozen ground with the team (by hand with manure forks); and in the spring, the land was disked and sown (always with more seed than is required in better conditions). We did all this to feed our livestock, the basis of our life, but the path was rough: Every season we fought marsh grass and moss, goldenrod and knapweed. We were surrounded by the wild, by untamed nature with a capital N. We were there, out in it and living from it. Who needed a wild garden?

Yet we were refreshed by the natural beauty around us, fascinated by its colors, forms, and harmony of design. In the spring on our daily walks to and from the mailbox (a one-mile hike twice a day), we looked forward to the succession of wildflowers in light woodland along the lane: exquisite lilac-pink rhodora flowers—so brilliant on hard, bare stems—clumps of nodding yellow clintonia, drifts of low, white bunch-berry, colonies of unfolding ferns, and deeper in the woods, solitary pink moccasin flowers. Down by the pond we took note of each plant—those at the water's edge such as yellow cinquefoil, the skullcap that squirmed through the boards of our rough dock, those in the water such as bright yellow bladderwort embellished with bright blue dragonflies, and by summer's end, the cattails, swamp milkweed, dusty pink joe-pye weed, and white boneset in the bog. We knew nature intimately as a force to fight and as a force that refreshed and delighted us. Was there a lesson here we had failed to understand? Another way to enjoy and work with the surrounding natural world?

Our experience with yellow flag was so successful we could no longer resist the obvious: By returning vigorous cultivated plants to wild or semiwild conditions, we could, with little effort, add significantly to the beauty of our landscape, letting nature itself do most of the work. Within a season, the yellow flag had settled in, grateful for evenly moist conditions, for generous room to spread, for accommodating and complementary wild companions: native wild iris (*Iris versicolor*) in varying shades of blue and purple, sheets of shiny bright yellow buttercups (plentiful in our poor, wet land) with a delicate understory of tiny-flowered white stitchwort and pale blue forget-me-not. This maintenance-free "planting," dispersed throughout the open land that encompasses cabins, house, and pastures, enhances what is already there, giving it more color and definition, definitely wild in appearance, *but removed from the untamed nature of the wholly wild.* We were learning that there are degrees of naturalizing, from very close to the wild (what we would call semiwild) to natural effects in an otherwise controlled landscape. The design and complexity of each planting would be dictated by the land itself, by the types of plants suited to each habitat.

When we built a bridge to the big cabin over a marshland drain, we created two areas, one on either side of the bridge, that appealed to us as naturalizing sites because of their prominence in the landscape and their difficult growing conditions (Figure 41). We discerned two distinct habitats here, one wet and sunny, the other damp and sunny, offering the opportunity to establish diverse flora. On the wet side, where yellow flag was already thriving, we added chives (divisions from the Harvest Bed), surprised to see that in wet conditions their flowers were rosier; spearmint from the mint beds, spreading as wide as it liked and allowed to produce its attractive lavender flower spikes; double-flower meadowsweet (*Filipendula ulmaria* 'Flore Pleno'), an original source of salicylic acid, with frothy, vanilla-scented plumes; and vivid purple

Figure 41.
Naturalized bridge plantings.

loosestrife (*Lythrum salicaria*), which in over twenty years has barely spread from its original planting, perhaps because it's so hedged in by other vigorous plants. All of these were shoved into puddles in the same way as yellow flag (the pros call it notch planting), where they joined wild iris (*I. versicolor*) and wide, arching mounds of marsh grass. Here the distinctive shape of marsh grass, an enemy plant elsewhere, is an asset all season, even in the fall with its tan leaves and tiny nodding flower clusters in matching color.

On the drier site opposite, we established blue comfrey, bistort, and elecampane from the Flowering Herb Garden, white-flowered meadow geranium (*Geranium pratense*), yellow-spiked loosestrife (*Lysimachia punctata*), queen-of-the-prairie (*Filipendula rubra* 'Venusta')—an oversize meadowsweet with frothy pink plumes—*Achillea ptarmica* 'The Pearl', sprays of long-lasting fluffy white pompons, impossible to grow elsewhere because of its creeping roots, and obedient plant (Physostegia), so called because when you push back one of its bright pink florets, however lightly, it remains in that position.

After these plantings proved successful, we turned our attention to the raised bed in front of the log cabin porch, where we had tried unsuccessfully to grow roses (only one 'Therese Bugnet' bush remained), and where we had persisted, year after year, always with indifferent results, in trying to grow hollyhocks, sunflowers, morning glory, marigold, sweet William, bachelor's button, larkspur, cosmos, nasturtium, godetia, poppies, and scarlet runner bean—it's embarrassing to recall such folly. Down came the log barriers, in went vigorous perennials on the wild side, of which we had a plentiful supply, only too happy to grow in the rich, moist, sunny conditions here that had discouraged or killed other types: white Siberian iris, sweet rocket from the Flowering Herb Garden, as well as blue comfrey and bistort, of which there was no end of extra roots, more double meadowsweet, the humble but ever useful tawny daylily (*Hemerocallis fulva*), and star of the planting, false lupine or Aaron's rod (*Thermopsis caroliniana*), an underrated native with showy spikes of densely packed, pealike flowers over gray-green foliage. As the plant spread, its early summer show has assumed spectacular proportions, with tier on tier of lemon-yellow stalks in a stunning mass.

Maintenance at these sites is minimal: When new plants are notched or heeled in, we trim the surrounding area so they won't be lost in the general picture or overwhelmed by their vigorous neighbors; plants are cut back (or left to form pods if these are interesting); the area around the planting is mown with a scythe or mower to emphasize its presence in the surrounding growth.

We discovered, quite by chance, that we could introduce an element of the natural in an otherwise traditional flower bed under three old lilac trees on the knoll opposite the house. After years of struggling in moist, weedy shade with hostas, bistort, and Solomon's seal, we confined our cultivation efforts to the front of the bed, the side that faces the house, leaving toughies like lungwort, double meadowsweet, orange daylilies, ribbon grass—creamy flowerheads in maturity—white and purple Siberian iris, wild bleeding heart, and star of Bethlehem (all adaptable to sun or shade in moist soil) to fill in at the back, to gradually merge with the pasture below; the pasture side is mown once a season, providing the only care the back of this garden now receives. This bed, like all our plantings, is fully packed with plants—hostas have spread wide, so there is no room for weeds—that merge seamlessly from cultivated at the front, to naturalized at the back and sides, no apparent division between them. Such a technique could be very useful in any area of a cultivated garden difficult to reach or where a softening effect is desirable.

Over time we have developed these and other methods to suit a variety of habitats in marginal land or in areas where traditional gardens would be unsuitable. In light woodland just beyond the Harvest and Rose Beds, we began to notch in woodland plants among those already there. Here, beneath the limbs of old apple trees, herb robert (*Geranium robertianum*) is a natural ground cover of light green ferny leaves and pretty little pink flowers in early summer, followed by fruits in the cranesbill design—round and puffed, with a reddish-tipped beak. What an inviting setting for extra lungwort, cowslips, violets, Solomon's seal, and ginger mint, the latter so invasive it can be grown only in a container elsewhere. No need to worry here, where it expands to its heart's content, creating a low mat of small pointed leaves splashed with cream. We find it soothing to take shelter beneath the trees on a hot June day, to walk down the path between the Harvest and Rose Beds and enter a quite different atmosphere, cool and refreshing, where we come not to work but to gaze in admiration. This place, where we neither cut back plants, nor weed, water, alter the soil, or otherwise interfere with nature, pleases us more than we could have imagined. Who needs a wild garden? As we discovered, we do.

We never thought we would so enjoy releasing garden plants to the wild (from which they originally came), to watch approvingly as they spread out the way nature intended; one can almost hear their collective sigh of relief from constraint. As for naturalizing subjects, we make no distinction among native and introduced, provided they meet the conditions for survival in the semiwild; nor do we select only unimproved or unaltered species if there are more suitable cultivars. *Polygonum bistorta* 'Superbum', or bistort, for instance, is an improved form of the wildflower, at home in both a traditional bed and a "wild" planting. We incorporate the wild plants already growing at our chosen site rather than removing them from their natural communities and adding them to our own, treatment they rarely survive. In any case, we prefer to enjoy them in their natural state, as in the wild flowers along our lane. In this, as in everything we pursue, we are pragmatic.

Although there are significant differences among our plantings—from iris heeled into ooze and left to themselves to more managed sites—they share two characteristics: They look natural, unforced, as if they belong where they are, and they blend in gently with the domesticated environment around them to create a balanced, harmonious scene. We did not understand these important principles of naturalizing when we began because the subject is rarely treated in any depth. We had to learn by doing, and we had a large canvas on which to work, but our experiences suggest that a semiwild planting—once you add to nature, the result can hardly be called wild—could be as small as a few plants in any unused corner. It is a mistake to think that you can or should bring the truly wild into a domesticated environment, as in the idea of substituting a wild meadow for a suburban lawn, the "meadow-in-a-can" phenomenon. Not only is such a thing out of place, it is wholly artificial. The beauty of a truly wild meadow is transient, and when flowers are spent, when growth is mature, it requires mowing to renew itself. The amount of labor to establish—and maintain—a wild meadow defeats the desire to introduce a sense of the natural world into a highly controlled environment. It is far easier and more satisfying to work with nature by adding a few vigorous types to a wildflower or two already growing at the edge of your property, to let them grow together in such a way that they appear unrestrained, yet are managed, however lightly, by your own hand.

We would need all the knowledge we had gained about naturalizing for the next and most ambitious project, reclamation of a steep slope we call The Bank.

One cold, windy winter evening, Jigs came to bed announcing, "We've got to do something about the unsightly places!"

His enthusiasm for improving neglected areas was inspired by recent nightly readings from the work of Gertrude Jekyll of Munstead Wood, mistress of the painterly eye, who held that nothing unsightly should be visible in the landscape. She was a gardener with a vision of harmony that encompassed the entire landscape—what we would call the integrated landscape—not just the garden itself, but the house, outbuildings, and even the surrounding woods, each of which she regarded in its own right and in relation to the others. Whatever detracted from a pleasing effect, she preached, should be banished or transformed.

During the decades we had been developing the farm—clearing and improving fields and pastures, rebuilding a tumbledown barn, adding the smokehouse and shop with attached woodshed, establishing vegetable, flower, and herb gardens, shrubs, hedges, and vines—we had neglected odd corners here and there. Through laziness or lack of imagination, we had allowed weeds, brush, and unpruned trees to take over, accepting their presence as inevitable. It was Jigs, captivated by Miss Jekyll, who galvanized us to tackle The Bank.

Seventy-five feet long and twelve feet wide, it rises steeply behind the repair shop and attached woodshed, leveling off at the top where a narrow path separates it from the vegetable garden. For years we trod this path, a shortcut to the barn, at least three times a day. We could see how the two old apple trees below, at either end of the bank, had spread their limbs and myriads of suckers, ungainly and twisted, over what had become a darkened thicket of tangled brush, weeds, and wild raspberries. We could see, but until Miss Jekyll made us realize that we should do something about it, we passively accepted its unattractive gloom.

In late winter, Jigs pruned heaps of overgrowth from the trees, opening the bank to the sun, a great improvement. By spring, as soon as the soil had thawed, the wild vegetation was killed with Roundup, then hauled off, revealing soft friable soil. It would be impressive to say we had a grand plan that we instantly and successfully carried out, but except for an initial planting of perennial ground covers at the top of the bank and a seeding of annual poppies (*Papaver somniferum*) for quick cover, we let this area evolve over several seasons as we found our way.

There were difficulties here we had never encountered. For one thing, the area was much larger than any we had dealt with, and while all our other naturalized plantings could be regarded as group accents within the larger landscape, the bank was an integral part of our domesticated environment: fruit and vegetable plantings above, shop-woodshed, hotbed and cold frame below, as well as the Apothecary's rose hedge that leads on to the Flowering Herb Garden and the house itself. The bank would require a different approach to naturalizing and we could not expect quick results (see Part One illustration, on pages 12–13).

The first winter after the perennial ground covers were planted at the top of the bank—ajugas, pulmonarias, lamiums, phlox, sedum, veronica, golden alyssum, cerastium—we discovered our first mistake. By removing all the weedy growth at once, we had exposed the bank to erosion from runoff rainwater and melting snow. Precious earth was washed below, carried in rivulets between the ground covers (these had not yet spread wide or thick enough to offer protection), leaving the upper bank nearly bare of decent topsoil; what remained was hard and, in drought periods, cracked, an impossible medium for notching plants or growing them. To remedy this, the following two springs, we lightly scattered compost and rotted sawdust over the top area. We had no desire to cultivate the bank as in a garden; we weren't trying to improve the soil, just replace some of it.

At first, confronted with so much bare ground, we were confounded. What to plant? Our job was easier when we recognized a variety of habitats (something our previous experiences had trained us to do), each one subtly different from the other because of its distinctive features: thin soil at the top of the bank; partial shade under trimmed apple limbs in the middle area; dark, dank, moist conditions at the very base of the bank; dry and exposed on the west and east slopes that extend beyond the shadow of the shop-woodshed (Jigs plants pumpkins, squash, and melons on the east slope toward the barn). Each of these microclimates, calling for different plant communities, allowed us to direct our energy to the development of one section at a time, to move steadily from one area to another without losing our connection to the site as a whole.

Of them all, the most difficult conditions to satisfy were those at the base of the bank. While the wall of the shop with its woodshed extension defined the back end of the planting, it also added the very darkness and gloom we had set out to dispel. We needed plants that would brighten the area, bringing light from shadows, that would grow willingly in shady, close conditions (little air circulation), in moist, rich, bottomland soil. Fortunately, nature supplied precisely what we were looking for in yellow jewelweed or touch-me-not (*Impatiens capensis*), which thrives in just the circumstances we offered. It grew there already, spontaneously and with abandon: three and one-half foot succulent leafy stems bear a multitude of pendant, golden orange, sharply spurred flowers in midsummer, each splotched with reddish-brown. When their pods are touched, seeds shoot forth, thus assuring prolific reseeding. Observing nature's gift, we encouraged jewelweed (gardening friends were appalled), helping out with a seasonal thinning to encourage a rough hedge effect. The suckering shrub, golden currant (*Ribes aureum*), planted just above the jewelweed, brings more light and needed grace in its dipping, floppy stems, covered in early summer with narrow, yellow, clove-scented trumpets, and in fall with burnished red foliage.

The two old apple trees, transformed by close trimming, now dominated the whole bank, giving it focus and character. With a well-defined shape, tall and handsome, they rise straight up, well above the shop roofline, the high limbs topped by a towering canopy of blossoms in early summer; then by fall the boughs are weighed down with a large crop of apples, a symbol of the bank's new fruitfulness. Partial shade beneath their spreading limbs called for bright yellow narcissus in spring, followed by sweet violets, lady's mantle, columbines (*Aquilegia* sp.), sweet cicely, bistort (the "everywhere plant"), and native wild anemone (*Anemone canadensis*)—so hard to control in a garden setting, so lovely when given room to form an extended, unhindered drift of pure white, goblet-shaped flowers in midsummer.

Near the top of the bank, in spaces free of ground covers, we planted tough, self-seeding annuals such as echium, nigella, calendula, California poppies, lilac and bright blue phacelias (*Phacelia tanacetifolia* and *P. campanularia*, both California natives), and in their midst a few low to medium-tall tough perennials like white musk mallow and mountain bluet, well able to fend for themselves. Because of the sharp drainage it afforded, the bank became home for several perennials we had been unable to grow elsewhere—"Try The Bank!" was our solution for creeping thymes, white and pink; for native Liatris 'Kobold', compact and striking with rose-purple fluffy spikes; and for foxglove (*Digitalis purpurea*), at home in these conditions as nowhere else in our landscape. Wildflowers volunteered in niches: buttercups on a steep section of the slope where they were left to prevent erosion; wild strawberries, a weed-smothering ground cover (their sweet berries a bonus); field daisies (*Chrysanthemum leucanthemum*) here and there in thick bouquets for most of the summer (since we have never succeeded with cultivated daisies, we were thrilled).

As the bank began to take shape, as plant communities evolved, we considered adding more "bones," basic structural elements like the apple trees. Yes, we are advised to establish these first, but as even the most sophisticated gardeners acknowledge, sometimes they are added only as the garden develops and as the gardener becomes more aware of design possibilities. Adding strong, complementary shapes and forms to the bank was part of our growing appreciation of their positive role in the winter scene. We were becoming keenly aware of the landscape as a four-season phenomenon, one that nourishes us every day of the year. Too often, gardeners focus all their energy on transient flowers without considering the importance of brilliant fall foliage or the clean outlines of trees and shrubs against the winter sky.

At the end of the woodshed, in poorly drained waste ground, we planted staghorn sumac (*Rhus typhina*), regarded elsewhere as a weed tree but prized here for its ability to thrive in adversity. Growing to about six feet in this region (in better conditions as high as thirty feet), it is attractive at all seasons, even when bare. The spreading branches, covered with reddish velvet hairs (some call it the velvet tree), give it a pleasing distinction in spring and winter. Terminal clusters of small green flowers in summer become ornamental reddish fruits by fall (they can be used to make a tart-flavored juice), when its canopy of long, deeply cut green foliage turns yellow.

Then we thought about shrub roses, the tough ones we were already growing elsewhere. Several years before we had begun work on the bank, we had planted the elegant double white rugosa, 'Blanc Double de Coubert', on the weedy, exposed slope where the bank begins, where it is clearly seen from the roadway below. At this perfect site for late winter and spring small bulbs—when the soil is still moist—we added snowdrops under the rose bush, then wild tulips—the stripe-leaved *Tulipa bakerii* 'Lilac Wonder', *T. kaufmania* 'Gaiety', and ground-hugging yellow and white 'Tarda'. By incorporating the exposed slope into the bank planting, by embellishing it with bulbs, ground covers, and flowers, we extended the bank's visual impact, integrating it into the general landscape of house and cultivated gardens. In summer, an Oriental carpet, edged with Lamium 'Beacon Silver', spreads out and rolls down the slope, now bright with red poppies (the Israeli 'flower of the field' poppy—blood red, unsplotched, and similar to the European *Papaver rhoeas*), calendulas, and nigella, shocking pink catchfly, blue cornflowers, black-eyed Susan, and a white froth of bedstraw—like baby's breath—self-seeded at the base of the rose. All of these thrive in full sun and dry conditions.

Two more roses in the same line of vision were added near the top of the bank. 'Dart's Dash' is a low, wide rugosa, as tough as they come, with large scarlet flowers (well scented) beginning in midsummer, and healthy dark green foliage. Beyond that, near the beginning of Jigs's pumpkin patch, we established a dog rose (understock from a failed, grafted rose), to grow up the nearby apple tree on its long, spreading stems. Its single pink flowers pass by soon enough, but its bright green foliage lasts into late fall, its clusters of polished red oval hips remain all winter. These roses of different and complementary shapes carry the eye forward to the pasture gate, where the rail fence just to its right is adorned nearly all summer with the abundant red rose clusters of Canadian Explorer 'Henry Kelsey' (see Figure 36, on page 161).

Miss Jekyll was right. Whatever detracts from the pleasing effect should be banished or transformed (and to succeed, you don't need a staff of helpers or piles of money). We could not have imagined the bank's metamorphosis, nor how it would influence the way we feel about our landscape—its beneficial impact in our lives. We used to follow the path along the scruffy bank because it was a shortcut to the barn, but now we take this route deliberately, because we enjoy seeing the progress of growth and bloom, because we are refreshed by the lively mixture of colors, because beauty always pleases.

On a hot summer day after noon chores (feed the chickens, collect the eggs, and clean the horse stables if they need it), carrying our basket of eggs, we push through the pasture "rose gate"—a pleasure in itself—and enter what feels like another world, almost dreamlike in its perfection (if we care to look closely, we can see its flaws). On the narrow path to our right is the pea fence, its green plastic netting now covered with climbing pea flowers, white ones and purple rose (these will be soup peas), and by poppies (*Papaver somniferum*), watermelon pink and raspberry, that sow themselves in the pea soil compost. So many poppies bloom here in early July that we call this the Poppy Walk (Figure 42). Just to our left, at the top of the bank, ground covers are past their bloom but foliage is still fresh and lush—bronze, silver, striped and frosted

Figure 42.
The Poppy Walk.

green; at the foot of an apple tree, phacelia's fuzzy lilac flowers uncoil above dainty fern foliage, paired as if by design with field daisies in the classic form; scarlet pinks, white mallows, and mountain bluet mingle together in the sun; pink, purple, and white foxglove, in partial shade, bear swaying towers of speckled fairy's thimbles; and further on, we see that on the lower part of the west slope a colony of golden sundrops is flowering with deep-purple clustered bellflowers. Just before we leave the path, we pass the white rose in its aura of intense perfume.

What have we created? Is this a wild garden? Of all our naturalized plantings, The Bank is the least natural. Does this make it artificial? Yes, in the sense that we have intervened in nature's work here far more than elsewhere by imposing a community of plants for our own aesthetic enjoyment rather than adding to one that was already there. But there was nothing inherently beneficial about the jumbled growth we removed, and after the first few seasons, The Bank has become virtually self-

Figure 43.
Big cabin with Marigold, Brownie, and Pookie.

sustaining. Maintenance is confined to cutting back perennials, a rough weeding twice a season, and a spring pruning of the roses. As in our other efforts, we matched plants to habitat and took advantage of spontaneous wild growth by incorporating it into our design. We mixed species with improved cultivars, we planted both native and introduced types. We used all our artifices to create a planting that appears natural.

From each of our varied experiences we have learned something important about the art of naturalizing, primarily about working with nature to create low-maintenance plantings. We have learned from the differences among them that there are degrees of management, from none (yellow flag and woodland plantings) to some labor (The Bank), yet their impact is similar: They appear natural, they merge with all the other elements in our landscape—beds, borders, buildings, pastures. Yet if we compare them with the truly wild, we recognize their difference. Unlike untamed nature—beautiful and compelling in its own way—our efforts are closely integrated into our domestic, cultivated landscape, and they do not seem to be at odds with it; on the contrary, each semiwild planting enhances the whole picture of what we see every day. From their impact on our own lives, lives lived in the midst of the real wild, we believe everyone who can manage it should reserve a bit of space for a garden on the wild side (Figure 43).

Sampler of Tough Plants

We believe the ultimate pleasure of naturalizing lies not in its undeniable ease of maintenance but in the opportunity it gives us to establish a satisfying partnership, on a modest scale, with the natural world in which we live. Our experiences suggest that anyone with a small plot of ground can use our simple techniques to create corners or oases of wild plantings that appear natural, as if they spontaneously arose without any help from the gardener's hand.

The secret of success is to choose plants that are able to survive on their own once they are established, and to match them to the growing conditions in which they thrive in the wild. Of course, candidates should be beautiful in some way so they add to the overall landscape, whether by strong forms, foliage, or flowers. We focus here on types suitable for poorly drained soil (wet or damp) and ground covers. With a few exceptions—noted with an asterisk—we wouldn't let them loose in the garden, but have no hesitation in recommending them for naturalizing. Some would say our choices are "garden thugs," and in the traditional confines of a garden, most of them are. It stands to reason that invasive plants can ruin a garden planting, but when you create situations where they can grow unhindered (with a little direction), they are plants to be admired for their toughness, adaptability, and unique beauty.

FOR MOIST OR WET CONDITIONS; SUN OR PARTIAL SHADE (MOSTLY PERENNIALS, HARDY TO ZONE 4)

Anemone canadensis, **Canada anemone,** 2 ft. A native plant in light woodlands we've found useful to brighten shady areas. A spreading canopy of deeply divided leaves is enhanced by long-blooming pure white goblet flowers in midsummer. For moist, rather than wet conditions, with columbine, bistort, and mountain bluet.

Filipendula rubra **'Venusta' (Martha Washington's plume), queen-of-the-prairie,** 8 ft. Blooming after its closely related cousin, this aptly named native is invaluable in wet ground. Martha Washington's sweet-scented, peach-rose plumes rise from coarse, deeply divided leaves to tower over our naturalized bridge planting.

Filipendula ulmaria **'Flore Pleno', meadowsweet,** 4–6 ft. We love this plant for its adaptability to sun or partial shade in heavy damp, even wet, soil. Hollow reddish stems growing up from handsome dark green leaves produce terminal clusters of tiny, crowded, cream-colored flowers (rosy in bud) in fluffy, sweet-scented clusters by midsummer. Foliage has a sharp wintergreen aroma when bruised, and when dried, a sweet scent from the presence of coumarin (as in freshly mown hay). An Old World herb with many household and medicinal uses, it was an original source of salicylic acid, later synthesized into the familiar aspirin.

Geranium pratense **'Flore Pleno', meadow geranium,** 3 ft. We got ours from the Newfoundland Botanical Garden's Heritage Garden, where every plant had been discovered in an old garden. Geraniums are popular now, but we never hear the virtues of this cottage garden favorite, willing to grow in moist garden soil or on its own in a naturalized planting in damp ground (where we prefer it). Ours is the double form, cup shaped and white—its natural shade is blue—with deeply cut foliage.

Hemerocallis fulva, **orange daylily,** 3 ft. Look into the face of this common (some would say too common) plant, and see the extraordinary beauty of its design: a large orange trumpet, about five inches across, of flared-back petals with darker zones and stripes in tawny shades of red and mahogany (fulva means tawny). If it weren't so common, it would be more valued for its vigor and adaptability to grow in dry or damp soil in sun or partial shade; very effective in preventing erosion on a steep bank.

Impatiens glandulifera, **policeman's helmet,** 6 ft. Annual. Sow seeds in late spring. Naturalized from Ontario to Nova Scotia and down to Massachusetts, this flamboyant, irrepressible plant is regarded as a treasured heirloom by gardeners with a penchant for the unusual. We love its large, spurred flowers in the shape of an English bobby's helmet, variable in color from deep rose to pink, peach, and white, spotted within and lightly scented; bees hover over them for weeks beginning in midsummer. Policeman's helmet will grow in sun or partial shade as long as the soil is moist; it is useful as an informal hedge or striking accent.

Inula helenium, **elecampane,** 6 ft. An Old World herb whose roots were once very important in medicinal preparations especially for horses (its older name is horseheal), elecampane is a Cinderella plant, transformed in summer from gawky basal growth of oversized light green leaves to a charming version of a sunflower, with fringed rather than straight rays, a valued vertical accent in a damp meadow planting.

Iris pseudacorus, **yellow flag iris,** 4 ft. We have already extolled the virtues of this moisture-loving iris (wet feet are o.k.), best grown in near-wild conditions. Its bright yellow flower heads are lightly veined, the falls a violet-brown, and stems are heavily sheathed in swordlike foliage—handsome all summer—as high or higher than the flowers.

*I. sibirica, **Siberian iris,** 2 ft. A few delicate plants established in damp soil in sun or partial shade soon produce sizable mats of narrow foliage that send up a mass of slender stems topped by pristine white or purple flowers in the classic iris design. They can be fit into the smallest naturalized planting.

Lysimachia punctata, **yellow loosestrife,** 2½ ft. Another cottage garden favorite we think best naturalized (in almost any soil, damp or dry) where it makes a splash of color in midsummer when a multitude of deep yellow florets open all along its stems; effective when grown as a hedge or screen to hide (or enhance) "the unsightly."

***Mentha spicata,* spearmint,** 2½ ft. For use, we grow this mint in a plastic-lined bed to prevent its creeping roots from roaming, but for pleasure we allow it to form beautiful drifts in a wet meadow of long slender spikes of pale lilac flowers by late summer above toothed leaves (we may harvest leaves if we need more mint). We are so used to thinking about mints as foliage plants that we forget they have pretty flowers, too.

***Phalaris arundinacea* 'Picta', ribbon grass,** 3 ft. Long before grasses became fashionable, ribbon grass was favored for its arching mound of green and cream-striped leaves. Plants form tight mats of growth from underground creeping roots that quickly overrun their neighbors in a garden, but in a naturalized setting of equally tough plants, they don't have much room to move. Grows well in sun or partial shade in damp soil with daylilies, meadowsweet, and Siberian iris. The tiny wheat-colored flower clusters on thin stems dry well for winter bouquets.

***Physostegia virginiana,* obedient plant,** 3 ft. A very desirable native plant for moist soil (but not, in our experience, in a traditional garden), with showy pink snapdragon-like florets in well-packed spikes that bloom in late summer; we have not found any of the cultivars (pink or white) to be less invasive.

****Sanguinaria canadensis,* bloodroot,** 4–12 in. An exquisite native wildflower ideal for growing in evenly moist soil and partial shade in light woodland or beneath a tree. In mid-spring when lungwort is in full bloom, we begin to look for the grayish-brown emerging leaves, so hard to see against brown earth. As the leaves unfurl, the flower stems uphold short-lived, solitary, white goblet flowers with many golden stamens within. If you miss the first flowers you'll have another chance—although each bloom is quickly transformed into a seedpod, new buds continue to open for almost three weeks. Once established, leave it alone or you might inadvertently destroy the planting (we speak from experience). It increases slowly by seed and rhizomes.

Thermopsis caroliniana/villosa, **false lupine/Carolina lupine,** 3 ft. An underrated native that produces stiff spikes of densely packed lemon-yellow pea florets by midsummer (similar in appearance to lupines). We allow it to form a spectacular mass of bloom in front of our big log cabin in moist meadow ground. If grown from seed, soak them for twelve hours in hot water before sowing to break the seed coat.

PERENNIAL GROUND COVERS FOR MOIST TO DRY CONDITIONS; SUN AND SHADE

Ajuga reptans, **bugleweed,** 6 in. Forget the "weed" in its name. This is a terrific ground cover (not garden plant) with rosettes of bronzy green leaves that form a tight carpet. In late spring plants produce spikes of powder-blue flowers that gain impact by their numbers; best in partial shade or where soil is evenly moist. 'Burgundy Glow', an elegant variation with garden possibilities, is less invasive; its foliage changes over the season from deep red to dark pink, variegated with creamy white (flower spikes are also blue); 'Alba' has all-green leaves and white flowers. We let these run down the bank together, and elsewhere we plant 'Burgundy Glow' and 'Alba' to light up dark corners or to form carpets under shrubs. In early spring, discard worn-out mats in the center of plantings.

*Alyssum saxatile, **basket of gold,** 6 in. Common in rock gardens but always striking, this short-lived perennial produces large tufts of long silvery leaves, crowned by late spring with bright yellow flower clusters. Full sun and well-drained soil will ensure self-seeding.

Campanula rapunculoides, **creeping bellflower,** 2½ ft. A nuisance in the garden, this irrepressible bellflower is an advantage on a dry, sunny slope where it goes about its business of extending its range, bearing toothed green leaves and light purple bells all along its stems over many weeks in the summer.

Cerastium tomentosum, **snow-in-summer,** 9 in. Best in sun, where its mats of gray-white foliage cascade down a rocky slope (overrunning most plants in their way), decorated in late spring and early summer with a multitude of small white flowers resembling a snowdrift. We like to pair the foliage, an asset all season, with bugleweed, but care must be taken to ensure neither smothers the other.

*Geranium macrorrhizum, **big-root geranium,** 10–15 in. We value this geranium for its ability to thrive in dry shade, and for its lemon-rose scented leaves. Plants form a dense mound of lobed foliage that turns reddish by fall. Magenta flowers with prominent pistils rise just above the leafy mound by midsummer; their buds and seed heads, in the cranesbill design, extend the beauty of their brief flowering (about two weeks). We grow big-root geranium as an accent at the back of a traditional island bed where, under the shade of an apple tree, it merges into a semiwild planting of ground covers and shrubs. To propagate, gently pull a stem with piece of root and replant.

***Lamium maculatum,* spotted dead nettle,** 6–8 in. Its odd name refers to its lack of stinging characteristics, in contrast to true nettles. Growing well in sun or shade, and in most soils from moist to dry, plants produce a low mat of heart-shaped, soft green foliage, spotted white along the midribs. Flowers, white and showy, are borne in whorls by late spring. 'Beacon Silver' with purplish-pink flowers, and similar cultivars ('White Nancy', 'Pink Pewter') are green-leaved types overlaid with a white sheen, resulting in a marbled appearance. If controlled, they could be grown in a garden.

***Lysimachia nummularia,* creeping Jenny,** 2 in. Where nothing else will grow in dense shade and poorly drained, moist conditions, this is the ground cover of choice, but think before you plant it since it suppresses surrounding growth (the job of a ground cover) with a vengeance; single stems can extend five feet. By midsummer spreading mats of rounded, coinlike green leaves are nearly obscured by long-lasting, bright yellow cupped flowers. This is a good choice for growing among stones where soil is too moist for creeping thyme.

***Ornithogalum umbellatum,* star of Bethlehem,** 6–12 in., bulb. Blooming in sheets of white stars in sun or shade in most soils, this too-willing plant is a menace in the garden but a great asset when naturalized. In partial shade and moist soil, it combines well with a gang of lovely toughies in early summer here: Geranium 'Johnson's Blue', *Hosta undulata* 'Medio-Picta', ribbon grass, and Siberian iris. Plant clusters of small bulbs 1–2 inches deep.

****Phlox subulata,* moss phlox,** 4–6 in. Valued for its dense mat of shiny, narrow green leaves and mass of white, pink, or lilac flowers by late spring, it needs well-drained soil and full sun to thrive. Nice on a rocky slope.

***Sedum spurium* 'Dragon's Blood',** 2 in. A friend gave us a small piece and we have found it very useful in dry, exposed areas. Its creeping roots send out long stems covered with fleshy, drought-resistant green leaves, and by midsummer it produces flat, blood-red flower clusters.

***Thymus praecox* subsp. *arcticus*/*T. serpyllum*, creeping thyme,** 3 in. We failed with this desirable ground cover until we could offer it light, fast draining soil (enhanced with gravel) and sun on our bank. There it forms tight mats of tiny green leaves and a multitude of little flowers, lavender-purple or white, in early summer.

***Viola odorata*, sweet violet,** 6–8 in. For many years we carried on a war with sweet violets, ripping them out of the Flowering Herb Garden where they increased without mercy in its deep, moist soil. We tossed them in a pile outside the garden where they gradually took hold, producing a beautiful carpet of glossy, heart-shaped leaves, and in late spring and early summer a mass of delicate white flowers resembling a stationary flock of butterflies. We fail to detect much fragrance, but they have a crisp texture and sweet floral flavor, a nice embellishment not only for chocolate cake frosting but for fruit salad. They will grow in sun or shade if the soil is evenly moist. ●

CHAPTER NINE

The Contained Garden

—

WE GROW PLANTS IN CONTAINERS not for want of space but for other reasons: the need to have herbs handy for daily use; as a way to grow tender types that need some coddling (we have room in our hearts for more than self-sufficient toughies); to bring hummingbirds and scent closer to us; to produce arresting accents within a garden or just outside its boundaries; to observe new plants that might be lost in a garden setting. It all started with basil.

In Vermont, we took basil and other flavoring herbs, like thyme, for granted as regular garden plants planted in long rows, but here in cold, heavy soil and cool summers, often into July, there was no way we could grow basil in the ground. A tropical plant, it requires steady warmth at all stages; any interruption retards growth. There's nothing more dismaying for a basil lover than to watch seedlings, so lovingly nurtured, visibly shrink into cold ground after they are planted. Our solution to this vexing problem—simple and guaranteed to bring results—has cheered fellow gardeners who could not find answers in conventional garden literature.

Figure 44.
Basil sown in buckets.

Our lean-to greenhouse of single-paned, secondhand storm windows and scrap barn boards may be leaky, but it serves its purpose well, even providing temporary quarters for day-old chicks in the spring. Why not start basil seedlings here after the chicks' departure?

People are surprised—until they use the method themselves—that we don't sow basil seeds until late June, but by this time even a little sun can warm the greenhouse to near-tropical temperatures, creating very favorable conditions for rapid germination and growth. Seeds are sown directly into their permanent summer home—leaky buckets formerly used for collecting maple sap—thus avoiding unnecessary transplanting (Figure 44). We use compost-enriched potting soil with extra perlite for drainage and vermiculite for holding moisture; then the tubs, set in a long row on the floor of the greenhouse, are lightly covered with a sheet of thin plastic. It's always a thrill to see the soil surface covered with forests of light green and purple seedlings within four days (expected germination time is fourteen days). Thick plantings of 'Genovese', 'Siam Queen', 'Cinnamon', 'Sweet Dani', 'Purple Ruffles', and others are thinned over several weeks (these give delicious, delicate basil flavor to salads). We wait until temperatures outdoors are in the 70°F range before we move the buckets outdoors, where they are arranged together on the wide stone walkway in front of the house (near a rain barrel for convenient watering). Basils-in-a-bucket do not yield as much as basils in warm ground elsewhere, but we are able to harvest each bucket twice a season and have enough to satisfy our own needs as well as to produce basil vinegars, jellies, and teas for sale.

The contained garden "just grew" as we found it an advantageous way to grow other herbs, especially the salad types we use every day. No need to run out to the garden when there's a little garden-in-a-tire right outside the front door.

A tire? Down-country friends are incredulous when we tell them about our tires, about Jigs's ninety-six-tire vegetable garden, about Jo Ann's tire herb garden. We first learned about the benefits of tire planting from a Dutch friend who knows of many inventive ways to grow plants. He showed us how to turn a recycled tire inside out (it takes heft) and set the resulting urn shape on the tire rim to make a container stand; he embellishes the edges of his tires by cutting them into scallops (Figure 45), but we leave ours plain. The tires not only resemble elegant cast-iron planters, but they draw and retain needed heat, discourage weeds, and because of their expanse of soil surface do not dry out as readily as smaller containers (Figure 46). We lay a plastic grain bag in the bottom of each tire before we fill it with compost dirt. If the tire is very large and deep (as in a truck tire), we use sawdust or newspapers at the bottom, then add enough soil to create a six-inch-deep bed. For a garden of salad herbs, we sow fernleaf dill directly, then when it is growing we add several plants each of sweet marjoram, salad burnet, and curled parsley.

Mints are especially suited to containers because their creeping roots are impossible to restrain in a garden among other plants. We were

—

Figure 45.
Cutting a tire to form a container.

Figure 46.
A tire planter.

already growing blocks of spearmint, peppermint, and apple mint in plastic-lined beds, separated from one another by large log barriers. These, with a fish tub (a 3' x 2' x 2' container) planted to ginger mint, produce two crops a season, enough for us to add a small dried handful every day—with catnip and lemon balm—to our Pekoe tea, and for Jo Ann to produce a range of herbal tea blends. But when an old oil drum cut lengthwise for an animal watering trough had rusted out, we claimed it for a peppermint planter closer to the house, so our favorite strain of peppermint—brought from Vermont—would be near at hand to add to cold drinks in the summer. The trough was settled in the shade of the summer apple tree at the back of the Tulip Bed just opposite the back kitchen door. Nestled between a wide mound of rose-scented big-root geranium (*Geranium macrorrhizum*) on one side and a low, dainty carpet of white-striped lamium (*Lamium maculatum*) on the other, its fresh-picked sprigs are the perfect last touch to a tall, refreshing glass of iced tea mixed with chilled rhubarb juice (stalks are cooked up with oranges and lemons) on a hot summer day (see "Fruit Garden Sampler," on page 87).

Nasturtiums, which produce foliage at the expense of flowers in rich soil, are ideal for containers, where soil can be modified (lower the compost, add more perlite and vermiculite). Since we require an abundance of flowers for salads, vinegar (a spicy note for our goose-berry chutney), and general fresh flavoring, and because we love their wonderful mixture of bright and soft colors in shades of yellow, scarlet, and orange, their classic spurred or heavily ruffled styles, we plant assorted types in containers from small to large, near the house and also in our working environment. An old barrel by the corner of the garden shed, next to a rough hedge of golden glow (*Rudbeckia laciniata* 'Hortensia') gives the trailing or climbing type—said to grow to ten feet, but in our experience seldom exceeding six feet—more height, while its succulent vinelike stems find their own support clinging to the wall's rough slab boards (Figure 47). In this way, nasturtiums can climb unaided to the top of the shed roof, a charming distant accent, a source of nectar for hummingbirds, and large flowers for stuffing (the ultimate appetizer).

These versatile plants add another welcome element to the contained garden that we had not considered—scent. When we became aware of their freely wafted perfume—sweet, spicy, and warm—we planted other scented types. We added nicotianas, acidanthera (a type of wild gladiolus), four-o'clocks, pansies, and pinks (*Dianthus superbus*) in half-barrels, sap buckets, tires, and wooden nail kegs, placed wherever their perfumes float our way—by the back kitchen door, on the stone walkways opposite the driveway, at the front of the house, and on the front porch itself.

Except for a few treasured terra-cotta pots saved for rosemary and rose geranium (these winter indoors, then spend the summer outdoors), containers come to hand from suitable objects that are no longer useful for any other purpose, such as the leaky maple-sap buckets. Although we generate many cracked teapots and pairs of worn-out work boots,

—

Figure 47.
Climbing nasturtiums on shed.

we have never been tempted to use them as containers because they add a false note, a self-conscious jokiness—"garden whimsy" in the phrase of current fashion—to the landscape. Our goal is to create as beautiful a setting as we can for our plants, not to distract the eye with coy artifices. If our containers are humble objects, old and rusting, we do little to gussy them up beyond painting the sap buckets—yellow, blue, gray, whatever paint is in supply—and an old milk can, painted a bright red, that has been planted to trailing white sweet alyssum every summer for the last twenty-five years (a perfect pairing).

As we added containers, most of them grouped together around the house where they are easier to tend, we noticed design possibilities similar to our plantings in the ground. These vague observations were deepened and clarified when we read a chapter called "I Giardinetti," or "little gardens," in *Betty Crocker's Kitchen Gardens*. Although the subjects—indoor herbs, suitable outdoor trees—were irrelevant to our vision, the Italian phrase *i giardinetti* suggested what we had been unconsciously creating: little gardens of contained plants. With the plants so close at hand, we had become more sensitive to their diverse forms and contrasting foliage and flowers, as in a real garden. In short, we began to regard container plants as aesthetic garden subjects. When a wide flatbed wheelbarrow that had been used to cart scythed grass to the horses was no longer needed, it was parked on the stone walkway directly opposite the front door, where it began a new life as a platform for our first little contained garden.

We placed containers on the flatbed—three feet long, two feet wide at its narrow front end, spreading to three feet wide at its handles—as we would in a traditional border: taller plants at the back, shorter ones up front, accents here and there of varying heights to relieve uniformity and add interest; where necessary, we set bricks under pots to raise them and give them more prominence. With the exception of very large containers—the herb garden-in-a-tire—we grow only one or two types together in a single container because in our experience plants grow better, look better, and create a stronger visual impression when each has more room to grow in these conditions (this goes against the current fashion for very busy mixed plantings). In any event, the containers are grouped closely together, so the effect is similar to the tightly layered, colorful tapestry of our beds and borders.

Such a contained garden has advantages over a planted garden. When the season advances and plants change in appearance as they mature, they can be moved—brought to the fore, retired to the background, or moved elsewhere. Pots of cold-resistant types, for instance, like *Dianthus superbus* 'Crimsonia'—fringed, jasmine-scented flowers—can replace containers of frost-sensitive ones. The contained garden, we were learning, can be extended well into late fall (November). And plant combinations unlikely in a garden setting can be tried without having to uproot those that offend the eye. We've enjoyed creating unusual associations of rosemary and purple velvet 'Fantasy' petunias, a small-flowered ground-cover type; pastel 'Whirlybird' nasturtiums with Greek oregano; burgundy and chartreuse coleus with sapphire blue trailing lobelia; bright red Texas sage, *Salvia coccinea* 'Lady in Red', with bright green 'Bravura' parsley.

Forced to find more space for our growing garden, we noticed that the ground in front of the wheelbarrow could accommodate a complementary grouping for the containers above. One season we may grow four-o'clocks (the plants grow from tubers) in several of our widest and deepest buckets to form a thick front hedge; another season, we alternate tubs of green and purple basils, then give them a front ruffle of nasturtiums in their range of creams, golds, scarlets, and orange (Figure 48). What a wonderful new world of plant design!

It was inevitable that we should begin to regard the entire surrounding area with a new perspective. Since we could not colonize the whole stone walkway—after all, we had to walk around the side of the house to attend to the west beds and the poultry—we confined our efforts to

Figure 48.
A wheelbarrow grouping of herbs and flowers.

the small corner garden by the front door—four feet deep, eight feet wide, shaped like a wedge where the side wall of the greenhouse meets the house (Figure 49). It was here that we first discovered the trick of placing containers in the midst of a garden so the containers themselves are hidden but the plants in them appear to be growing in the ground like those around them. Here, shrubby white mugwort (*Artemisia lactiflora*) and red monarda form a background for southernwood, lady's mantle, coral bells, single white peony (*Paeonia* 'Krinkled White'), double peach poppies (*Papaver somniferum*), double white feverfew, tall 'Golden Beauty' calendula, lamb's ears, and dwarf Hosta 'Ginko Craig'. But there was enough foliage cover to insert a sap bucket of gray-white beach wormwood combined with small neon purple-pink wild petunias (*Petunia integrifolia*), another of tall, heavily scented white nicotiana (*Nicotiana alata*), and a tub of Cleome 'Lilac Queen', its spidery flowers on long wandlike stems in full bloom by mid-August among the creamy white sprays of white mugwort (for early cleome bloom here, we push its growth along in the greenhouse until late July).

We were pleased to see how this garden was enhanced by containers, and how we were able thereby to site plants in situations where normally they would not be able to grow. By giving beach wormwood, a low, spreading plant usually reserved for hanging baskets or the front of the border, extra height in a sap bucket, it added its singular color and texture (smooth like felt) to the middle of the bed in front of red monarda, an otherwise impossible combination. The old-fashioned nicotiana, droopy during the day when it is barely noticed in a crowd of plants, is transformed by late afternoon, when it lifts its pure white trumpets and pours forth an enveloping aroma, sweet with a hint of spice.

Figure 49.
The front of the house.

Encouraged by these innovative "planting" techniques, we expanded our activities further afield. In the Harvest Bed, we added a container of fernleaf tansy to a close planting of garlic chives and echinacea, and in the Flowering Herb Garden, we added tree wormwood (*Artemisia arborescens*), a frost-tender shrub with deeply fringed silvery foliage that we'd never grown before, to consort with sprays of red velvet 'Champlain' rose.

We observed that a strong, single, contained accent outside the garden proper could improve the garden's overall design, thus extending its beneficial influence within the whole landscape. An old wooden wheelbarrow beyond repair was parked alongside the Tulip Bed's thick hedge of common lungwort (*Pulmonaria officinalis*). The wheelbarrow, filled deeply with rich, moist compost soil, provides favorable conditions for our favorite strain of large-flowered pansies, the reliable 'Swiss Giant', which blooms in shades of yellow, burgundy, wine, and cream by early summer when the glossy ground cover, *Viola odorata*, upon which the wheelbarrow rests, produces a mass of complementary small, crisp white flowers. This is also the time when the lungwort hedge is crowned with hundreds of azure-blue trumpets, while in the garden proper, clouds of sky blue forget-me-not weave among pale yellow tulips. To complete this container "planting," a low accent is achieved by setting a shallow metal tray of unknown origin on a nearby tree stump. Here we combine silvery false licorice (*Helichrysum petiolare*) with trailing lobelia (long-blooming in partial shade) for all-season interest. As with the wheelbarrow pansies, these are plants and combinations that would be lost among the vigorous types in the tulip bed, but in containers they are raised above the others and shown to advantage.

The care of these containers is not as labor intensive as it might seem. With so much field- and farmwork, with the need to make some form of dairy products—butter or cheese—nearly every day, to harvest berries and fruits as they ripen and turn them into hundreds of jars of jam and jelly, with all the gardens to maintain, we do not have time to pamper plants, even those in containers.

We mulch all the containers, either with grass clippings, moss, or rocks (these are for small planters, especially those in exposed sites), and only water them in extended dry spells. Plants are further protected from drying out by the canopy of foliage that results when containers are grouped together and by the large surface areas and deep soil beds of tire, barrel, or wheelbarrow plantings that don't dry out as fast as smaller containers. Since the soil mix is made from composted barn waste, flowering plants are fertilized only once or twice during the summer with liquid fertilizer high in phosphates and potash (Rx-15) to encourage bloom; herbs like basil are fertilized after their foliage is cut back, to stimulate another flush of growth. Flowers are deadheaded, if needed, as we pass by on the way to somewhere else. Plants like nicotiana are very much appreciated for their ability to bloom all summer without any cosmetic attention.

Nor do we fuss about adding gravel or other drainage material in the bottom of containers as usually advised; with the exception of the terra-cotta pots, all of them are leaky and already drain well. If the containers are tall or wide, necessitating a great amount of top soil, we fill the bottom third with a lightweight, organic substance such as well-rotted sawdust or wood shavings. This has the added benefit of not adding much weight to containers we may want to bring indoors for the winter.

The same sort of pleasure we derive from walking among the conventional gardens—delighting in their scents, shapes, harmonies, and contrasts, observing visits from the butterflies, hummingbirds, and bees that come to gather nectar—is intensified in the contained garden, where these same attractions are just beyond the kitchen door, visible from the kitchen itself.

In midsummer, the show begins at 8:25 in the morning, after we've gone up to the barn to milk the cows, returned with the milk pails, strained the milk into a large cheese pot (this is a cheese-making day), prepared breakfast at the woodstove, and sat down to eat it at the massive wooden table. It's while we are discussing the day's work over a last cup of morning cocoa (Jigs) and mocha (Jo Ann) that we see through the kitchen window the first hummingbird of the day hovering around the showy flowers of bicolored Texas sage, *Salvia coccinea* 'Coral Nymph', a background plant on the wheelbarrow flatbed. We watch for several minutes as he (brighter than the female) visits each of the small tubular flowers with protruding stamens that grow in loose whorls around the plant's top stems. When we step outside on the porch, the air is still sweet from open nicotianas and four-o'clocks, and bees are busy in the lilac flower spikes of *Hosta* 'Ginko Craig' at the edge of the corner garden.

By ten in the morning, with the cheese packed into a mold and the mold placed in the old wooden press to squeeze out whey, with the dew off the hay tumbles in the field, we are ready to hitch up the horses and bring in a load, and in passing the little contained garden, we observe that the hummingbirds are back (husband and wife this time), making the rounds of Texas sage (both red and coral) and the four-o'clock hedge in tubs on the stones below the wheelbarrow.

Back home by noon for lunch after a quick swim to wash our hot, itchy bodies, we notice that the nicotianas (the tall white and 'Crimson King', a compact heirloom from the 1930s) and the four-o'clocks are sleeping, as befits plants that work so hard all night. By 3:30, in the heat of the afternoon, a time to laze around with a tall glass of iced tea–rhubarb juice, the hummingbirds are at work in the red and white nicotiana, both now awakened and perky. As the afternoon cools, we go out to the vegetable garden to pick weeds for the laying hens in the barn, to check for ripe tomatoes (not yet, but turning), to bring back pickling cukes to make a crock of kosher dill pickles, and before you know it, it's five o'clock, the start of the most exciting show in town, when the four-o'clocks open (we are in the Atlantic time zone). (Figure 50.)

Figure 50.
The beautiful and fragrant four o'clock.

The first to open are fuchsia trumpets at five sharp, followed by the other colors—soft pink, pure white, and yellow with red-tipped anthers—over the next thirty-five minutes, when we observe a small flying insect deep within a flower, its legs covered with pollen. So much work to do on a summer's day!

At six, we go out to the pond pasture to bring in the two milk cows, and after we milk them, we return them to the pasture, take the team to theirs for the night, go back to the house to strain the milk once more (there will be no cheese tomorrow), and prepare supper. The salad of assorted leaf and head lettuces, arugula, and cress was picked, washed and sorted in the afternoon, so now all we have to do is snip fresh herbs from the tire garden just off the front porch by the Virginia rose hedge. To complete our herbal bouquet, we need a few nasturtium flowers and basil leaves from pots on the stone walkway in front of the wheelbarrow, and as we reach down to pluck them, spicy whiffs of four-o'clocks drift around us. How enjoyable it is to become immersed in the beauty, touch, and smell of these engaging plants.

After washing up and heating the day's cheese in a pot of its whey—a part of the curing process—it is 8:00 P.M., time to take our cups of hot tea to the front porch, to sit on our old wooden camp chairs in the gathering twilight and enjoy our fabulous night garden (Figure 51). We have never tried to establish plantings based on a single theme, as in a moonlight or scented garden, or as in a conventional herb garden, because even if we wanted to, our growing conditions do not allow it. The closest we have come to a theme garden was an attempt to grow silver and blue plants in a small raised bed against the west side of the house. Since the soil tends to be moist and the site a mix of sun and partial shade, we have been forced to confine the silvers and blues (the vast majority of which like sun and fast-draining soil) to a few accents here and there. We find it much more satisfactory to match plants to habitat rather than to consign them to sites based on a single idea.

But here, in a collection of containers on the wheelbarrow, on the stone walkways, and in the corner garden, we had unwittingly created an evening garden, one where scent is the dominant theme. We bring out a book or magazine to read, but find ourselves absorbed in the heady aromas, and when it's too dark to pretend to read, at precisely 8:25 P.M., we turn indoors, but not before we see our hummingbirds return, first to the red monarda in the corner bed, then to the salvias, one by one, on the wheelbarrow, twelve hours after the show curtain was raised.

Like pieces of a puzzle, each element in the landscape has found its special place for which it seems (after the fact) destined. Each planting, no matter how broad and sweeping, as in naturalized effects, or small and intimate, as in the contained gardens, complements the others, creating a scene of harmony and balance. Growing plants in containers, while only a very small part of our landscape, is invaluable, because it brings us so very close to a variety of flowers and herbs that we might not otherwise be able to know and enjoy. It brings them directly and intimately into our everyday existence, where we make no fine distinctions between the ones we use—the salad herbs, for instance—and those we enjoy for their presence or scent. Each of them fulfills a need. Just as we have learned

Figure 51.
Enjoying the night garden.

that there are many ways, none of them difficult or expensive to carry out, to improve the larger landscape, there are compelling reasons to create contained gardens. Their beneficial impact, far greater than their size suggests, is surely the most compelling reason of all.

Sampler of Scented Plants

We began to cultivate plants in containers close to the house because it was a practical and convenient way to raise types with special soil or climate needs (basils, nasturtiums, tender perennials) and to have herbs nearby for daily use. Although we hadn't planned it that way, many were freely fragrant or released their scent when lightly brushed or rubbed, and as a bonus, they attracted hummingbirds. We soon realized how much we enjoyed having refreshing aromas in our midst (especially in the evening when we relaxed on the front porch). Of course, it's convenient to step just beyond the kitchen door and pick fresh herbs and flowers for salad and flavoring, but even if we never picked a single sprig of basil to toss into a salad, we would still want to grow all the different kinds in containers where we can gaze on their lustrous, perky leaves and smell their spicy perfumes every day. We prize these plants for the pleasure they give us just by being.

Each season our potted collection varies, but we almost always include the ones described below. Even if you already grow some of these in your garden, once you have grown them in containers where you will be certain to notice them during the day and in the evening— near a porch or patio, doorway or path—the contained garden will become an essential feature of your landscape, as it is of ours.

HERBS AND FLOWERS (FOR SUNNY CONDITIONS UNLESS OTHERWISE NOTED; HEIGHTS ARE SHORTER IN CONTAINERS)

Anethum graveolens **'Fernleaf' dill,** 18 in. Annual. Dwarf bushy plants are bred for foliage, so they are slow to blossom. We sow seeds directly in the container outdoors when we sow lettuce seeds in the garden, then cut the green ferny foliage all summer for salads and Herbal Confetti (see page 237). Their fresh fragrance, released by rubbing or close sniffing, is summed up in the word "pickles."

Artemisia stelleriana, **beach wormwood/wild dusty miller,** 6 in. Short-lived perennial. Found growing wild in sprawling patches on beaches in the Northeast, its distinctive foliage is thick, felty, and white, while in cultivars such as 'Silver Brocade', foliage is more deeply cut and habit is more uniformly spreading; aroma is lightly camphoraceous when leaves are rubbed. Difficult to winter over in the ground unless given light soil with perfect drainage (as on a sandy beach), its container soil can be adjusted to include a little grit and extra perlite; we winter containers in our unheated greenhouse. Plants should be trimmed back in spring to encourage fresh growth and can be propagated by stem cuttings. Beach wormwood can be grown effectively in a hanging basket and combines beautifully with the small-flowered purple 'Fantasy' petunia.

Cleome hasselerana, **spider flower,** 3–5 ft. Annual. We used to admire these tall, airy tropical flowers in fall gardens but could not grow them ourselves until we learned how to germinate seeds and give plants a head start in our greenhouse so they would bloom before frost. Seeds should be prechilled for two weeks in the fridge before sowing on the soil surface (they also need light to germinate); or you can sow seeds as we do directly in the container, cover it with plastic, then place it outside *before the last frost*; after germination occurs, we bring the container indoors to grow in the warmth of the greenhouse until plants are mature enough to put outside (mid-July here) for the rest of the summer. Ours are descendants of 'Lilac Queen', a lovely shade of lilac with rose-colored buds in large round clusters—six to eight inches across—and gracefully protruding stamens; fragrance is pleasantly pungent. Plants get their name from the long spidery seedpods that dangle down along the stem.

Dianthus superbus, fringed pink, 12–15 in. Short-lived perennial. We adore the warm jasmine fragrance of these pinks and find it easier to grow them in containers where we can give them the fast-draining soil they require. 'Crimsonia', ruby red and sweet, blooms the first year from seed sown indoors eight to ten weeks before the last frost. 'Rainbow Loveliness' (*D. allwoodii* x *D. superbus*) includes carmine, pink, lilac, and white flowers with darker bands, all heavily fringed and strongly perfumed. We winter over containers in the unheated greenhouse, and after they have flowered the following season, we make new plants by pulling off side shoots from the mother plant—with a bit of the main stem—and planting them.

Gladiolus communis/Acidanthera bicolor, peacock orchid, 2 ft. Bulb. If you avoid glads because of their stiffness and artificiality, you will love this graceful wild type with clove-scented two-inch-wide star flowers, creamy white with purple at their base, opening in succession all along the stem; their strong aroma is most noticeable in the evening. We plant bulbs outside in a tire as soon as the soil warms (the tire holds the heat these plants need to bloom by fall); then we cover the tire with plastic until bulbs sprout. The sword-shaped foliage is a handsome accent all summer, ringed with vining petunias (see below).

***Melissa officinalis,* lemon balm,** 2 ft. Short-lived perennial. We grow this as an annual because of a problem with white fly, which winters over in established plants. Seeds sown indoors six to eight weeks before the last frost produce fast-growing seedlings that we plant outside in tires after the last frost. Foliage is light green and scallop edged, and most lemony when harvested from lush, not woody, growth (close sniffing on a sunny day, or rubbing leaves releases aroma). We dry large quantities for winter and summer teas.

***Mentha longifolia,* horsemint,** to 3 ft. Perennial. We grow two types: Silver Mint and 'Habek' (Bible mint), both derived from the Middle Eastern species, a rangy, coarse, strongly scented mint covered with tiny hairs that give the leaves a grayish cast and drought resistance. We grow the variants in five-inch-wide terra-cotta pots, a pleasing contrast to their gray-green foliage. Silver Mint has oval, veined, silvery green leaves; 'Habek' has very narrow, curling foliage and a semitrailing habit (at least in a cramped container). We like these for their strong fragrance (released by brushing) and soft green leaves among bright potted flowers at the front of our contained garden. Plants should be trimmed several times during the summer (use the trimmings for hot or cold tea) and fertilized. Both make fine winter houseplants.

***Mirabilis jalapa,* four-o'clock,** 2–4 ft. Annual. We have already praised these bushy plants with spicy evening scent and tubular flowers, white, pink, red, or yellow (or bicolor and all mixed up on a single plant if you're lucky) by midsummer. We sow seeds indoors four to six weeks before the last frost in a fifteen-inch-wide, deep container (two to three plants in each), then set them outdoors when temperatures are consistently warm. Over the summer, the roots expand, and by fall they form large, dark, rather menacing-looking tubers. Despite all our resolutions about digging them up and wintering them over (like dahlia tubers), we let them die and sow seeds again the following season. Hummingbirds are fond of this plant.

***Nicotiana alata,* nicotiana/flowering tobacco,** 15 in.–4 ft. Annual. We start seeds indoors six to eight weeks before the last frost. N. 'Crimson King' is an older compact strain with velvety red flowers (moderately fragrant) that never needs deadheading and combines beautifully in a half-barrel with white sweet alyssum. *N. alata,* Edna St. Vincent Millay's old "dumb white," is tall and embarrassingly gawky during the day but richly perfumed by late afternoon, when its creamy tubes, tinged with rust or chartreuse on their undersides, perk up and pour forth their sweet-spicy, powerful fragrance. We plant three seedlings in a twelve-inch-wide tub with several clumps of trailing blue lobelia (*Lobelia erinus*) for companions. All nicotianas benefit from partial shade and will self-seed given the opportunity. These are also hummingbird plants.

***Occimum basilicum,* basil,** 8–18 in. Annual. We have already described our unusual method for raising basil successfully in a cool climate; plants are in lush foliage by the time we set them out, and their distinctively different aromas (described here according to taste) are released by light brushing or sniffing.

    'Cinnamon', 18 in. A vigorous ornamental type with purplish stems and flowers, and a sharp spicy flavor; we dry leaves to use in a tea mix (see pages 236–237).

    'Dark Opal'/'Red Rubin'/'Purple Ruffles', 15 in. 'Dark Opal', the original purple basil, is the most vigorous, but seeds produce about 25 percent green seedlings; 'Red Rubin' is an improved version; 'Purple Ruffles' is heavily fringed and ruffled, very ornamental. All purple types have purple-bronze, shiny foliage, and if allowed to flower, produce purplish-pink flower spikes, striking above their foliage. We preserve their spicy, rather than sweet, flavor in jelly and vinegar (see below).

'Genovese', 1–2 ft. Vigorous, with large leaves and a sweet, light clove taste, this is the best for general flavoring (terrific for salads and pesto), and it dries well for winter use.

'Lettuce Leaf'/'Mammoth', 2 ft. These are extra-large-leaved types with quilted or dimpled leaves, mildly flavored. A single leaf will cover half a slice of bread and can be substituted for lettuce in sandwiches.

'Siam Queen', 2 ft. This is a vigorous Thai basil, very decorative, with purple stems and flowers. We dry its licorice-flavored foliage to use in our special tea blend (see pages 236–237).

'Spicy Globe', 6–9 in. Characteristic of the dwarf bush type (*O. basilicum* 'Minimum'), it has a multitude of small, pointed, nutmeg-flavored leaves that form a compact, dense mound that shows off well at the front of a contained garden. We winter over the most immature plants (before they become woody) and use leaves in egg dishes.

'Sweet Dani', 2 ft. An improved, vigorous, lemon-flavored basil we dry for tea (see pages 236–237).

***Origanum majorana*, sweet marjoram,** 12 in. We sow seeds four to six weeks before the last frost (they need light to germinate) and transplant the tiny seedlings by clumps into containers, then place them outdoors when temperatures warm. Semitrailing plants bear a profusion of small, gray-green leaves, sweet with a hint of camphor; great for using in all tomato dishes. Remarkably hardy, sweet marjoram will survive frosts well into the fall; an attractive and useful plant for the winter windowsill.

***Pelargonium graveolens,* rose geranium,** 18 in. Tender perennial. If you've ever pined for a scented geranium but don't think you have the knack to grow them, we urge you to try rose geranium. It will be your friend for life however you abuse it (forget to water, expose to frost), as we know from experience. A handsome shrub to five feet in its native South Africa and similar climates (California), the potted plant is considerably dwarfed, but then you have the chance to closely observe and smell its abundant foliage: a canopy of velvety, light-green, divided leaves with a strong rose scent. It shows off well in a terra-cotta pot. We dry foliage for potpourri and use it fresh to flavor jellies.

***Petunia* sp.,** 8 in.–3 ft. Annual. Sow seeds indoors ten to twelve weeks before the last frost. We've always been partial to old-fashioned, open-pollinated petunias in the classic single-trumpet design, sweetly fragrant (especially in the evening) and more graceful than the current petunia flower machines. In recent years, seeds of wild and semiwild types have become available through seed exchanges and specialty seedhouses. *Petunia integrifolia/violacea*, one of the parents of modern hybrids (and chief contributor to the 'Wave' series), carries inch-wide dark rose trumpets with a purple throat. A lax plant with a vining habit, its small flowers climb up through the creamy sprays of white mugwort (*Artemisia lactiflora*) when a container is carefully "planted" in a traditional garden; these petunias are also very showy in a hanging basket.

Seeds sold as "Vining Petunias" produce two-inch-wide fluted trumpets, rose, pinks, purple, and whites—both pure white and buff (the latter close to the other parent of modern hybrids, *P. axillaris*). In this type, outer petals are flushed with violet, centers are sometimes black eyed, surrounded by a yellow ring. We like to grow the whites separately for their spectacular effect in the evening when they perk up and glow in the fading light, pouring forth a lightly spiced sweet aroma. They always elicit admiration.

Poterium sanguisorba, **salad burnet,** 12 in. Biennial. We sow seeds indoors four to six weeks before the last frost, excluding light, then plant seedlings in two-inch plant cells where they form a solid block of roots that can be transplanted into a container without being disturbed. Plants form basal growth of dainty, wavy-edged leaves, rather long. Those with the best flavor—like cucumber—are in the middle of the clump, short and bright green; rub them to release their unique scent. These are the ones we prize for using in Herbal Confetti (see page 237). Second-year flowering plants have ornamental value for a short time in early summer but lack flavor.

Salvia coccinea **'Lady in Red', Texas sage,** 2 feet, native. Tender perennial. Sow seeds twelve weeks before the last frost, but do not set out containers until temperatures are consistently warm or plants will not thrive. This is one of our favorite salvias for its whorls of bright red tubular flowers (very attractive to hummingbirds) above musk-scented, light green foliage; 'Coral Nymph' and 'White Nymph' extend the color range (hummingbirds like these, too). In our contained garden, they sow themselves into nearby pots so we always have seedlings to winter over on the windowsill, where they bloom for months. To ensure that we have plentiful blooms early the following season, we winter over a few mature plants.

Tropaeolum, **nasturtium,** 6 in.–6 ft. Annual. When outdoor temperatures are 60–69°F, sow seeds in containers, in unenriched, well-drained soil. Garden nasturtiums are hybrid forms of two species, low-growing *T. minor* and tall, scrambling *T. majus.* We plant all the types—dwarf, semitrailing, and tall—because we love their spurred flowers in shades of red, rose, mahogany, orange, yellows, and creams with light green round foliage, and their warm spicy aroma. Our favorites are 'Dwarf Double Jewel' in the whole color range; the heirloom 'Empress of India' (1884), a scarlet large-flowered type with blue gray foliage; the semitrailing 'Gleam' series (large-flowered doubles or singles in soft colors); and the large-flowered climbing types in bright colors. Since these only grow to six or seven feet, we plant them in a barrel to give them height (stems are lax and must be supported or plants will grow as a ground cover). Summer is synonymous with abundant nasturtium bloom to use in salads and Herbal Confetti (see below); we also use the flowers to make vinegar and sauces. A hummingbird favorite.

DIRECTIONS FOR GREEN BASIL TEA; HERBAL CONFETTI; PURPLE BASIL JELLY; PURPLE BASIL VINEGAR

Green Basil Tea

We seldom think of basil as a medicinal, but it is a natural digestive, and when combined with spices, orange peel, and lemon balm (a natural sedative), it makes a soothing, relaxing, and delicious tea. Combine the following:

1 cup dried green basil leaves

('Cinnamon', 'Siam Queen', and 'Sweet Dani')

1 cup dried lemon balm leaves

2 tablespoons each whole cloves and crushed cinnamon

1 tablespoon dried and broken orange peel

Store in a covered tin or jar in a cool cupboard. To make one cup of tea: Steep 2 teaspoons of this mixture in a cup of boiling water for a few minutes; strain and add honey to sweeten if you want. The mixture can be used twice (steep longer for the second cup).

Herbal Confetti

For general flavoring in salads or to add to cream cheese spreads or dips. It is colorful and very tasty.

Gather the following on a sunny day:

1 large green basil leaf

2 nasturtium flowers in different colors (inspect for insects)

A few sprigs each of fernleaf dill, salad burnet, and marjoram

Make sure all herbs are fresh and clean. Spread out basil leaf, place herbs and nasturtium flowers on top; tightly roll up leaf, cut in fine pieces with kitchen scissors: the result is Herbal Confetti.

Purple Basil Jelly

Makes about ten ½-cup (125 ml.) jelly jars

Place 1½ cups freshly picked purple basil leaves in a saucepan. Cover them with 3¼ cups water, and while bringing the mixture just to the boiling point, gently bruise leaves with the bottom of a glass to release their color and flavor. Turn off heat and let herbs steep for 10 minutes, bruising the leaves occasionally. Strain mixture and discard leaves (they will have lost most of their color). Reheat liquid (you should have 3 cups; if not, add water) with 2 tablespoons vinegar and 1 box pectin crystals. Mix, then bring to a boil that can't be stirred down; add 4 cups sugar, stir in, and bring back to a boil that can't be stirred down. Boil for 1 minute; remove from heat, let mixture settle, then pour into sterilized glass jelly jars and seal at once. Try with cream cheese on whole-wheat bread or muffins.

Purple Basil Vinegar

Makes 1 quart.

Loosely fill a sterilized widemouthed quart jar with freshly picked leaves, then pour white vinegar over to cover (a smaller amount of leaves will make a weaker flavored vinegar). Cover the jar with a nonreactive cover; if in doubt, cover the jar opening first with plastic wrap. Leave the jar in the sun for two weeks or until the solution is rosy pink and the foliage has lost color. Strain and pour into a clean, sterilized jar; cover again with a nonreactive cover and store in a cool, dark place. We combine this with olive oil for salad dressing (see "Kitchen Garden Sampler," page 64). ●

CHAPTER TEN

In the Cottage Garden Spirit

⁓

VISITORS SOMETIMES GAZE at our gardens and ask, "How can we make a cottage garden like this?"

We could answer, "Just buy a rundown farm in the middle of nowhere, have little income, and develop the art of self reliance."

But that wouldn't be very helpful. Although we never set out to create a cottage garden (about which we knew nothing), we inevitably followed its ways—in the plants we grew, in our extended use of them throughout the landscape, in the rustic framework that surrounds them. What impresses visitors is the ambience of the place, its homeyness, the lack of pretension, and an appealing sense of the well worn—in contrast to its opposite: shiny, slick, new, and fashionable. In practical terms, this means an absence of hard, perfect edges, as in the concrete of "hardscapes": Building materials are wood, rough and ready, often reused, and built with human hands rather than by machines or in a factory; paths are dirt, grass, or sawdust; plantings are soft rather than stiff in appearance and so crowded that no earth is visible, thus creating a picture of natural, unforced abundance.

How did we get to where we are? How did we unwittingly create a cottage garden, or its aura? For us, there was no choice. Our circumstances dictated the path that generations of people with limited means have pursued instinctively wherever they live. Occurring away from the centers of sophistication, often in remote places, the characteristics of a real, as opposed to mythical, cottage garden are humble means and materials, the creative use of a limited plant repertoire—mainly from noncommercial sources—a thorough knowledge of cultivation and propagation (especially the latter), and the patience taught by a life lived in daily struggle with the natural world, the kind it takes to nurture a six-inch softwood stem cutting into a mature lilac bush. The garden that results from such an approach—more accurately termed "folk garden" for its universality—evolves naturally over time from the gardener's life and what comes to hand in materials, in shared roots, slips, and seeds. It is the very antithesis of the installed garden of instant effect with the latest in plant-product fashion. The plants at the heart of a true cottage garden may be limited in scope and imperfect, yet they have an appeal that more tailored, restrained, and refined forms do not quite possess. There are, for instance, new, compact, long-blooming rudbeckias, but none that look better against the naturally weathered boards of an old shed than old-fashioned golden glow (*Rudbeckia laciniata* 'Hortensia'), whose mass of small tightly doubled yellow daisies atop too-tall lanky stems are produced in abundance by late summer. Although golden glow inevitably bows down before wind and rain, old-timers rarely stake it. "I just let it take care of itself" is the most common response of gardeners in the cottage/folk mode who know when to interfere with nature and when to let it have its way.

There is no doubt that the look of our gardens is greatly influenced by the hand-me-down plants that are the backbone of all our plantings. For the first fifteen years, when there was no extra cash to buy mail-order perennials, we relied solely on those that were here when we came, the few we dug from the wild (like the Virginia rose and the now fashionable musk mallow, *Malva moschata*, a field weed here), the ones we found in old and neglected gardens, assorted plants and seeds passed along from neighbors, friends, and gardening acquaintances, and purchased seed, mostly of annuals. We have no regrets; these were our first teachers in the skills of growing, propagating, and landscaping.

When we moved to the farm over thirty years ago, we had some rhubarb roots, choice peppermint, and a clump of chives from a friend, and a few herbs Jigs had raised—the indomitable blue comfrey, elecampane, and hyssop. These joined the plants we found here, all grown

Figure 52.
Lungwort tulips and spurge.

from neighbor's slips and bulbs in the 1920s and 1930s: lilacs, mock orange, the old double white narcissus, *Narcissus albus plenus odoratus* (late blooming and intensely fragrant), the Loyalist rose ('Banshee'), Solomon's seal, yellow flag iris by the back door, and common lungwort (*Pulmonaria officinalis*), in a wide circle around an overgrown clump of orange daylilies (*Hemerocallis fulva*) on the knoll in front of the farmhouse. These formed the basis of our early landscaping efforts.

It was a fortunate beginning, for they taught us to respect and be grateful for vigor in plants (as in many things) and forced us to find inventive ways to extend their uses in our landscape. When we were looking for suitable plants to enclose the Flowering Herb Garden and adjacent Tulip Bed, we eyed the thick circle of lungwort and thought it might serve our need for the hundreds of roots it would take to establish a living frame (Figure 52). We learned that despite being recommended for growing in shade—where its flowers do last longer—our new planting thrived because its need for moist soil conditions, the most important factor in its growth, was satisfied. In this single effort, we learned how to divide rhizomatous roots—untangle and replant them—and how to care for the resulting hedge: cut it back after flowering to produce new, fresh foliage. Most important, our success encouraged us to explore other imaginative ways to realize the full landscaping potential of all of our plants, thereby magnifying our relatively small plant palette. We did not know then that using such robust, easily propagated types for hedging is a classic folk-gardening strategy, one that employs the most unlikely plants, as we were to discover.

We first saw variegated goutweed (*Aegopodium podagraria* 'Variegatum')—normally regarded with suspicion as a too-aggressive ground cover—grown as a neat hedge in a backyard planting from the 1920s, where it was used to divide garden "rooms" of shrubbery, border, and rock garden. Growth was controlled simply by mowing the grass on both sides of the hedge, and by trimming back its early summer flowering of white umbels—a dainty form of Queen Anne's lace. The effect was lovely and far easier to establish and maintain than a woody hedge. The gardener, not knowing it had never been done, took the plants at hand—perhaps a generous clump from another garden—and saw in them the possibility for creating a low mounded wall of soft, emerald-green leaves, irregularly edged with white. A word of caution: There is a world of difference between variegated goutweed and its plain, even more invasive cousin with shiny green serrated leaves, the wild form of *A. podagraria*. This plant, associated with monasteries and church buildings because of its reputed healing properties for sore joints, is sometimes found growing unchecked in old, neglected gardens and it can be a real problem for anyone who inherits it. If its roots are growing in a cultivated flower bed, we advise the selective use of Roundup or moving the flower bed to another site and controlling the goutweed by mowing.

We begged a few roots of variegated goutweed (not hard to part with) and established a small planting in a dank, shady corner between the cellar door and the back wall of the kitchen, where nothing but weeds flourished. Over several seasons, plants spread to form a mounded carpet of handsome foliage, shaped by mowing to form a curving wedge shape that leads from the entranceway to the back kitchen door. We were delighted by the ease with which we had brought light to a dark, uninviting area and transformed it into a low-maintenance landscaping feature. Care is confined to mowing the carpet down nearly to the ground

Figure 53.
A cottage garden sampling at the back kitchen door.

with a long-handled sickle in early June, and mowing regularly around the planting with the gas-powered mower whenever the grass is cut, our standard procedure for curbing such wayward growth. Several years later, when this spot became the site for a large, ugly propane gas tank (we eventually bought a small gas stove for summer cooking), we placed a white trellis in front of the tank to support orange and yellow 'Dropmore Scarlet' honeysuckle, a dwarf form of the species (we have nothing against improved cultivars if we can get them). Since the vine could not compete with goutweed in the ground, we planted its roots in an old nail keg set up on a brick platform. Now the corner is a positive asset, a step away from the back kitchen door (Figure 53).

The development of the area on the other side of the back kitchen door, partly in the shade of an old apple tree, exposed to wind, proved more difficult to carry out. When we noticed that the potted impatiens we had set on top of the goutweed carpet across the way (a trick we had observed in our Dutch friend's garden) were triple the size of those grown in exposed sites, we erected a protective slab fence, trimmed so the top boards formed a graceful curve, to back a plank-enclosed raised bed—four and one-half feet deep by nine feet long—and we began to experiment with our limited plants. We thought cottage pinks would be nice near an entranceway for their scent, but they proved short-lived because of the overly moist and heavy soil conditions. We improved it by the addition of our composted soil and rotted sawdust, but it still did not provide the sharp drainage that all pinks need. Once we'd got it firmly into our minds that plants do best when they are grown where *they* like to grow, rather than where *you* think they should grow—a lesson we found hard to accept—we began to solve our problems at this site.

The community we established here, while hardly color coordinated, is pleasing in a cottage garden way, with its diversity of forms and colors tightly packed together within a small area. Dominated by some of our oldest and toughest plant acquisitions, it includes the shrub golden currant (*Ribes aureum*), grown from a tiny slip Jo Ann begged from a gardener on the mainland where she went to give a workshop on heirloom flowers. Its floppy-stemmed form at the back of the bed in the partial shade of the apple tree is ideally suited for cottage garden ambience. Superhardy and amenable to virtually any growing conditions except under water, golden currant blesses us first with fresh green leaves at a time when all other trees and shrubs are bare, then in early summer, with masses of golden, scented trumpets that attract early visiting hummingbirds (after they have dined on lungwort nectar). An important landscape feature all season, its lobed, nearly heart-shaped foliage turns a burnished red when most other plants have faded. Easily propagated by suckers, it is now established at the base of the bank in dark, dank conditions, and under the shade of the apple tree at the back of the Tulip Bed. Both here and by the back kitchen door, its dipping branches provide an appealing setting for snowdrops, scilla, and hyacinths to push through a ground cover of dusty pink bleeding heart (*Dicentra formosa*) and white-flowered ajuga (*Ajuga reptans* 'Alba'). It would be unusual to find so many attributes together in even the most highly bred shrub.

We added the "old red lily," which Jo Ann first saw at the same mainland workshop when the group visited a fifty-year-old garden established on a steep hillside. Wholly maintained by an elderly woman, with occasional help from her husband, an incredible wealth of flora flourished in near-naturalized conditions. Jo Ann noticed the lily for its compact growth, early summer bloom, and vivid fire-red, up-facing flowers, similar in appearance and color to nasturtium-red 'Enchantment', one of the earliest lily hybrids (1947). Asked its name, her hostess said, "Oh, that's the old red lily," implying with a dismissive wave that it was so familiar what more could you want to know? Native to the European Alps, *Lilium bulbiferum* var. *croceum,* also called fire lily, is the orange or saffron lily of history, a familiar garden plant throughout Northern Ireland because its flowering coincides with the victory of William of Orange in

1691 (perhaps it was planted in Protestant settlements in Nova Scotia for the same reason). Garden historian Ann Leighton describes it as an old favorite, like the tiger lily, in eighteenth-century American gardens, noting that both lilies are able to take care of themselves. We can vouch for that, for even in less than ideal conditions, the old red lily steadily increases, nestled between chives and blue catmint (*Nepeta* x *faassenii* 'Dropmore Blue'). The best, and perhaps only, place to find it is in an old garden.

If we couldn't have pinks by the back door, we would plant other scented types to take their place. Sweet rocket, scarlet bee balm, and double soapwort—all of which thrive in heavy, moist soil—extend the season of pleasant aromas to late summer.

Of these, soapwort is too invasive to grow within the bed itself, so we plant it just beyond the wooden plank barriers to form a wide, lax swath near a well-used path, and we contain its growth by mowing. When a friend, a retired postmistress, gave us a small bunch of roots she called "London pride," we were pleasantly surprised to discover it was the double form of soapwort, or bouncing bet (*Saponaria officinalis* 'Rosea Plena'), regarded as a choice heirloom elsewhere, but a ditch weed here. Commonly grown in Cape Breton gardens in the 1930s, then neglected when vigorous perennials were supplanted by tame, disposable annual bedding plants in the 1940s and 1950s, our soapwort clump was a direct descendant of plants established in the late 1800s by prosperous Captain Ross (in whose imposing house the postmistress now lives), who had sailed his schooner about the Maritimes' waterways, selling, trading, and buying whatever surplus the people had; perhaps he got the soapwort roots in trade. We like to think of him sitting on his spacious front porch on a humid evening in late summer to enjoy double soapwort's floating sweet-spicy scent.

Maybe he caught a fleeting glimpse, as we have, of a whirring hawkmoth, hovering around its flowers.

We did not set out to create a cottage garden atmosphere by the back kitchen door, but by using simple means—a plank-enclosed bed, slab fence, nail-keg planter, and vigorous old-fashioned types, the area inevitably conveys the impression of unforced charm that we associate with a cottage garden. Its small size is enhanced by nearby plantings— the variegated goutweed wedge, the facing Tulip Bed and the Flowering Herb Garden—separate but integral parts of the whole landscape.

Some of our most interesting plants have come from pass-along seeds. What cottage garden is complete without hollyhocks? All of ours—tall and single flowered—are from local strains traced back to the 1920s garden of Elizabeth MacDonald, whose faded photograph shows a still-handsome woman at ninety, standing tall and erect in front of a magnificent stand of her favorite flowers. We traced the passing of her seeds from hand to hand, from generation to generation, until we were directed to a large white farmhouse, where the recent construction of a deck had destroyed most of Elizabeth MacDonald's descendant hollyhocks.

Even as we were discovering a wealth of desirable plants—now referred to as heirlooms—they were going down before the Three Ds: the (satellite) dish, the (bull) dozer, and the deck. Because of its isolation, untouched by fashion or development until relatively recently, the peninsula on Cape Breton Island was like a window into the past, where the cottage garden style was a living memory: the sharing of vigorous plants, a preference for showy and scented types, the tradition of 'bride's plants'—usually a rose or peony, a piece of which was taken by a bride to her new home as a memento of her past home and associations.

People remembered the last trip of the plant peddler in 1940 (not seen in developed areas for more than a century) and could show you the very shrubs—lilacs, Peegee hydrangea, weigela, spirea—their mothers or fathers had bought from him. Every old plant had a lineage—from so-and-so's garden—and a story to tell. Until recently, the area was a rich hunting ground for desirable perennials, bulbs, and shrubs where old plantings up deserted mountainsides, at the edge of woodland roads, in lonely glens where no one had lived for over forty years had been left undisturbed. But now all that was changing. Old houses—with their gardens—were bulldozed to make way for the new: Fashionable decks (on which no one sits in the evening because of mosquitoes) and satellite dishes displaced vintage shrubberies and borders. Change is inevitable, but it gave a sense of urgency to the pursuit of heirloom plants.

The remaining hollyhocks by the old farmhouse (where we were shown a grove of trees from the plant peddler's stock), were of fairytale beauty, a dark purple strain with nearly black, wide open, glistening trumpets crammed on thick stems to eight feet. Seeds collected here gradually produced variants in colors (from cross-fertilization) ranging from white to shades of dark-eyed pinks, reds, and purple-black; we maintain favorite shades by growing new plants vegetatively from offshoots at the base of the selected mother plant. Although some of the hollyhocks appear to be resistant to rust, most are afflicted from time to time, depending on the season (the fungus is brought on by wet conditions). We limit its damage by changing sites, providing good air circulation, and reducing thick populations. When infestations are severe, we treat them with agricultural sulfur powder (see Chapter Eleven under "Disease and Insect Control").

We did not immediately fall in love with every old plant that was given to us. Conservative to a fault, we seldom discard what may be of possible use, but we were dismayed by the startling growth of a clump given to us with the assurance that it would produce beautiful flowers. Advised to grow it in moist ground in sun or shade, we dug it in at the back of the Flowering Herb Garden, where its thick, watery, red stems grew upward with no promise of bloom. We did not see any advantage in letting such unattractive growth take up so much valuable room without any benefit of bloom (or beauty of form or foliage), so it was tossed onto the compost heap. But our adventures with *Impatiens glandulifera,* a self-seeding annual also known as policeman's helmet, red jewelweed, Himalayan balsam, jumping jack, and jump seed, had only begun.

Later in the season when we visited a friend in her new home and saw it in full, flamboyant bloom in the center of her newly established backyard garden (very much in the cottage garden spirit), we regretted having discarded it. Tall and shimmering in full sun, full of bees visiting its mass of hooded pink flowers (its peculiar stems barely visible), it could not have been more desirable for a cottage garden or for any other. When we compared notes, our friend's experience had been very similar to ours, but with a true gardener's curiosity, she had let the plants grow on.

Now that we had rediscovered policeman's helmet, it turned up everywhere, as if parading its beauty—"See what you missed!" On a trip to Toronto among a group of professional horticulturalists, we were bemused when no one knew the name of the plant that formed a glorious informal six-foot hedge, also shimmering with bees in full sun, in an otherwise overcultivated, professional landscape of stiff bedding plants. As if an electric current had passed through them, everyone

Figure 54.
Policeman's helmet.

suddenly awoke from the stupor of our plodding tour to stare in disbe-
lief at the glorious flowering hedge before them, its dramatic effect
magnified by everything we had seen before. We have since read of
similarly dramatic encounters, as in Margaret Brownlow's classic *Herbs
and the Fragrant Garden:* "The pursuit, some 15 years ago, of this exotic
affair, inaccessibly tantalized me; flaunting its glories, it was glimpsed
from suburban trains. . . . The search ended by stopping a taxi somewhere
in Devon where sprays of a single plant of this lovely vagrant, growing
by a roadside rivulet, could be picked and examined."

Our story has a happy ending. More than a decade after we had so
thoughtlessly thrown it away, we carefully planted pass-along seeds of

policeman's helmet at the base of our sumac tree on the steep bank. By midsummer, plants produced a profusion of spotted helmets in the full range of colors—rose-lilac, salmon-rose, blush pink, white, and "peach ice cream" (Jigs's well-chosen name). (Figure 54.) Look for seeds in specialty catalogs or in an old garden.

Except for this adventure and a period when we were researching the history of local flowers, we did not actively pursue plants—we had so much else to claim our attention and energy on the farm. We did, however, hanker for a hardy vine, but all our efforts ended in failure (clematis, honeysuckle, and climbing roses were added later). We had given up when an acquaintance with a large, rambling hillside garden gave us roots of the hop vine with the admonition to "watch it."

We had by this time enough experience with vigorous, even rampant plants to take the warning seriously, and we recalled Kenneth Roberts's account of how his house in the country had become engulfed in a tangle of hop vine that he innocently supposed would create, unattended, the archetypal cottage garden he envisioned. How our dreams are so often spoiled by reality!

Growing to twenty feet in a single season on weak, twining stems, the hop vine produces almost heart-shaped, finely toothed leaves and cone-shaped flowers (the source of bitter hop flavor) that turn from chartreuse to golden amber by early fall. Once popular for providing dense shade for porches and verandas, it passed out of fashion when tamer, showier vines like clematis were introduced. In Cape Breton, where it was grown from the time of the first settlers for making barm— a form of yeast to raise bread—old hop vines can still be found in the countryside, growing neatly up a tall pole by the side of the house. We planted ours at the base of the shop's front wall, along which we nailed a World War II cargo net horizontally for its support. The second season, it shot up, framing the shop doorway in a "bosky dingle," spreading sideways along the wall as it twined itself around the netting. An annual thinning of roots (some extras were established to grow over our wide, wooden arbor by the raspberry and rhubarb beds), and regular mowing of the grass around it has kept the hop vine within bounds.

We had not foreseen that the hop vine and repair shop were meant for each other, that when paired together, their countrified air is intensified. Built in 1974 along the roadway that leads up to the barn, from boards sawn from our own logs (hauled to the sawmill three miles away with the team), the shop's clean, uncomplicated lines were dictated by our resources, the purpose of the building, and our aesthetic preferences. Without electricity, the only light inside comes from three nine-paned recycled windows along the front wall that look out to the blueberry hedge and pasture beyond; and two against the back wall, which look out onto the steep slope behind. Wide double-front doors—embellished above with a huge double daisy Jigs fashioned from rusty horseshoes—allow entry to horse-drawn vehicles for repair and horses to be shod; the narrow doorway to the right, now adorned with the hop vine, leads inside to the forge for shaping ironwork and horseshoes, a dim interior of horsey, woodsy, musty aromas.

The only flaw in this marriage of building and vine was the weedy growth along the front shop wall, beyond the hop vine, that we were unable to discourage. The solution, one we have used wherever this is a problem, was to supplant the weeds with tougher and far more attractive plants, of which we have an abundant supply. When we built a narrow, plank-enclosed bed here and filled it with our compost soil, we extended the hop vine accent, first with a massed planting of the nineteenth-century 'Pheasant's-eye' (*Narcissus poeticus recurvus*), a late-blooming, intensely scented, dainty daffodil with glistening, flared-back white petals and a small ruffled cup, green-eyed and rimmed bright red (Figure 55), to which we

Figure 55.
A combination of narcissus and hops (behind) on the trellis.

added a group of indestructibles that bloom, in turn, all season: Sedum 'Autumn Joy' below the hop vine, followed by lilac wild monarda, blue and bicolored monkshood, yellow daylilies, and white and pink phlox from local deserted gardens, plants that are repeated down the line in a colorful border.

The repair shop, once a single element in bare surroundings, has become a valuable landscaping asset suggestive of a cottage garden in its simple form and weathered boards, in its vine-draped doorway, and in the crowded, colorful flower border that edges it. In the winter when we stop by the woodshed with the team sled to load firewood for the house, the horses, Pookie and Brownie, lean forward to nibble seedheads and stems, so we don't need to do much plant trimming in the spring. And we leave some of the old, bare hop vines, still wrapped around the netting, to help support next season's growth (see Figure 4, on page 21).

From our own experiences, the process of creating a cottage garden (or its atmosphere) is built up slowly over time, based on a personal vision that grows directly from one's needs, desires, and resources. A cottage garden cannot be rushed, its plans do not come ready-made, as in garden blueprints, planting by numbers, or by current fashion. Its main characteristics are simplicity of design: the use of unpretentious materials and vigorous plants, and well-defined, densely packed, colorful plantings. Its effect is a landscape that seems natural, unforced, inevitable, relaxed, and abundant. We think that anyone can establish such a cottage garden however large or small the area, in town or country, and we offer this guide to help you get started.

Keep it simple. Simplicity of design is at the heart of the cottage garden. Don't try to do too many things at once. A cottage garden is by definition on a small scale, with the house at its center. Begin by establishing a planting or accent outside your front or back door and see where it leads.

Vertical accents, a traditional feature of the cottage garden, are charming, but avoid senseless clutter. Well-clothed arbors and trellises are appealing and evocative, but they should be integrated into the general landscape design and not there just for looks (arbors should lead somewhere). Always have purpose in mind: A single corner accent like a lush climbing rose, for instance, can transform and soften the hard lines of a modern house and suggest an extended planting.

Materials should be functional and unpretentious, and should complement the garden and blend with the general setting of existing features, especially the house. Wood, used, mellowed bricks, and stone are desirable building materials; avoid installing hardscape, that is, cement walks or walls, unless they already exist. Hardscape not only looks hard and out of place in a cottage garden atmosphere, it takes a lot of effort to dismantle if you don't like it.

Vigorous plants are the hallmark of a cottage garden because they possess the untailored forms and exuberant good health that convey a sense of the natural. They are generally adaptable to sites (sun or shade) and can therefore be used in different situations, extending their uses. They are low maintenance (not maintenance free), disease and insect resistant, or robust enough to survive infestation. But don't be slavish about confining your plants to unimproved species or open-pollinated seed. Many fine cultivars and seed strains are well suited to the cottage garden (see the "Sampler of Old Favorites" on page 258).

Well-defined boundaries, crowded and colorful plantings are important elements in the cottage garden. Plantings gain impact when they are tightly bound within a framework so they overflow its edges. The term "gay abandon," sometimes used to describe a cottage garden, is misleading; a cottage garden makes careful use of limited space by the use of edging plants, barriers (such as our wooden planks or logs), and hedges. It is the crowded, dense plantings within these boundaries that give the cottage garden the impression of artless "abandon," as colorful blooms, rather than subdued foliage, give it a bright, charming air.

Look for old-fashioned plants (perennials, annuals, bulbs, roses, and shrubs) surviving in old or neglected plantings. You may be surprised to discover byways and odd corners at the edges of developed areas or an old farmstead or graveyard where a few neglected plants linger. Keep an eye out for indicator plants such as daffodils, lilac, orange daylily, or rhubarb that suggest the remnants of a garden; return at different times of the season to see if anything else is growing.

Always get permission before you dig up anything. Mark daffodils and return later to dig them up after the foliage has turned brown; take only small pieces of plants (divisions, roots, or stem cuttings) or a small handful of seeds. Whatever you take, the original planting should look undisturbed.

Seek out old-time gardeners and benefit from their wisdom about growing. They often lavish attention on their favorites that they will gladly share with you. Preserving out-of-fashion plants that might otherwise be lost is a major legacy of cottage garden culture.

Avoid plant fashion. If you like grasses, by all means incorporate them in your design (but don't overdo it). Fashion by its nature is a fleeting phenomenon. The cottage garden should convey stability and enduring values.

Above all, have patience, a virtue worth cultivating in an age of instant gratification. By developing the garden slowly and thoughtfully, by mastering the art of plant propagation and seed germination, for instance, you will have the satisfaction of nurturing plants from their very beginnings—a process that teaches valuable skills—and from this experience you will become more aware of the slower rhythms of the natural world.

Beyond the cottage garden's outward forms, there is the very personal matter of its inner life, the special way each gardener looks at his or her creation. For us, it is the human associations that give our landscape transcendent meaning. Most of our plants are common sorts, readily available from commercial sources, but these could never mean as much to us as the ones grown from roots, divisions, and seeds from the hands of people we care about, perhaps long dead, whose memory is bound to what they gave us. In them, we remember not only their gifts, we remember them. Such gardens, built up over time from intimate connections and memories, rather than from plant nursery shelves or catalog listings, embody for us the unique spirit of a true cottage garden.

Sampler of Old Favorites

Although we have twenty acres of cleared land, we are restricted (except for wide sweeps of naturalized plantings in out-of-the-way places) to gardening in relatively small spaces that don't interfere with horse passageways and the tethering of livestock. The largest plantings are the sixty-foot-long Harvest and Rose Beds; the smallest, a narrow strip in front of the greenhouse. The effect of scattered gardens could have been disastrous, yet they complement one another, thereby magnifying their individual presence. It is as if a large garden had been broken up into pieces and distributed in such a way that the spaces between the gardens are a natural part of the grand design, as each small garden leads inevitably to the next.

Aside from the attractive framework of apple trees, shrubs, weathered buildings, and other fundamental features, what gives separate plantings coherence is their common style and the repetition of certain types of plants: ordinary, old-fashioned, and beautiful. The fact that we didn't have many plants to work with turned out to be a blessing, for by repeating them wherever we could, they created a balanced, harmonious landscape.

There are a few plants not yet discussed in detail that should be mentioned here because even though they have great value for general landscaping, they may be neglected in favor of the latest in plant fashions. Do not be afraid to grow the most vigorous in confined spaces. As we learned with variegated goutweed—the mother of all spreaders— there are simple controls, such as mowing around them. It is not the nature of the plant but how it is handled that is significant. With a few noted exceptions, these are perennials, hardy to Zone 4.

Aconitum sp., monkshood, 4–6 ft. Most of our monkshoods are variants of *A. napellus,* an upright plant for background or hedging, with shiny, palm-shaped leaves and many-branched stems that carry loose spikes of variable purplish to azure-blue flowers shaped like a hood, blooming from midsummer. Later blooming *A.* x *cammarum* 'Bicolor' is an exquisite heirloom with large white hoods darkly edged with purple-blue. We grow these in moist ground and partial shade where clumps increase slowly (in rich ground plants will need staking); contrary to standard advice, monkshood is easy to divide in spring with a ball of earth. Every part is considered poisonous, so wear gloves for this operation.

Cosmos *bipinnatus* 'Sonata Hybrids', 2 ft., annual. Sow seed outdoors in full sun in well-drained soil, or start indoors six to eight weeks before the last frost; barely cover seed. It may seem sacrilegious to include a new version of this old favorite, but we think 'Sonata' is a vast improvement. For many years we grew 'Sensation', a 1936 introduction that set the standard: wide daisylike flowers with silky, serrated petals—pink, crimson, and white—overlapping and radiating from a raised golden center, and borne on tall, branching stems with feathery foliage. The problems with this type are that in colder climates it doesn't start producing flowers until the days get shorter in the fall, and its tall, branching stems bend before wind. As much as we admired this striking annual, we gave up growing it until we discovered 'Sonata Hybrids', which bloom early and bear larger flowers (and more of them) on a shorter, compact plant that doesn't need staking. Who could argue with such merits? We grow cosmos in a showy mass in front of the greenhouse, where it is edged with silvery lamb's ears. Cosmos will self-seed, but if you want the choice white (it seems to glow at twilight), save its seed or buy 'Sonata White'.

Dianthus *deltoides*, maiden pink, 6 in. A truly diminutive plant that does a great job filling in and softening hard edges, maiden pink spreads in a dense mat of dark green leaves covered with a profusion of bright crimson, but scentless, flowers in a dazzling early summer display. Extra growth is easy to pull out.

***Dicentra spectabilis,* bleeding heart,** 3 ft. x 3 ft. Although it has the old-fashioned look, bleeding heart wasn't introduced to American gardens until the mid-1800s, when it became instantly popular. And no wonder: In late spring, arching stems bow to the ground, laden with dangling racemes of dark pink, white-tipped hearts; the white-flowered version, *D. spectabilis* 'Alba', not quite as vigorous, is elegant. Once established in partial shade in evenly moist ground, plants can be left to increase slowly. Their form is wide, but accommodating to controlled ground covers and tulips. In midsummer or whenever the deeply divided foliage looks tattered, cut it back and let late-flowering phlox (planted nearby) take over.

***Euphorbia polychroma,* cushion spurge,** 18 in. x 3 ft. We never fail to be impressed by cushion spurge's spectacular wide dome of chartreuse-golden bracts among spring tulips. Although recommended for dry, sandy soil, ours grows in heavy, moist conditions (and full sun) but spreads slowly. The best method for propagation is to dig up its stubby shoots as soon as they emerge and replant them. Cushion spurge is flashiest in the spring, but even when its top bracts turn green with the onset of hot weather, the plant retains its neat cushion form and its leaves turn rosy by fall.

***Hosta* 'Royal Standard',** 2 ft. x 3 ft. There are many hostas available today, but none gives us as much pleasure as 'Royal Standard', a hybrid of the less hardy *H. plantaginea*. Plants maintain large, heart-shaped, glossy green foliage all summer, then by August produce spires of intensely fragrant, fresh white flowers—like miniature lilies—when new bloom is rare. We grow it in sun or shade, wherever the soil is evenly moist, siting plants at garden edges where extra growth can be mown during the summer or chopped out in early spring as soon as leaf tips emerge.

Lilium Hybrids, 2–6 ft. We have already described our adventures with the "old red lily" (*L. bulbiferum* var. *croceum*), and if you can find it or the similar up-facing 'Enchantment', plant the bulbs in well-drained, enriched soil (the same as for potatoes) in full sun—or partial shade in warmer gardening zones—and leave them undisturbed. The bulbs themselves take up little room, nor do the narrow flowering stems, and when they are spent, nearby plants will fill in. We also like the old favorite 'Citronella', which blooms by midsummer with blue borage. Its four- to five-foot stems bear many down-facing golden flowers—as many as thirty flowers per stem—covered with small black dots; the later-blooming 'Mrs. R. O. Backhouse', an old Martagon Hybrid, has small yellow down-facing flowers, flushed magenta-rose with slight spotting. Of more interest is its rising, rocket-shaped sheath, which is a focal point in the Tulip Bed long before its leaves and flowering stems emerge.

Malva sp., 2½–3 ft. Musk mallow, *M. moschata*, a field weed here, thrives in a garden with well-drained soil and sun, where it produces translucent, light pink or pure white loose bells in clusters at the top of the plant, while buds for later bloom are forming at its base among downy, musk-scented foliage. It outblooms most other perennials, starting in midsummer and lasting through late fall, creating striking contrasts among bright colors and pleasing harmony among pastels. Cut back after flowering or expect an army of seedlings; these should be pulled out before tough taproots form. Hollyhock mallow, *M. alcea* 'Fastigiata', is a different proposition. As wide as it is tall, it rolls over the opposition but is very effective when grown outside a garden barrier and controlled by mowing. It blooms all summer from head to foot with glistening pink bells. Cut back after flowering.

***Malva sylvestris* 'Zebrina',** 3 ft., annual. Sow seeds outside when soil is warm. The 'Zebrina' mallow is a tamed version of the wild mallow with upright, self-supporting stems, lobed leaves, and distinctive, mauve to pink bell-shaped flowers, delicately veined with purple, that open from midsummer to late fall. It is best grown in unenriched, well-drained soil in sun or partial shade; in rich soil it will produce too many leaves, and stems may need staking.

***Oenothera fruticosa,* sundrops,** 18 in. Bright yellow, saucer-shaped flowers bloom in profusion by midsummer over a rosette of red-tinged foliage (especially in early growth); foliage turns scarlet in the fall. It combines well with bright purple clustered bellflowers (*Campanula glomerata*), which bloom at the same time. Sundrops grow in sun and well-drained soil and are unmatched in dry, exposed conditions. Extra growth is not difficult to pull out.

***Papaver somniferum,* opium poppy,** 2½–3 ft., annual. Sow seeds outside before the last frost. In polite circles these are called "lettuce-leaved" or "bread-seed poppy," double forms are called "peony poppies," but all are variants of the opium poppy grown by Thomas Jefferson for beauty alone. Petals of the single type are translucent, in luscious shades of watermelon, raspberry, and pink, splotched with dark gray at their base. Double types range from red with feathery petals to shades of pink, mauve, and peach (white and "black" are rare). We can't say we planted them in every garden, but they are there and always welcome in midsummer. In the spring or early summer, we thin seedlings, making sure they are where we want them (among other flowers to hide their stalks and foliage); Jigs discovered that you *can* transplant them in clumps with as much soil as possible, then water well. When they are finished blooming, we pull up most of the plants to control seeding; we preserve special strains by saving their seeds and planting them in separate places. (*Note:* The California Department of Agriculture has declared that growing this plant in California is illegal.)

***Phlox paniculata,* garden phlox,** 3–4 ft. Ours are from old local gardens and range in color from bright pink, soft red-eyed pink, lilac, and lilac-eyed white to pure white. They bloom in very showy, pyramidal heads—six to ten inches wide—by late summer, and some are especially fragrant (musk and sweet at the same time). We plant them in full sun and well-drained, evenly moist soil, which helps to discourage powdery mildew. Their slow growth allows room for earlier-blooming plants. We divide plants every three or four years depending on need (some authorities advise reducing plants to five stems every season but we think that's stingy).

***Sedum telephium,* live-forever,** 2 ft. While every gardener knows about 'Autumn Joy', few know about this old garden sedum, a slender neat plant with similar fleshy leaves and crimson flower heads (it is also regarded as a medicinal herb). It can fit into the smallest planting in full sun and most soils (except wet), and it makes an attractive hedge that is very effective for smothering weeds in problem areas. Plant in dry, exposed ground and at garden edges.

***Trollius* sp., globeflower,** 2 ft. This underused flower with virtues and no vices asks for nothing more than moist soil and a shady spot. In early spring, its oversized, double buttercups—yellow-orange to primrose—burst open in bouquet sprays, lighting up the darkest spot.

Their early bloom is an asset among hostas, which have only begun to show through the soil. Clumps can be left undivided for four or five years. A good cut flower.

***Valeriana officinalis,* valerian,** 4–5 ft. We can't imagine early summer without experiencing the heady musk aroma of valerian floating above bellflowers, iris, Oriental poppies, peonies, and foxglove. If you want to convey the spirit of the cottage garden, valerian is indispensable for its massed clusters of white or washed-out pink flowers—like miniature Queen Anne's lace—atop waving, wandlike stems that grow up from clumps of long, ladderlike leaves. It grows in most soils and in sun or partial shade. Whenever it becomes overbearing, chop out extra clumps. The odd-smelling roots are the source of valerian's sedative properties.

PART THREE

The Integrated Landscape—
Practice & Philosophy

*Dazzling displays of color
line the side of house.*

CHAPTER ELEVEN

Growing Guide

—

Hardiness Zones

NORTH AMERICAN HARDINESS ZONE numbers are based on the average minimum winter temperatures across the United States, Canada, Alaska, and Mexico. Zones are numbered from 1 to 12, with the lower numbers representing the coldest winter regions, and the higher numbers the warmer winter regions; in Zone 1, for instance, the average minimum winter temperature is –50°F; in Zone 12, along the California coast, average minimum winter temperatures are above 40°F. These Zone numbers are meant as a guide in selecting perennials suited to your area. If you want to grow bleeding heart, for instance, and you live in warm-winter areas (Zones 8–12), you will probably have to grow it as an annual since it requires winter dormancy, but if you want to grow the old orange daylily, you can grow it virtually anywhere.

We had been growing perennials for many years, oblivious of our Hardiness Zone number because we rarely bought plants, and the roots, slips, cuttings, and seeds that were passed along were never labeled, unlike most plants from reliable mail-order sources. We knew, however, that if we gave these plants the right soil and site, they would succeed as they had been doing for decades in local gardens, some of them abandoned. We knew our plants were tough.

When the latest North American Hardiness Zone Map was issued in 1990, the first update in twenty-five years, we were astonished to learn that we gardened in Zone 6 (–10°F to 0°F), or in Zone 5b according to a Canadian version. In practice, all of our perennials—except those we describe as tender—are hardy to Zone 4 (–30°F to –20°F). The reason for the discrepancy is that the official zone designations do not take into sufficient account other factors such as wind, soil, and site and their combined effect, which may be more important in determining plant hardiness. Take the case of lavender (*Lavandula officinalis*, the hardiest type), an herb we love but find very difficult to accommodate. According to authorities, it is hardy to Zone 5 (–20° to –10°F), within our hardiness range, but even after providing it with improved soil drainage and protection from wind, we failed many times in wintering over plants because in our climate, where spring is nonexistent and early summer temperatures are cool, plants do not grow fast enough during the summer to develop the protective hardwood they need by fall to withstand freezing temperatures; friends in the city, where the density of buildings or trees or altitude ameliorate these conditions, have no problem as long as they provide lavender with well-drained soil and sun. Wherever growing conditions allow lavender to develop hardwood before frost, even if it is in northern Vermont where winter temperatures dip to –35°F, success is virtually assured.

Consult Hardiness Zone Maps and read the tags on purchased plants (if a Hardiness Zone number is not given, be sure to ask about it), but

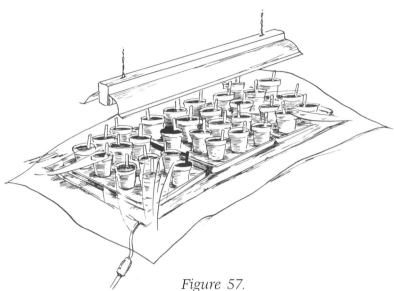

Figure 57.
Germinating seeds indoors.

draw on accumulated garden wisdom, the sort available from keen gardeners in your area, and observe the perennials surviving in old gardens. But don't be afraid to stretch the recommended hardiness limits of a plant you want to grow. Authorities do not always agree on plant hardiness; the hardiness of newly introduced plants is unknown; by planting in protected microclimates (either natural or those you have devised) and mulching heavily, even wrapping plants, you may succeed.

Successful Seed Germination

An embarrassing problem rarely discussed among gardeners is seed germination failure. While nothing is more thrilling to observe than the emergence of new life from sown seeds, nothing is more disheartening than their death. We, like many gardeners, accepted our losses (too numerous to contemplate) until we read the work of Professor

Norman Deno, whose self-published study of seed germination, *Seed Germination: Theory and Practice,* revolutionized the way we think about seeds. They are not inert, as we thought, just awaiting water and warmth to spring to life; they are already alive—in a chemical sense—but they are protected against germinating until conditions are most favorable for their success. Even the most common seeds among vegetables and flowers do not germinate until they have spent time in those little packets you buy every season, a period of about six months that is essential for breaking down the seed's natural inhibitors. The process the gardener uses to overcome these inhibitors is called conditioning. We attribute our phenomenal success in seed germination (when contrasted to past efforts) to using these simple conditioning techniques.

1. For germinating seeds indoors that require 70°F temperatures—the vast majority of seeds—we provide bottom heat in the form of an old heating pad (for bad backs) set on medium (Figure 57). We fill recycled Styrofoam cups with premoistened, sterilized seeding mix, sow the seeds, cover the containers with dry-cleaning-bag type thin plastic, then set them on the heating pad—wrapped in a plastic bag—which rests underneath a 40-watt fluorescent bulb. This ensures steady warmth from above and beneath the seeding containers and steady moisture. Under these conditions, germination is extraordinarily rapid; some seeds like 'Lady' lavender have germinated in twenty-four hours, others in forty-eight, and most of the rest within a week. After seeds have germinated, they are removed from the heat and placed under grow lights until they are ready to be hardened off in our unheated greenhouse.

2. For seeds that need stratification or prechilling, we spread them on one side of a folded, premoistened paper towel, fold over the unsown side as a cover, then insert the damp towel in a loosely closed and labeled sandwich bag, and leave it in the fridge for the recommended time, usually from two days to two weeks. This method is surer than sowing seeds outside in the fall and letting nature do the work.

3. For seeds that need light to germinate (this usually includes prechilled seeds), we press them into the premoistened soil surface; for those that require darkness to germinate, we put tin foil over the plastic cover to exclude all light.

4. As an alternative to sowing hard-coated seeds outdoors in the fall or in the spring before the last frost—a method we use for lupine—we soak them in warm water so the coat breaks down and water can penetrate them (you can also chip seeds, but we've not found that as successful). Some seeds, like parsley, require long soaking (forty-eight hours) with a change of water.

5. As for how deep to sow seeds, the rule of thumb is to cover them with soil twice their thickness; when in doubt, we use the minimum amount.

Our experience suggests the following reasons for seed germination failure:

        a. Seeds are planted too deep.

        b. Soil becomes dried out or soggy.

        c. Temperatures are too cold for germination.

        d. Seeds are poor quality (old or dead).

It isn't necessary to do everything right, because often germination will occur whatever you do (but rates will be low and the resulting seedlings may be weak), and authorities don't always agree on the conditioning required to encourage germination. There is still a lot of mystery

about the process. The best advice is to follow the greatly improved directions on seed packets and to consult a reliable guide (see Bibliography).

Seed Saving

With a few exceptions—shell beans, pumpkins, garden cress, arugula,
and potato tubers—we don't save many vegetable seeds, since some of
them are hybrids or difficult to process. We do, however, save a lot of
flower and herb seeds for our own use and for Jo Ann's Kitchen &
Garden seed line of hardy herbs and heirlooms. During late summer and
fall, seeds are drying on trays in the greenhouse, on windowsills, or
upstairs on newspaper or in boxes. When they are completely dry, we
process each type to reduce chaff. Our methods are crude but effective
and include rubbing seeds through strainers and colanders, hand picking,
and winnowing (blowing across piled up seeds). We store seeds in a cool
place away from light, either in labeled jars or in envelopes filed alpha-
betically in an old shoe box. Saving seed has become a fall ritual, and
even if we didn't need to save them, we would feel compelled to pluck
ripened heads just because they are there and hold so much future
promise. Although we sometimes save seeds of hybrids just to see the
outcome (second generation are most like the first), most of our saved
seed comes from open-pollinated types whose progeny may vary
somewhat but usually come true to type.

Our general method is to gather the seed in as clean condition as
possible and to keep each type in separate, prelabeled envelopes. Some
with "shakers" (like poppies) are easier to harvest with their stems on,
and they are placed head first in a paper bag, where seeds are released
at the bottom of the bag when the shakers are fully dried; these are

marked with an asterisk below. The others have seeds in heads (sunflower) or pods (scarlet runner) or are nutlike (nasturtiums).

Calendula

Columbine*

Cosmos 'Sonata' (dwarf type)

Feverfew

Foxglove*

Garlic chives*

Hollyhock

Love-in-a-mist*

Mallows (all kinds)

Painted sage

Poppies*

Nicotiana ('Crimson King' and the old white)*

Nasturtium

Rose and white campion*

Scarlet runner bean

Silver dollar

Sunflower

The Compost Heap

So much has been written about this over the last thirty years that we will describe only some of our practices that are unusual and might suggest adaptations to the reader. We explained, in Chapter 3, "The Kitchen Garden," how we made soil for the large raised beds by accumulating summer manure from pigs, hens, and horses. Bedding material for pigs is unshredded newspaper; the hens have sawdust, shavings, old hay, and newspaper (which they quickly shred); the horses have sawdust. The pig and horse stalls are cleaned daily, the hen pen only three or four times during the summer. One or two wheelbarrows full of this material are dumped in a log enclosure in the barnyard every noon from the end of May until late September and is covered at once with sawdust or shavings or old hay from piles nearby (Figure 58). By October, manure is being spread on the fields again, and then we turn the summer manure pile. The most resistant stuff is newspaper from the pigpen, and we shake out the thick accumulations, spreading it out in the new pile. If the compost is heavy and dank, the manure ratio is too high, so we add sawdust, and so forth, as we go along, and of course we cover the whole pile that way when we're done.

By the next spring, that compost will be ready to use on the gardens, but the newspapers, only partially rotted, must be separated out to be used as weed-suppressing mulch around bushes like blueberries or currants, or they can be returned to the unused heap. The compost is rough, but we break it up as we work it into the soil of the raised beds with a deep rake. If we want fine compost for seeding, we sift it through three-eighth-inch mesh hardware cloth on a frame over a twenty-gallon tub.

Readers without animals can often get manure for the hauling from riding stables, racecourses, dog kennels, zoos, and even farms; shredded newspaper and grass clippings can be used instead of sawdust; and city street cleaners are happy to get rid of leaves. Jigs once worked at a plant nursery where all the soil was made from leaves the city dumped in huge piles. By adding plenty of material that isn't manure, the amount is stretched and the mixture is lighter and easier to handle. If you have the time and energy to turn the heap more than once, it will rot faster.

No-Dig Gardening: Raised Beds

Even if our poor, heavy soil didn't dictate using raised beds to grow most of our plants, we think it is an excellent way to garden for other reasons: They take up less space than traditional gardens because they can be more densely planted and are more productive; weeds are shaded out; soil can easily be adjusted to meet special needs; their design and the way they elevate plantings is an asset in the general landscape. And, of course, no digging is required.

Raised beds may be used for nearly anything (Figure 59). We have one for peas that's twelve inches wide and forty feet long; the rhubarb

Figure 58.
Manuring.

bed has a two-foot depth of soil; and our flower beds are all shapes and sizes. Vegetable beds should be about four feet wide and six to eight inches deep, which means the enclosing material (logs in our case, and old telephone poles are great) has to be at least eight inches high, while the thick plastic underneath should be six to seven feet wide, depending on the width of the enclosing material—you want a six-inch apron sticking out. In the case of deep-rooted perennial flowers, herbs, or roses, lay several thicknesses of newspaper over sod ground instead of thick plastic.

When the logs or whatever you're using are firmly in place on the plastic or newspaper, fill the bed with six to eight inches of rotted manure or compost. Add sawdust if the texture seems dense. Except where potatoes are to be grown, sprinkle lime over the surface. Add 6-12-12 fertilizer. If the soil mixture is manure and fairly fresh, use 0-20-20 instead. Work the whole bed thoroughly with a deep rake—we do it twice—and then smooth it with a regular rake. If the surface texture is not very fine, use sifted soil to cover seeds, pressed firmly.

To maintain the level of the bed, add compost or manure, rotted or fresh, as well as sawdust, in the fall. Work it in then or wait until spring. To discourage weeds along the outside edge where the lawn mower doesn't reach, spray *closely* with Roundup early in the season, and depending on growth, once again later.

No-Dig Gardening: Direct Sod Planting

To plant directly in sod ground, choose vigorous perennials or bulbs. Make a slit with a sharp spade or trowel, then push in the roots; firmly close up the slit. Place several layers of newspaper on top of the ground around the slit to smother weeds, heap a thick, wide circular layer of

Figure 59.
Raised beds.

compost on it, then add a top cover of old hay or sawdust. Once plants are established, the initial mulch will become friable soil and you can proceed as you would with any planting, mulching (or not) and fertilizing it every season. Tough bulbs like narcissus do not need anything after planting except a seasonal top-dressing of bonemeal.

Plant Maintenance

We don't pamper our plants, but we don't ignore them either. A friend with a demanding schedule and a beautiful garden once observed that it's not the amount of time you spend in the garden, it's what you do when you're there. We often think of him as we cast our eyes about the gardens in early morning when we are feeding the chickens, at midday when we return from the barn or field through the vegetable gardens, or at dusk when we stroll down the path between the Harvest and Rose Beds, all the while making mental notes on what needs to be done; then whenever there's a moment to spare, we go straight to cutting back plants, or staking them, or removing spent blooms.

At the top of the list is cutting back herbs and flowers to encourage foliage regrowth or rebloom, a job we do about three times a season—in early summer, midsummer, and late summer. To make the best use of our time, we wait until there are several plants to trim at once.

With a few types such as white mugwort and golden glow, we cut them back midway through their growth to reduce their height, but generally we let plants grow naturally. An exception is borage, which in rich soil becomes overbearing without severe trimming; we do this at any time in its growth, whenever it is needed. Sometimes you have to be tough with tough plants. We rarely pinch growing tips to encourage bushiness, but plants are kept in healthy trim because we harvest them for use or for bouquets. We do deadhead (remove spent blooms) if appearance is greatly affected or if this will encourage more flowers.

We dread staking and avoid it where possible by growing weak-stemmed plants like monkshood in thinner soil where their growth is somewhat subdued. When there is no alternative (Oriental poppies and hollyhocks come to mind), we stake as early in the plant's growth as possible so that developing stems and foliage will obscure supports; these should be about three-fourths of the plant's expected height. For hollyhocks, we tie stems to wooden stakes with strips of pantyhose in a loose figure eight; for Oriental poppies and peonies, we construct a corral of strong sticks (three to four per plant) and baling twine; for shorter floppy plants, we insert twiggy willow brush among the stems.

At the end of the growing season, if there are any plants not yet cut back, we trim stems leaving "arms" (up to two feet) to catch the snow—

a great insulator. In late fall or early winter, when the ground is frozen, we drive the team wagon as close to plantings as we can to fork off manure onto the beds. Like snow, this helps protect them from alternate freezing and thawing, and, of course, it breaks down to enrich the soil.

Propagation

We propagate our plants because we have many uses for them in the landscape and we enjoy extending their lives. The easiest technique is to divide overgrown clumps by chopping them into sections. The nature of the clump—whether it forms mats with dead centers as monardas do, or is attached to deep, fleshy taproots that are difficult to dislodge, as with comfrey—dictates how we will dig it up, entirely (monardas) or in parts (comfrey). A sharp spade combined with a digging shovel works in even the toughest cases. We divide plants whenever they are dormant, which means that early growing plants like lungwort are divided in the fall, while phlox is divided in the spring. The following are very easy to divide: mints, sorrel, oreganos, chives, sweet woodruff, 'Silver King' artemisia, and lemon balm.

Layering is useful for increasing fruiting shrubs (gooseberries and currants) whose flexible basal branches can be bent to the ground. If they haven't layered themselves (black currants do this readily), we bend a branch to the ground and weight it there with a rock six inches from the end. The following season, or whenever top growth appears, we sever the newly rooted plant from its parent and grow it in a cold frame, or we plant it at its new site.

In the traditional version, root cuttings are made in the fall with a single root, cut into two-inch sections; these are placed upright in a four-inch pot of soil and covered with one-half inch of soil. After the pots are watered, they are stored in a cold frame or cold place over the winter, and in the spring, rooted shoots are replanted. In our version, rather than dig up roots, we chop off pieces of root with top growth from the mother plant, then replant these close together directly in the soil of a cold frame and proceed as described. This simple procedure works well with hollyhocks, sweet rocket, and perennial mallows.

In midsummer we make tip cuttings of tender perennials like rose geranium, false licorice, and tree wormwood that we need to winter indoors. It's a lot easier to carry these over in small pots on a windowsill than to lug heavy, container-grown plants indoors and try to find a sunny place for them (sometimes we do both). To make tip cuttings, we select green, nonblooming, nonwoody stems and make a sharp cut at an angle just below a node about three to six inches from the stem's tip. Then we remove the bottom leaves, dip stem ends in rooting hormone powder, and insert stems in a small pot filled with potting soil amended with extra perlite (crowding stems together encourages rooting). We cover the container loosely with a plastic bag, then place it out of direct light until the cuttings root, in six weeks or less. For best success, the surrounding temperature should be in the 70°F range.

Some plants will root in water, even in a bouquet (purple basil). If stems show signs of root growth, change water every day and when the roots are one-half inch long, pot them up and keep a wary eye on them. Roots that form readily in water must be coaxed to settle into soil.

We propagate roses by pulling up suckers from nongrafted specimens. We detach them from the mother plant by clipping them with a bit of the main root. The suckers are cut back to about six inches, then potted in a soil mix amended with perlite, watered, and kept in a protected area out of direct sun until they show signs of growth, when they are repotted. We make stem cuttings about six inches long anytime during the summer and early fall from green-wood stems with buds or those that have produced blooms. Stems are treated the same as tip cuttings; if they have not produced roots by late fall, we leave them in pots on the floor of the greenhouse over the winter, protected with a loose plastic covering to maintain moisture.

Managing Water Resources

We have a surface water well near the vegetable gardens from which we bucket out water for young plants—tomatoes, peppers, the cabbage family, cucumbers, melons—when we set them out, and if we have a prolonged dry spell, we water the plants from there until the well runs dry. If drought persists, we spread sawdust mulch over the beds, and then we carry buckets from the four rain barrels around the house. When that's used up, we pray. We have had two summer-long droughts here, so dry that we were hard pressed to find water for the livestock, but our gardens have always made it through. Of course, it would be better if we had a reliable water source, but if plants are liberally supplied with water when they're starting out and if they're mulched, they should be all right. We also use wastewater from the kitchen, but only on full-grown plants, especially on shrubs and roses; it will eventually kill young plants.

Harvesting

We eat so well all year round not because we produce so much, but because we know how to make use of everything at every stage of ripeness, irrespective of blemishes. How tomatoes are harvested and sorted has been told in Chapter 3, "The Kitchen Garden," and that may be taken as a paradigm. When rhubarb becomes tough and stringy, it goes into juice and wine, and the same is true of small fruit—under-ripe for jelly and jam, ripe for eating, overripe for juice and wine and drying. Small potatoes may go to the pigs, but just as often we boil them with their skins on for supper. Beans are eaten fresh and dried, corn fresh and canned, peas fresh and dried for Hopping Johnny, and so on. Apples are sorted for different purposes and different keeping properties, so we have them fresh from late August until May, and in all kind of ways—jelly, apple sweetmeats, dried, juice, pies—throughout the year. Jo Ann's book *The Old-Fashioned Fruit Garden* tells how to use fruit at all stages, and old cookbooks can give helpful advice.

Disease and Insect Control

The notion that healthy plants, grown "organically," are not bothered by insects is moonshine. Disease in our vegetable gardens has never been a problem, but Colorado potato beetles, cabbageworms, cutworms, root maggot, slugs, corn borers, tomato hornworms, ravens, and deer have visited us, some regularly, some intermittently. For more years than we care to remember, we spent hours conscientiously squashing potato beetles and their larvae and eggs between our fingers, with the only result that the ones we missed eventually built up a huge residual population. Dusting with rotenone at the first sight of a beetle was the answer, and we have not seen a single one for six years. If you have only a small planting of cabbage, Brussels sprouts, broccoli, and cauli-flower, it is possible to control cabbageworms by inspecting each plant every day to squash the green worms on the leaves and the egg clusters on the undersides, but the worms are hard to see, and if you have 100 or more plants, as we do, dust them with rotenone as soon as you see those pretty white butterflies fluttering about. Watch for damage—holes in the leaves—and dust when you see it.

Cutworms wreaked terrible destruction, both when we planted in the ground, and to a lesser extent, in the raised beds, until we learned to sprinkle cutworm poison over the beds before the final raking. Root maggots infest radishes and carrots. Dust the furrow with wood ashes before you drop in the seeds. Slugs we have always with us. As Jo Ann works in the flower gardens, she carries a covered plastic container with her as a repository for slugs, and we watch for them whenever we turn over a stone or bit of wood, but the best control is slug bait sprinkled over the soil, covered with a chip of wood or bark.

Corn borers can be controlled by weekly spraying with Sevin once the corn is knee high, but we don't bother, even though they are found in nearly every ear we pick. Since they seldom do any damage beyond the tip of the ear, we simply cut that off when we husk them. Infestations of tomato hornworm, very damaging to the fruit when they occur, have struck us only twice. Weekly spraying with Sevin controls them.

We finally gave up growing an acre of field corn for the livestock because ravens pulled up every single plant. The only surefire solution was to shoot one and hang it on a stick in the field, but because they are extremely wary, and spending an afternoon with a shotgun up a tree at the edge of the field finally came to seem an unprofitable exercise, we gave up. Then they turned to the sweet corn seedlings in the garden. If we were unable to shoot one, we learned to cover the plants with netting until they were a foot high. We still have to shoot one raven every spring, because they prey on our baby chicks in the turkey pen.

Coyotes have so decimated the deer population here in recent years that they are no longer a problem, but they used to be thick in our gardens at night in late summer. We tried all the preventive measures so confidently advanced in garden publications, but in the end we found shooting at them with bird shot on a few evenings banished them.

Hollyhock rust is the only serious disease among our flowers. Signs of fungus attack are raised, bright orange pustules on the back of leaves, causing them to droop, then fall. Rust attacks hollyhocks as well as most mallows whenever there is an encouraging environment: periods of steady moisture from heavy dew, fog, rain, or cloud cover, and temperatures between 60°F and 70°F for a period of two to four hours ("organically" raised plants are not immune, as has been suggested).

We fight rust by planting hollyhocks in full sun with good air circulation and thinning overcrowded populations so any moisture that collects on their foliage will dry as quickly as possible; we reduce mallow populations, which may be carrier plants; we look for rust-resistant strains among established hollyhocks; where rust is persistent and damaging, we dust plants with agricultural sulfur according to the following plan: When the first emerging leaves show signs of disease, they are removed and burned. The new set of leaves is dusted at once, then again every ten days unless the weather is exceptionally dry and hot. In the fall, plants are cut back and all fallen leaves and debris around them are removed. ●

CHAPTER TWELVE

A Summary of Practical & Aesthetic Principles

⁓

THE GARDEN PANORAMA WE HAVE DESCRIBED has been thirty years in the making. For much of that time, we were so involved in developing the farm and trying to make a living that our efforts at creating individual plantings of use and delight were largely unexamined. It was only when we became conscious of each one as an essential part of the whole that we began to consider how we had achieved the harmony of design we call the integrated landscape. We view our experiences in the light of certain practical and aesthetic principles that can be applied to any garden, whatever its size.

Underlying all our ideas about how to go about developing a landscape is the fundamental one of letting it evolve over time from life and needs rather than from a blueprint, because we think that such an approach, allowing for growth and change, is more satisfying in the long run. If in the beginning you install elaborate hard structures, you may regret these later when they will be difficult and expensive to alter. By contrast, our approach stresses the establishment of soft features that can be easily changed according to need (grass paths and wooden fences, for instance). Not only is this approach cheaper—within every gardener's reach—but it limits the garden's infrastructure or basic framework to unobtrusive supports. While the framework is essential, it should not overwhelm and dominate the garden itself. Keep it simple.

The principle of simplicity also applies to the design of the garden. Pretentious, complex designs overwhelm the garden's content—the plants themselves. Our straightforward oblong raised beds, as well as island beds and traditional borders, are laid out to show off the plants within. The gardens' visual impact is derived from a combination of easily achieved elements—tightly confining wooden barriers or low hedges, surrounded by trimmed grass and paths. These simple devices draw our attention to, rather than away from, crammed plantings, rich in form and color. The effect is one of unforced yet overflowing abundance, as true of the Kitchen Garden as of the Flowering Herb Garden. Semiwild plantings follow a similar plan, except that surrounding wild grasses are roughly, rather than neatly, trimmed (Figure 60).

The success of individual plantings depends on matching plants to habitat, rather than forcing them to grow in unnatural conditions. Plants grown this way will never achieve their potential as positive elements in the landscape; they will always be in marginal health, subject to early death from disease and insect infestations. By matching vigorous plants to sites they prefer, we were able to transform even the most unpromising areas of our landscape—dank corners, dry shade, swamp, and dry slopes—into assets. There was, moreover, no expense involved since we

Figure 60.
Bull standing in the rough wild grasses.

used easily propagated types we were already growing elsewhere. From this experience we learned to appreciate every plant in our repertoire, even the rampant ones. Do not despise the common and unfashionable if they are beautiful in some way and can be grown to advantage.

The creative use of space is very important, especially where it is limited. Many of our plantings are relatively small, but they gain impact by their connection to one another. An intimate dooryard garden, for instance, can be appreciated in its own right but also regarded as a related part of nearby plantings. It is not only plants in the ground that count, however, but the vertical effect of trees, shrubs, and climbing vines, or any plant with a strong, upright form. By thinking vertically about space, we can open the landscape to another dimension, one freed from the constraints of limited ground. Vertical plantings also transform dull areas, create distant views, and carry our spirits upward in soaring tree lines and high canopies. Wherever we are, our eyes are drawn to tall accents that help us to see the landscape in a new and refreshing way. Elegant effects can be achieved by the most humble means when an old rhubarb plant (Figure 61) is allowed to send up its tall, cream-colored plumes in a distant area dominated by green shrubbery. How our view is altered and refreshed! Once ignored, the old coarse rhubarb plant now attracts our eye with its rising creamy plumes in their surrounding greenery.

Adding "bones" in the form of shrubs and trees to the landscape as it is developed, rather than in its initial stages as we are advised, may sound like heresy, but it is the way most of us go about it. Confronted with bare ground, we spend time getting to know its contours, we fit plants to the site and change them around until we create harmonious communities. As these develop, we feel the need for more structure and for focal points that will enhance the whole picture. Take time to think about adding shrubs and trees to the landscape (unless they are already there). Although easier to move than hardscape (cement walls, for instance), they will be difficult to move nonetheless if they have been wrongly placed.

Another heresy worth considering is to think of your landscape as composed of fluid outdoor living spaces rather than as "rooms." To achieve an integrated landscape, one where every element seems to be inevitable, natural, and an essential part of the whole, it is better to think of the spaces you develop as linked to one another rather than as a series of unconnected theme gardens that just happen to share the same ground.

—

Figure 61.
Blooming rhubarb plant.

The maintenance of an integrated landscape need not be daunting if you stick to essentials. With limited time, we decided to do only what was necessary to keep our plantings healthy and attractive at all seasons. Basically, this means cutting back plants (since many are harvested for use, this is no extra effort), trimming grass, pruning roses as needed, and applying a seasonal top-dressing of manure or compost in early winter. For what we get—foliage and bloom from spring through fall—that's not a lot of work. Whatever success we have achieved in creating a harmonious setting can be attributed to following simplicity in methods and design, without exception, throughout the entire landscape. However different, the plantings are linked together by a unity of vision apparent in their style—full and natural rather than tailored—in the repetition of similar and complementary materials (wooden fences, arbors, barriers), and in the plants themselves (sturdy, old-fashioned, and adaptable). That we make no distinction between what is useful and what is beautiful helps to meld the elements, not only in our own perception but in the landscape's meaning for others. It looks lived-in, used, and comfortable. In creating your own landscape, do not force its development and do not be swayed by passing fads. Life itself, combined with a love of growing things, will push you in the right direction. We hope the principles we have discussed will be a starting point. ⬤

Epilogue

—

Jigs wrote this prophetic essay twenty years ago:

THINGS

One generation passes away, and another generation comes: but the earth abides forever. Yes.

And time and death happen to us all. Yes.

And all things pass away. Yes.

But there are things about us, things we briefly hold, things that then are passed to others who keep them and use them in their turn, so that a thing may pass through many hands, many lives, bearing to us in its cracks and patches and stains and worn edges other times, bearing away from us to others, our times, our ways.

Disregard the new, the boughten, and the ceremonial gifts; consider only those things that have been much used, that were freely given, and that, used by us, have become part of our lives.

Like those old, old quilts of Lily's, with which she parted so regretfully. Was it her great-grandmother who made them? Lily had used them and looked after them with so much care, so much love—showing me where she had repaired one when her son, twenty years ago, had ripped it—and now she was surrendering them to nothing more than a friend, not even a relative, giving away a portion of her memories, her past, her self.

So it is with things: They possess us. Our lives have been woven around them; to give them away is more than generosity.

Lily and Fred gave us many things, at one time and another, especially when a few years ago, Fred retired and they moved to the West Coast. Humble things that have become so useful to us every day: a heavy red plastic bucket in which we carry whey to the pigs, a record player built by their eldest son, two shovels, a ladder, the pot we cook our cocoa in every morning, our roasting pan, a duffel bag, rugs, and much else I cannot even remember now as specifically theirs.

We cannot assume the burden of life that charges the object; once given, it begins a new life, invested now with our feelings. Lily's quilts, which meant so much to her, play a less significant part in my life than her heavy red plastic bucket.

Things become memorials. When I use what were once their things, I think of Lily and Fred. I imagine them using the things: I see Lily as a young mother, repairing the quilt. I remember them when they gave me the things, and I think of them now, our relations reduced to a few letters crossing the nearly 4,000 miles between us.

In the midst of my life, pouring out whey from the red bucket into the pig's trough or using the ladder, I am handling memorials, doing my work with votive offerings to old associations.

So many things, so many people.

The small blue-and-gray butter crock and the cast-iron doughnut pot, solid, practical, homely, remind me of Alice Burroughs, thrifty farmwife who gave them to us quietly, shyly, deprecatingly, and above all, nervously, not sure how we would receive what she called "just some old family things I don't use anymore."

Harry sold everything—antiques, farm equipment, old junk—from a house and barn and yard crammed full, and I've bought things from him, but what I remember are the things he gave me. I tried to buy his cabbage cutter, but he'd only lend it to me at sauerkraut time, until one fall when I came to get it, he gave me a beautiful machine, better than his own. Or the fine, heavy, antique cleaver he just handed to me with a smile, a year after I'd asked him to look out for one. Or the two double beds with hand-carved chestnut headboards.

Seller of things, intermediary between one user and another, I remember him for what he sweetly gave.

If so many of the things in our household have been used and worn and given and often given again, I cannot work around the farm without touching things handled by men and women long before I was born, things that were given me by people who knew their value not just in dollars once paid, but, more important, in the work the men and women had done with them over the years. Labor that I can see today in the wear marks—the smooth edges, the grooves and hollows worn into the iron or wood, the leather worn thin.

Mrs. Jackman, when she sold the farm after her husband died, gave me a truckload of old work harness, which is nearly all we have. Murdoch MacGinnis, who only met me once when he came to look at our horses, gave me his sulky plow. Richard Ide gave me his chick brooder. Mrs. Bartlett gave us her grandfather's dump cart, work sleigh, spring wagon, and several sets of shafts. Floyd Hall gave us a set of work harness and our butter churn. Pat Sweet gave me a bridle. Jim Kempton gave us our cider barrels. Alex Gillis gave us our one-horse wagon.

When I list the things like that, remembering the people who freely gave them, thinking of the burden of life they bore before they passed into my hands, I am ashamed of the little I have given away.

But I know my time will come.

All things pass away.

As I grow older, my grip on things will weaken; I will no longer need them nor even want them. It is hard to admit now, but one day I will know I have plowed my last furrow, mowed my last swath, pressed my last barrel of cider.

Even before that, as our lives ebb, we will begin to part with those things that seemed once to mean so much to us, that seemed so indispensable for our work, that seemed such an integral part of our days; and one by one, we will give them into other hands and lives, bearing our burden of love and care and labor.

Then, may those who come after us into possession of these things remember us, both in our age and in the time when we used them in the vigor of our days!

—

Haying with horses, Jigs pitches the windrows of hay up onto the wagon with a long fork where Jo Ann spreads it around, tramping it down from end to end, making it a solid square load eight feet high that will lift off neatly in four or five huge bites of the horsepowered hay fork when we get to the barn and Jigs drives the fork's prongs deep into the load. The mounds of hay will rise straight up to the peak and then sway across the barn until, at a shout from Jigs and a jerk on the release rope, the hay will drop into the mow and Jo Ann will turn Pookie around and lead him back to the barn while Jigs pulls back the fork to drop it onto the load for another bite. Haying with horses is a job for many hands, but since the children left home at the end of the 1970s, we had been doing it alone. In the summer of 2000, we managed to gather in only four loads before we realized we couldn't do it anymore; in our mid-sixties, we no longer had the energy for such a task under the hot sun. We hired a crew with a baler.

―

"Tomorrow to fresh woods and pastures new."
—John Milton, *Lycidas*

We could have kept on in that way, of course, but the act of relinquishing one of the farm's central activities to others seemed to take the heart out of the enterprise. We decided to sell the farm. And so it came to pass that we gave away most of our equipment, animals, and things that had been the tools of our life for so many years.

At the end of June 2001, we left the farm forever, looking back for the last time on the beauty of the landscape we had created over thirty years. On a much smaller place in the Champlain Valley of New York, we have begun to re-create our gardens and our tiny farming operation. Writing this book, making conscious and articulate everything we learned over those years, should make the task easier, just as we hope it will guide and inspire our readers. ●

Bibliography

Bennett, Jennifer, and Turid Forsyth. *The Harrowsmith Annual Garden.* Camden East, Ontario: Camden House, 1990.

Bowles, Ella Shannon, and Dorothy S. Towle. *Secrets of New England Cooking.* New York: M. Barrows and Co., 1947.

Brownlow, Margaret. *Herbs and the Fragrant Garden.* Kent, England: The Herb Farm, Ltd., 1957.

Campbell, Mary Mason. Illustrated by Tasha Tudor. *Betty Crocker's Kitchen Gardens.* New York: University Publications, 1971.

Crockett, James Underwood. *The Time-Life Encyclopedia of Gardening: Annuals.* Alexandria, Va.: Time-Life Books, 1971.

————. *The Time-Life Encyclopedia of Gardening: Perennials.* Alexandria, Va.: Time-Life Books, 1972.

Deno, Norman C. *Seed Germination: Theory and Practice.* State College, Pa.: Norman C. Deno, 1993.

Farmer, Fannie Merritt. *The 1986 Boston Cooking-School Cook Book.* New York: Gramercy, 1997.

Fell, Derek. *Annuals: How to Select, Grow, and Enjoy.* Los Angeles: HP Books, 1983.

Gardner, Jo Ann. *The Old-Fashioned Fruit Garden.* Halifax, Nova Scotia: Nimbus Publishing, Ltd., 1989.

————. *The Heirloom Garden.* Pownal, Vt.: Storey Communications, 1992.

————. *Living with Herbs.* Woodstock, Vt.: The Countryman Press, 1997.

————. *Heirloom Flower Gardens.* White River Junction, Vt.: Chelsea Green Publishing, 2001.

————. *Herbs in Bloom.* Portland, Or.: Timber Press, 1998.

Griffiths, Mark, ed. *Index of Garden Plants: The New Royal Horticultural Society Dictionary.* Portland, Or.: Timber Press, 1994.

Harper, Pamela, and Frederick McGourty. *Perennials: How to Select, Grow, and Enjoy.* Los Angeles: HP Books, 1985.

Heath, Edward Harris. *The Wonderful World of Cooking.* New York: Simon and Schuster, 1956.

Hedrick, U. P. *Fruits for the Home Garden.* New York: Dover reprint, 1944.

Jekyll, Gertrude. *A Gardener's Testament* (first published by *Country Life*, 1937). Suffolk, England: The Antique Collectors' Club, 1982.

Lima, Patrick. *The Harrowsmith Perennial Garden.* Camden East, Ontario: Camden House, 1986.

Osborne, Robert. *Hardy Roses.* Pownal, Vt.: Storey Communications, 1991.

Phillips, Rodger, and Martyn Rix. *The Random House Book of Perennials.* Vols. 1 and 2. New York: Random House, 1991.

Powell, Eileen. *From Seed to Bloom.* Pownal, Vt.: Storey Communications, 1995.

Shepherd, Roy E. *History of the Rose.* (First published New York, 1954.) New York: Earl M. Coleman, 1978.

Verrier, Suzanne. *Rosa Rugosa.* Deer Park, Wis.: Capability Books, 1991.

Index